A GERMAN OFFICER DURING THE ARMENIAN GENOCIDE

A Biography of Max Von Scheubner-Richter

[based on *Posten auf ewiger Wache: Aus dem abenteuerlichen Leben des Max von Scheubner-Richter*]

by
Paul Leverkuehn

translated by Alasdair Lean
with a preface by Jorge Vartparonian
and a historical introduction
by Hilmar Kaiser

Gomidas Institute
London

A German Officer During the Armenian Genocide: A Biography of Max Von Scheubner-Richter is based on a translation of *Posten auf ewiger Wache: Aus dem abenteuerlichen Leben des Max von Scheubner-Richter* (Essen: Essener Verlagsanstalt, 1938).

Published by Taderon Press for the Gomidas Institute.

Printed at Gopsons, India

ISBN 978-1-903656-81-5

For further information please contact:
Gomidas Institute
42 Blythe Rd.
London W14 0HA
England
Email: *info@gomidas.org*
Web: *www.gomidas.org*

TABLE OF CONTENTS

Reference Map

RUSSIAN-OTTOMAN-PERSIAN FRONTIER AND SCHEUBNER-RICHTER'S ZONE OF OPERATION CIRCA 1915-16.

Foreword by Jorge Vartparonian

In my opinion this biography of Max Erwin von Scheubner Richter is important, not on account of its literary merits, but for suggesting important historical links between the first two major genocides of the twentieth century, shaking our parents and grandparents' world, and setting a terrible precedent for the future of our planet.

During World War II its author became chief of German military intelligence in Turkey, which lends his story credibility. When this book was published in 1938, its hero had already become a member of the Nazi pantheon, honoured in yearly public ceremonies, so barring anything critical ever being said of him. Perhaps our knowledge of the sinister web connecting the Armenian and Jewish holocausts may be of some use in preventing similar happenings in the future.

The adventures of Max Erwin von Scheubner-Richter vie with those of other contemporary characters such as Sidney Reilly, Bruce Lockhart, Trebitsch Lincoln, "Parvus" (Alexander Helphand) and Rafael de Nogales. Many of these passed through the same places and had the same friends or enemies. Born simply Max Richter in Riga, Russian Lettland, in 1884, he married countess Mathilde von Scheubner, 18 years older than himself, the daughter of an aristocratic industrialist (whose factory he had defended at the head of a Cossack detachment during the 1905 left-wing uprisings). At the time, he was studying chemistry at Riga University, and was a member of the "Rubonia" fraternity for Baltic Germans. This subsequently turned into a hotbed of Nazis, including prominent Baltic party members, such as Alfred Rosenberg, Arno Schickedanz, and Otto von Kursell.

On marrying, Richter was adopted by an aristocratic aunt of his wife, prefixing a "von" and adding his wife's aristocratic surname to his own, leaving his native Latvia to seek his fortune in Munich, where he studied engineering. When the First World War broke out, his patriotic spirit led him to enlist straight away as a volunteer in a Bavarian regiment of light cavalry, in which his excellent equestrian skills could be put to best use. He was a brave soldier and was decorated with the Iron Cross (second class) shortly after arriving at the front, in Lorraine. After this he spent over a year at the head of a joint Turkish-German expedition to the Caucasus, which failed to sabotage the Russian oil-fields at Baku, but succeeded in preventing the Tsar's army from aiding the besieged British troops at Kut-el-Amara (in present-day Iraq), where the British suffered their worst defeat in the Middle

East, losing 13,000 prisoners, most of whom did not survive their Turkish captivity. These prisoners replaced Armenians forced to work on the Baghdad railway in the Amanus mountains, who were immediately deported and massacred to a man.

During WWI, the Turkish armed forces were frequently headed by German officers, many of them as chiefs of the general staff. Among them we can mention Marshall von der Goltz; Fritz Bronsart von Schellendorf; General von Falkenhayn; Baron Kress von Kressenstein; General Otto von Lossow; General von Seeckt. Several of them participated, years later, in the events leading up to the famous Munich putsch of 1923, in which Scheubner-Richter lost his life. Adolf Hitler spoke glowingly of one of them, Marshal von der Goltz, during World War II, describing the drastic measures he had taken in Flanders almost forty years earlier (such as executing town mayors, putting villages to the torch, and deporting entire populations, in reprisal for actions perpetrated against his soldiers).

As German vice-consul in Erzurum, and one of the two chiefs of the expeditionary force, Scheubner-Richter was not only a witness to numerous Turkish atrocities against the Armenian population, but was also able to get on intimate terms with high officials in the Comittee of Union and Progress, who governed Turkey at the time through the triumvirate made up of Enver, Djemal, and Talaat – the War, Navy, and Interior ministers. The latter used to personally send telegrams to the interior of Anatolia and Arabia with secret orders to destroy the Armenian population. Scheubner-Richter's war reports to Constantinople and Berlin on the systematic campaign to exterminate the Armenians are today in the German Foreign Ministry archives. During the latter years of the war he participated in the German 8th Army's campaign against the Russians, in the course of which he was once more decorated with the Iron Cross (first class) just like his future idol Adolf Hitler. This campaign turned into an armed struggle against Leo Trotsky's Red Army, and against communist subversion in the German army. When the war ended, Bolshevism was threatening to destroy the very fabric of German society, and a series of events took place amounting to a genuine civil war, beginning with the suppression of the Spartakus movement in Berlin (January 1919), and ending with the overthrow of the Munich Soviet Republic (April-May 1919) by Reichswehr troops and "Freikorps" right-wing paramilitaries. These Spartacist-Communist uprisings were headed by revolutionaries who were frequently Jews. In fact many Bolsheviks, Mensheviks, and Social Revolutionaries in Russia had been Jews, and the same happened after the war in Germany, Poland, Hungary, and other central and eastern countries. In the Russian, German, and Hungarian civil wars, revolution implied the physical destruction of an entire social class – the bourgeoisie – and another – the aristocracy. As an example, the Commissar for Justice in Lenin's cabinet, Isaac Steinberg, asked Lenin if his title would not be more accurately expressed as "People's Commissar for Social Extermination," to which Lenin replied that indeed it would, but it could not be officially admitted. All this made a deep impression on the European middle classes at the time, channelling their fear of communism into a vulgar anti-semitism already in the air. Many Germans held the opinion that the Jews were behind all the woes they had to endure after Versailles, from the "stab in the back" which had supposedly brought about the collapse of their army, to economic exploitation and usury. What was remarkable was that in Turkey Scheubner-Richter had seen how a minority was blamed for every evil, and was then exterminated; his letters show his profound disagreement with this systematic policy of the Committee for Union and Progress, yet he shared the dislike for Jews and the desire for "ethnic cleansing."

In his reports Scheubner-Richter had mentioned Armenians as "the Jews of the East," "crafty merchants," "unscrupulous," etc., but was invariably opposed to the "final solution" of the Armenian question. He was unable to conciliate the idea of massacring defenseless women and children with the strategic necessity of removing potential subversives from the war scene. Scheubner-Richter arrived at the conviction that the left-wing Jews and their capitalist brethren (the so-called Golden International) intended to dominate the world and destroy his country. He ignored the fact that Russian Jews were natural anti-czarists, thanks to the pogroms they had suffered, and that they might also be inclined to persecute the bourgeois Jews who did not share their political views. Thus the head rabbi of Moscow declared: "The Trotskys carry out the revolution, and the Bronsteins have to pay for it." (Bronstein was Trotsky's real surname.) Scheubner-Richter had been captured in Riga by German communists in January 1919, while representing Reich interests there. The Bolsheviks wished to execute him in reprisal for the murder of Rosa Luxemburg and Karl Liebknecht (leaders of the Spartakus movement, both of Jewish extraction) in Berlin. He was taken four times before a firing-squad, and finally released on orders of the Russian People's Commissar for Foreign Affairs, Chicherin. The mass shootings of thousands of citizens in the Rumbula forests, on the outskirts of Riga, seem to have exacerbated his seething hatred of communism. Twenty-two years later, a good while before the Wannsee Conference sealed the doom of European Jewry, tens of thousands of Latvian Jews were to be murdered in the same forests by the SS, composed of Lettish soldiers and German officers. The intense hatred towards Jews which the white Russian exiles brought with them to Munich and Berlin encouraged resentment against this ancient nation in Germany. Scheubner-Richter was part of that exiled Russian society, and helped fuel antisemitic propaganda. His friend Alfred Rosenberg was a key factor in promoting the spurious "Protocols of the Elders of Zion," which purported to reveal a worldwide Jewish plan to dominate the planet. It was he who introduced his friend Max Erwin to Hitler in late 1920, and shortly thereafter both Scheubner-Richter and his wife joined the Nazi party. According to Georg Franz-Willing, it was Scheubner-Richter who exercised the most powerful influence on Hitler at a certain point at the beginning of the latter's political career. He and Rosenberg, besides Eckart, were the ones who determined Hitler's anti-Bolshevik and anti-Semitic bias, and from early 1923 on, managed the Nazi newspaper *Voelkischer Beobachter* pretty much as they pleased, to the extent that Hitler would jokingly refer to it as the "Baltischer Beobachter."

It remains a puzzle how a man with unquestionable humanitarian sentiments towards the Armenians, as evidenced both in this book and in his diplomatic reports, could have become a supporter of "ethnic cleansing" against the Jews. The scenes of cruelty Scheubner-Richter witnessed in Turkey, the Baltic countries, and in the struggles between Reds and Whites in Germany undoubtedly hardened him. The Russian Revolution had raised the hopes of many, and a wind of rebellion wafted throughout Europe. The old semi-feudal structures had proved their total inefficacy in the face of the millions of casualties the war had produced; and the conflict between new ideas, the reaction of the middle classes, and certain deep grudges, resulted in dangerous new political movements.

Scheubner-Richter sensed these influences keenly and felt drawn to a leader who was talking about a new Germany with a mixture of interesting though contradictory ideas, and possessing an extraordinary power of oratory that reached the ordinary man. Both Scheubner-Richter and his wife fell into the trap and forgot all about morality. They became the party's principal fund-raisers, and helped furnish Adolf the demagogue with a more "respectable" image. Their connections with the Russian and Bavarian royal houses, Marshal Ludendorff, the aristocracy in general, and powerful industrialists were essential in securing the money that made possible the party's amazing growth from 1920 on. Countess Mathilde and grand duchess Victoria Melita (granddaughter of Queen Victoria, former sister-in-law of Russian Tsarina Alexandra, and at that time the wife of

Grand Duke Kyril, the pretender to the Russian throne) were often seen together in Munich, watching the parades of SA troops. This helped make the Nazis fashionable among certain elegant circles in Bavaria.

Scheubner-Richter was also disgusted by the strategic alliance between Germany's socialist post-war government, rightwing officers and diplomats, and Soviet Russia. "National Bolshevism" was an idea espoused by General von Seeckt, officials Ago von Malzan and Walther Rathenau, under ex-Soviet envoy Karl Radek's influence. This made it possible for a "Black Reichswehr" to be equipped with poison gas, tanks, military aircraft, submarines, and an efficient body of officers, from Soviet Russia with love. However, the Nazi party's liaison with the Black Reichswehr happened to be Scheubner-Richter. If the occupation of the Ruhr by Belgium and France had led to a new war, the Nazi contingents in the Kampfbund and other paramilitary groups would have enrolled in this Black Army. Former Turkish war minister Enver Pasha, one of von Seeckt's proteges, was sent to Russia to organize this German-Soviet alliance, ending up in the secret clauses of the treaty of Rapallo, which challenged the limitations to the German armed forces imposed by the treaty of Versailles. Von Seeckt's other protege, Talaat Pasha, ex-Turkish interior minister, remained in Berlin, and was assassinated in March 1921 by Soghomon Tehlirian, an Armenian student. Scheubner-Richter should have testified in this trial, but for unknown reasons was not summoned. At this time he was able to organize the meeting of White Russians at Bad Reichenhall, where he once more failed in having Grand Duke Kyril declared official pretender to the Russian throne. When a Berlin jury acquitted Tehlirian in June 1921, Adolf Hitler was in the city. There is no way he could have been unaware of the Ottoman massacres of Armenians which led the jury to absolve Tehlirian. The headlines of every newspaper in the world carried the news about the extermination of the Armenians, on account of the unprecedented result of the trial: assassin acquitted, and victim condemned. The same lawyer that later coined the term "genocide" in 1944, Rafael Lemkin, was a law student in Lvov, Poland, when he read about this famous case, in which the killer was acquitted of murder after being caught in the act. He asked his law professor: "How can a whole race be murdered and no one punished for it?" His teacher answered: "How can you stop a farmer killing his chickens? The key word is SOVEREIGNTY." Since then society has changed and human rights are protected – in theory. But in practical terms this has not been very effective, and just a few years ago 800,000 Rwandan Tutsis were massacred in only three months, and at present thousands are dying in Darfur. The UNO has not proved to be a very effective institution, and we are still searching for ways for human rights to be respected, and efficient means to prevent petty dictators from destroying parts of their own populations.

Without doubt Hitler knew what had happened to the Armenians and, according to historian Marlis Steinert, his friend and confidant Scheubner-Richter was one of his best sources of information as to how a war situation could be used to destroy detested minorities with impunity. According to another historian, Ian Kershaw, "If the bullet that killed Scheubner-Richter had hit a foot to the right, the whole course of history would have been different." He was referring to the November 1923 "putsch", planned by Scheubner-Richter and a handful of others at the former's Wiedermaierstrasse apartment in Munich. When the march to the Feldherrnhalle began, Scheubner-Richter mentioned to Hitler his premonition that he would end up badly. Hitler linked arms with Scheubner-Richter on his left, and Marshal Ludendorff on his right; and when his friend received the fatal shot in his chest and fell, Hitler was dragged to the ground, dislocating a shoulder, but was saved from the ensuing volley of shots. The conspirators had neglected putting in practice one of Scheubner-Richter's maxims: "In order to be successful, the nationalist revolution should not come before the acquisition of political power, in which control of the police is the prerequisite for the national revolution."

Every book on the 1923 "putsch" contains abundant material about Scheubner-Richter's substantial participation in this fiasco. In October he had told his Führer: "In order to keep the men together we must do something, otherwise they'll become left-wing radicals." 1923 had been a traumatic year, with the Franco-Belgian occupation of the Ruhr, the dollar at trillions of marcs, uncontrollable inflation that brought about the destruction of the economy and of morality; and finally, in October, with a failed communist rebellion in Hamburg. Something had to be done, and the answer was the "putsch." It was to be Scheubner-Richter's last failure. His death was "a tragedy, but to face it is the life of a German officer," said his wife Mathilde, which suggests a fairly cold personality, if the story is true. (It was reported by Scheubner-Richter's butler, Aigner.)

The Fuehrer showed great fondness for Mathilde, who visited him during his imprisonment at Landsberg am Lech. During World War II Hitler saw to it that, when his friend's widow died, she should be buried at her husband's side in the mausoleums the Nazis built in Munich when they came to power. She died eight years after the end of the war, in an old people's home; however Scheubner-Richter's sarcophagus, together with the other fifteen dead of November 9th, was placed in one of the two Greek-style "Temples of Honour" at the Munich Königsplatz, in 1935. After coming to power, every year Hitler would lead a solemn procession from the Bürgerbräukeller to the Feldherrnhalle. On arriving there, a guard of honour would shoot a salvo of 16 shots into the air, and a band played "I had a comrade." Following this those present would remain in silence while Hitler placed a wreath on the altar, in honour of the sixteen fallen "martyrs," to whom he had dedicated the first volume of *Mein Kampf* eleven years earlier. At the "Temples of Honour" at the Königsplatz, Gauleiter Wagner would call out each martyr's name, and once more Hitler would place flowers in each temple "to decorate his comrades with the garlands of immortality." These "Temples of Honour" were destroyed by the Allies in 1947. But the damage had already been done. According to Hitler, the only irreplaceable one had been Scheubner-Richter. On August 22nd, 1939, in the Obersalzberg, Adolf Hitler declared to his assembled officers (including Admiral Canaris, Paul Leverkuehn's chief in military intelligence): "I have ordered my Death-head units to exterminate without mercy men, women, and children of the Polish race. Only in this way shall we be able to acquire the living space we need. After all, who today remembers the extermination of the Armenians?"

Historical Introduction

Max Erwin Von Scheubner-Richter and the Armenian Genocide[1]

by Hilmar Kaiser

For the past fifteen years, the policies of the Imperial German government during the Armenian Genocide have stood at the center of a lively debate. Reviving a much older debate, two scholars have suggested that Germans had participated in the crime. In his monographic study Artem Ohandjanian claimed that Germany had had full control over its genocidal Ottoman ally. Perhaps more importantly, Ohandjanian presented some Austro-Hungarian documents and concluded that Germany had more or less suggested the persecution of Armenians to the Ottoman government.[2] Christoph Dinkel followed Ohandjanian's line of reasoning and added further information from miscellaneous German sources. Dinkel summed his views up as follows:

> It is certain, however, that the measures against the Armenians (including the deportation) in the 3rd Army's region (beginning May 1915) were not a purely Turkish "solution" but were proposed and demanded by this circle of German officers. The same is probably true for the region under the 4th Army. ... The outcome of this counsel, that is, the measures against the Armenians which led to the Genocide, may thus be reduced to an "exertion of influence" by the German side. German officers proposed the deportations and also played a large role in ensuring that they were carried out against other German opposition.[3]

1   Material included in the present contribution appeared first in a case study focusing on the Armenians of Erzerum. Hilmar Kaiser, "A Scene from the Inferno.' The Armenians of Erzerum and the Genocide, 1915-1916," in *Der Völkermord an den Armeniern und die Shoah / The Armenian Genocide and the Shoah,* edited by Hans-Lukas Kieser and Dominik Schaller, Zürich, Chronos Verlag, 2002, pp. 129-186.

2   Artem Ohandjanian, *Armenien. Der Verschwiegene Völkermord,* Wien, Böhlau, 1989, p. 221.

While Dinkel based his argument largely on conclusions derived from fragmentary circumstantial evidence, he carefully worded his assessment of the German position. His reference to German opposition to the Armenian Genocide reflected earlier findings by Ulrich Trumpener and Wolf-Dieter Bihl. In their monographic studies, these two authors had offered more comprehensive assessments of the German and Austro-Hungarian policies vis-à-vis the Armenian Genocide while not directly focusing on the crime.[4] Analyzing several areas of German-Ottoman political relations Trumpener concluded:

> During most of the war period, specifically until the spring of 1918, the majority of the Turkish leaders, and Enver in particular, were prepared to collaborate closely with the Reich in the military conduct of the war, but they vigorously and, on the whole, effectively resisted all German attempts to meddle in the internal affairs of the Ottoman empire.

Ohandjanian's and especially Dinkel's studies provided a point of departure for Vahakn Dadrian.[5] In a series of publications, most notably in a monographic essay, the author asserted that the German involvement in the Armenian Genocide was much larger than other authors had thought. Dadrian argued that high-ranking German diplomats, politicians, and military officers in Berlin, Constantinople, and at their posts in Ottoman provincial towns had played a critical part in the planning and execution of the crime.[6] While referring to a substantial body of archival resources, the author took some license with the extant archival record.[7]

Hilmar Kaiser re-examined the earlier findings of Ohandjanian, Dinkel, and Dadrian. For instance, the files of the Baghdad Railway company provided detailed evidence not only on the company's policies toward Armenians but also on those of the German civil and military authorities. It appeared that no unified German policy existed at high levels. On the

---

3   Christoph Dinkel, "German Officers and the Armenian Genocide" in *Armenian Review* 44/1 (1991), p. 120.

4   Ulrich Trumpener, *Germany and the Ottoman Empire 1914-1918*, Princeton, N. J., Princeton University Press, 1968 Reprint: Delmar, N.Y., Caravan Books, 1989; Wolf-Dieter Bihl, *Die Kaukasus-Politik der Mittelmächte, Teil 1: Ihre Basis in der Orient-Politik und ihre Aktionen 1914-1917*, (Veröffentlichungen der Kommission für Neuere Geschichte Österreichs, 61), Vienna, Böhlau, 1975.

5   Vahakn N. Dadrian, *German Responsibility in the Armenian Genocide. A Review of the Historical Evidence of German Complicity*, foreword by Roger W. Smith, Watertown, MA, Blue Crane Books, 1996.

contrary, leading German diplomats, business men, and military officers were pursuing often antagonistic strategies.[8] In another case study, a German officer could be linked to the killing of Armenians at Urfa. Thus, for the first time, a German officer in Ottoman services had been directly implicated.[9] The officer was, however, punished for his role at Urfa by the German General Staff. More importantly, reviewing German decision making at top government levels, Kaiser published for the first time German chancellor's Theobald Von Bethmann Hollweg's authoritative decision on the Armenian Genocide and explained its importance.

6   Ibid., p. 186 "What stands out in that evidence is a central feature of German complicity, namely, the willingness of a number of German officials, civilian and military, to aid and abet the Turks in their drive to liquidate the Armenians. They thus qualify to be regarded as co-perpetrators and "accessories to the crime," the bearers of the onus of what the Germans call "*mitschuld*" (i.e., complicity). Subsumed in this general category of inculpation are those German officers who actually signed deportation orders and as such are in fact co-perpetrators; additionally to be considered are, however, the two major variants depicting the twin modalities of German involvement. One is described as "suggestion" (*anregung*); the involvement here is active as the actor is seen taking the initiative to sensitize or incite the Turks against the Armenians. The other is in the form of consent (*zusage*); the actor is in a passive role as he merely is responding, albeit positively, to the scheme presented to him by the Turks. This notwithstanding, the difference is such as to subside into insignificance, if not irrelevance, when one considers the oneness of the consequence resulting from the underlying indistinguishability of both types of roles, namely, the role of unscrupulous abettor in the Turkish enactment of the genocide against the Armenians."

7   Hilmar Kaiser, "Germany and the Armenian Genocide, A Review Essay," in *Journal of the Society for Armenian Studies* 8 (1995 [1997]) pp. 127-142; Hilmar Kaiser, "Germany and the Armenian Genocide, Part II: Reply to Vahakn N. Dadrian's Response," Ibid., 9 (1996, 1997 [1999]) p. 137. The latter text as well as the accompanying erratum was manipulated by the journal's editor, Dennis Papazian.

8   Hilmar Kaiser, "The Baghdad Railway and the Armenian Genocide, 1915-1916: A Case Study in German Resistance and Complicity," in Richard G. Hovannisian, ed., *Remembrance and Denial: The Case of the Armenian Genocide*, Detroit, Wayne State University Press, 1999 pp. 67-112.

9   Eberhard Wolffskeel von Reichenberg, *Zeitoun, Mousa Dagh, Ourfa, Letters on the Armenian Genocide*, edited and introduced by Hilmar Kaiser, 2nd ed. Princeton, NJ- London: Gomidas Institute, 2004.

"Our sole object is to keep Turkey on our side until the end of the war, no matter if Armenians perish or not. In the face of a longer continuing war we will still need the Turks very much."[10]

The present discussion continues this series of case studies on the German role during the Armenian Genocide.[11] It focuses on the role of Max Erwin Von Scheubner-Richter, a German from the Russian Baltic provinces, formerly serving as an officer in the Bavarian army and on duty in the Ottoman Empire from 1914 to 1916. Scheubner's activities in the Ottoman Empire can be divided into two distinct phases. First, he served as German Vice-Consul at Erzerum. Later he passed through some of the Armenian killing fields of the eastern provinces and into Persia.[12] One episode of Scheubner's service has attracted special attention within debates concerning the German role in the Armenian Genocide. When Scheubner's detachment was asked to join an effort to suppress a local Christian effort at self-defense, he declined. The matter was referred to the Ottoman Minister of War and de-facto Ottoman Supreme Commander Enver Pasha, and German General Colmar von der Goltz, and thus gained some importance. While Johannes Lepsius followed Scheubner's own reasoning and presented the case as an Ottoman attempt to compromise German armed forces, Dadrian who incorrectly claimed that a massacre had taken place, saw the episode as a proof for Goltz' complicity in the Armenian Genocide. Recently, Carl Alexander von Krethlow also asserted

10 Auswärtiges Amt – Politisches Archiv, Berlin, (hereafter: AA-PA) Türkei 183/40, A 36184, Metternich to Bethmann Hollweg, Pera, Dec. 7, 1915 No 711; Bethmann Hollweg, Berlin, Dec. 17, 1915; Türkei 183/40, A 36591, Metternich to AA, Pera, Dec. 18, 1915 telegram 2990; Hilmar Kaiser, "Le génocide arménien: négation 'à l'allemande'" in *L'actualité du Génocide des Arméniens. Actes du colloque organisé par le Comité de Défense de la Cause Arménienne*, Paris, Edipol, 1999, pp. 75-91.

11 Other aspects of German policies concerning Armenians were discussed in Harry Stürmer, *Two War Years in Constantinople. Sketches of German and Young Turkish Ethics and Politics*, revised and complete edition with annotations and an introduction by Hilmar Kaiser, London, Sterndale Classics, 2004; *Imperialism, Racism, and Development Theories. The Construction of a Dominant Paradigm on Ottoman Armenians*, Ann Arbor, MI, Gomidas Institute, 1997. Hilmar Kaiser (in collaboration with Luther and Nancy Eskijian), *At the Crossroads of Der Zor. Death, Survival, and Humanitarian Resistance in Aleppo, 1915 – 1917*, Princeton, NJ: Gomidas Institute, 2001.

12 Bihl summarized this effort first. Vol. 1 pp. 70-72.

that a massacre had taken place and proposed a new interpretation of Goltz' actions in regard to Ottoman Armenians.[13] This study will also take a closer look at Goltz's policies towards the besieged Christians at Hazik and Armenians in Mosul.

In sum, the material introduced here adds substantially to Paul Leverkuehn's earlier account of Scheubner's Iranian Raid.[14] Based on the same sources Leverkuehn, the military expedition into Persia will put into a proper context while correcting a series of Leverkuehn's misrepresentatons and errors. This expedition was, in fact, not a critical venture that determined events in that theatre of war but simply an episode and the fringes of a side-show.

I. German Plans and Failures to Revolutionize Trans-Caucasia.

At the beginning of World War 1, the Russian-Ottoman border region was of prime importance for German plans to weaken the Russian enemy in the Caucasus. Since the Ottoman Empire had not yet declared war or formally attacked Russia, German schemes focused on sending small groups of men into Russian territory with the goal of destroying Russian transport facilities and industrial installations. More ambitions projects were pursued by German agents who had been sent to Trebizond in order to organize a rebellion among Georgians in Trans-Caucasia. These projects were rather improvised and suffered from a lack of coordination with Ottoman operatives. The German agents also created concerns among local Ottoman agents. The latter not only lacked necessary information on German plans but also feared being compromised by German agents in an area that was under the scrutiny of Russian agents.[15]

---

13 Carl Alexander von Krethlow, "Colmar Freiherr von der Goltz und der Genozid an den Armeniern 1915-1916," in *Sozial.Geschichte* N. F. 21 (2006), p. 51.

14 Paul Leverkuehn, *Posten auf ewiger Wache. Aus dem abenteuerlichen Leben des Max von Scheubner-Richter,* Essen, Essener Verlagsanstalt, 1938. A recent article by Mike Joseph does not provide new insights and ignores a substantial part of the available published record. More critically, Joseph blurs the distinction between the historical record and his own imagination, disqualifying his work. Mike Joseph, "Max Erwin von Scheubner-Richter: The Personal Link from Genocide to Hitler," in Hans-Lukas Kieser, Elmar Plozza, eds., *Der Völkermord an den Armeniern, die Türkei und Europa. The Armenian Genocide, Turkey and Europe,* Zürich, Chronos, 2006, pp. 147-165.

For the Germans the city of Erzerum, strategically located and a main base for the Ottoman 3rd Army, was to become a second base for their cross-border operations, specifically for missions into Iran and against Baku. A German vice-consulate existed at Erzerum since September 1913. Unlike other German consulates, it had been explicitly established as a political observation outpost.[16] By that time, renewed international importance of the Armenian Question made a German representation in core areas covered by the Armenian reform scheme desirable. Edgar Anders, the German consular official, was particularly suited for the position. He was trained as an interpreter for Russian, French, and Turkish languages, and had served before at an important location in Cilicia. [17] Germany being a latecomer on the scene, Anders had to create a German intelligence network covering the whole region.[18] The process was still under way when World War I broke out in Europe. The war caught Anders by surprise in Tiflis on what was described as a "vacation." He was arrested, leaving his post vacant at a critical moment. With the disappearance of Anders, the German authorities had lost their only means of secret communication with the area. As an ally of the Ottoman Empire, the German diplomatic and consular service enjoyed the privilege of secret communication through coded telegrams and German military couriers, while German officers serving in the Ottoman army did not enjoy the same privilege.

With the pending attack on Russia, naming a new consul became an urgent matter complicated by the fact that the German Foreign Office was short of staff. At this juncture, an Austrian scholar, Dr. Victor Pietschmann, who had just returned from the area, appeared in Berlin and

---

15   In his memoirs, Arif Cemil [Denker] described in detail the operations of the Special Organization in this region. Arif Cemil [Denker], *I. Dünya Savaşı'nda Teşkilâtı Mahsusa*, Istanbul, Arba Yayınları, 1997. For the German activities see Bihl, vol.1.

16   AA-PA, Deutsche Konsulate Türkei, No 57, Konsulate, Erserum, Bd. 1, Ic 13840, Neurath to Bethmann Hollweg, Pera, Dec. 17, 1915 No. 11141. Türkei 183/29, A 7713, Wangenheim to Bethmann Hollweg, Pera, Apr. 12, 1913, No 106.

17   Edgar Anders, 1874 in Breslau (Wroclaw) – 1942 Freiburg i.B., had studied in Heidelberg. He worked for some time at the German Consulate-General Constantinople and for the German Consulate in Adana.

18   AA-PA, Türkei 183/35, A 13845, Mutius to Bethmann Hollweg, Therapia, July 10, 1914 No 186. Türkei 183/36, A 16307, Wangenheim to Bethmann Hollweg, Therapia, July 24, 1914 No 195.

submitted a memorandum offering his services. Pietschmann drew a simplistic picture of the political situation in the Ottoman eastern provinces. He claimed that wScheubner-Richterhile Kurds and Turks were inclined to be friendly towards Germany and its war effort, the opposite case applied to Armenians and Greeks.[19] Pietschmann was soon interviewed by another Austrian, Dr. Paul Schwarz who was a specialist on oil industries and had been entrusted with an attack on Baku.[20] Schwarz prepared a new memorandum that was based on some additional interviews but followed Pietschmann's outline.[21] While the outcome remained a mixture of generalities and even blatantly false gossip, it had some impact. Schwarz suggested transferring his basis for the attack from Constantinople to Erzerum. The German Foreign Office agreed and assigned Schwarz to the position of German consul at Erzerum. Soon Schwarz left for Constantinople where he arrived on November 5, 1914, continuing to Erzerum on Nov. 11, 1914.[22] At Erzerum, Schwarz recruited agents who were sent out to destroy the Baku-Batum pipeline.[23]

Incoming news from the Caucasus was promising. The German embassy at Constantinople estimated that the number of rebels had increased to 50,000 armed men and an electric plant at Batum had been destroyed. In view of this positive news, Enver believed that the time for an Ottoman

19 Universität Halle, Lepsius-Archiv, 90-1049, Pietschmann, Constantinople, Oct. 19, 1914. The text has also been reproduced in Hans-Lukas Kieser, *Der verpasste Friede. Mission, Ethnie und Staat in den Ostprovinzen der Türkei 1839-1938*, Zürich, Chronos Verlag, 2000 pp. 557-561. See also Bihl, vol. 1 pp. 65-66.

20 Paul Schwarz was an Austro-Hungarian subject. He had studied in Brünn, Leipzig, Berlin, and Breslau. In 1903 he defended his PhD thesis and became an oil expert. After his stay in Erzerum Schwarz joined German intelligence and stayed in German government employment for the coming decades. AA-PA, Personalakte Paul Schwarz. Weltkrieg 11d secr./5, A 14332, Wangenheim to Bethmann Hollweg, Pera, April 20, 1915 No. 246.

21 AA-PA, Weltkrieg 11d secr./1, A 28182, Paul Schwarz, "The present situation in Turkish Armenia" [Constantinople ?], 1914. The precise date of the memorandum is unknown but it must have been drafted between October 20 and 25, 1914.

22 AA-PA, Weltkrieg 11d secr./2, AS 2500, Wangenheim to AA, Therapia, Nov. 5, 1914 telegram 1241; AS 2583, Wangenheim to AA, Therapia, Nov. 11, 1914 telegram 1323; AS 2794, Schwarz to AA, Erzerum, Nov. 29,1914 telegram.

23 AA-PA, Weltkrieg 11d secr./2, A 34459, Wangenheim to AA, Pera, Dec. 11, 1914 telegram 1586.

attack had come. He left for the eastern front to direct operations together with his chief of staff, Bronsart von Schellendorf.[24]

In Germany, recruitment for the Caucasian operations had started as well. On November 8, 1914, Max Erwin von Scheubner-Richter reported at the AA and was appointed as Schwarz' consular secretary.[25] Scheubner reached Erzerum on December 19, 1914, where he learned about his assignment to destroy the Baku oil industry.[26] The next day, however, he took over the administration of the consulate as Schwarz joined the Ottoman 3rd Army's attack on the Russian lines the following day. Arguing that his position as secretary was not conducive for his task, Scheubner requested his appointment as a Vice-Consul. What appeared at the time as a temporary measure was to become in Scheubner's mind a long-term arrangement. He intended to take over the Erzerum post as Vice-Consul for the duration of the war. Meanwhile and without consulting the embassy at Constantinople, he already had labelled himself attaché.[27] His request was granted thereby establishing a pattern through which Scheubner repeatedly sought promotion and, if possible, independence from supervision.

At the time of Scheubner's request, rumors of a devastating Ottoman defeat had reached Berlin. The Ottoman authorities were still trying to keep the German embassy at Constantinople in the dark.[28] But within days, the extent of the disaster became apparent and with it the failure of

---

24 AA-PA, Weltkrieg 11d secr./ 2, A 33710, Wangenheim to AA, Pera, Dec. 6, 1914 telegram 1542.

25 AA-PA, Weltkrieg 11d secr./4, AS 2520. Wesendonk, Berlin, Nov. 8, 1914 and marginalia idem, Ibid. Nov. 9, 1914. Konstantinopel 943, J. No. 5446, Matthieu to Scheubner-Richter, Berlin, Nov. 10, 1914 No. Ic 15546/87852 (copy) enclosure in Matthieu to Wangenheim, Berlin, Nov. 10, 1914.

26 AA-PA, Ic Deutsche Konsulate No. 57 Erzerum, A 35620, Schwarz to AA, Erzerum, Dec. 20, 1914. Weltkrieg 11d secr./5, A 13936, Scheubner-Richter to Wangenheim, Erserum, Mar. 6, 1915 copy enclosure in Wangenheim to Bethmann Hollweg, Pera, Apr. 17, 1915 No. 240.

27 AA-PA, Konstantinopel 943, J. No. 174 , Scheubner to Wangenheim, Erzerum, Jan. 7, 1915 telegram. Scheubner argued that the position as a secretary was also inadequate with regard to his "social position." Weltkrieg 11d secr./3, A 955, Wangenheim to AA, Pera, Jan. 8, 1915 telegram 73. Konstantinopel 944, J. No. 9654, Scheubner to Wangenheim, Near Bitlis, Oct. 14, 1915 No. 1. Schwarz later supported Scheubner's move, Konstantinopel 943, J. No. 280, Schwarz to Wangenheim, Erzerum, Jan. 12, 1915 telegram. See also: Ibid., J. No. 2423, Scheubner Richter to Wangenheim, Erzerum, Mar. 6, 1915.

the German plans for Trans-Caucasia. Schwarz returned on January 10, 1915 to Erzerum in a deplorable state suffering from dysentery and a frost bitten right hand.[29] Given his poor state of health and the overall situation, his mission had become unlikely to succeed and Schwarz obtained the embassy's consent to return to Constantinople. For the time being, Schwarz and Scheubner concentrated on the care for wounded German officers and organized German propaganda efforts in the area.[30] It was decided Scheuber should take charge of the consulate until necessary reinforcements would arrive.[31] However, things turned out differently when the situation changed.

Following Schwarz' departure Scheubner took over affairs for good at the Erzerum consulate. For some time he promoted a plan to open a German school in Erzerum but failed due to Ottoman opposition. Bitterly, he complained about his low income as the absent Schwarz still received his full consular pay. Contacts with local officials turned out to be somewhat complicated as the latter did not drink alcohol, at least in his presence.[32]

A few weeks later, a certain Prince Emir Arslan Khan turned up at the consulate claiming to represent a Caucasian Muslim underground organization. Scheubner and Posseldt Pasha, a German officer who was in charge of the city's defenses, interviewed the man carefully. Arslan Khan told them that he could muster 500,000 armed men if Germany would

28 Bundes-Archiv, Abteilungen Freiburg, (hereafter: MA-Freiburg) W-10/50321, Wangenheim to AA, Jan. 8, 1915.
29 For Schwarz' account of the Sarikamish battle see AA-PA, Weltkrieg 11d secr./5, A 13937, Schwarz, Constantinople, Apr. 15, 1915 enclosure II in Wangenheim to Bethmann Hollweg, Pera, Apr. 17, 1915 No. 241.
30 AA-PA, Konstaninopel 943, J. No. 262, Schwarz to Wangenheim, Erzerum, Jan. 12, 1915 telegram. Weltkrieg 11d secr./8, A 28583, Scheubner Richter to Bethmann Hollweg, Erzerum, Aug. 7, 1915. The plan for the operations envisaged by Scheubner and the Austrian geographer Victor Pietschmann are found in Weltkrieg 11d secr./6, A 16890, Scheubner Richter to Wangenheim, Erzerum, May 1, 1915 J. No. 321 Secret Report No. 7, Pietschmann, Erzerum, Apr. 24, 1915 enclosed in Wangenheim to Bethmann Hollweg, Pera, May 19, 1915 No. 306.
31 AA-PA, Weltkrieg 11d secr./3, A 1717, Wangenheim to AA, Pera, Jan. 14, 1915 telegram 134; A 4506, Wangenheim to Bethmann Hollweg, Pera, Jan. 23, 1915 No. 513; Weltkrieg 11d secr./5, A 12936, Scheubner Richter to Wangenheim, Mar. 6, 1915 copy enclosed in Wangenheim to Bethmann Hollweg, Pera, Apr. 17, 1915 No. 240.
32 AA-PA, Konstantinopel 943, Scheubner to Müller, Erzerum, May 21, 1915 private.

meet certain political conditions. The news must have been most welcome to the Germans who anticipated a powerful Russian offensive following the Ottoman 3rd Army's catastrophic defeat.[33] As inquiries in Germany into Arslan's identity failed to produce any results, Berlin ordered further investigations in Erzerum.[34] Evidently, the German diplomats were interested.

The Ottoman authorities, for their part, were not idle in the matter either. On February 9, 1915, Tahsin Bey, the governor of Erzerum,[35] informed the Ministry of Interior that Arslan had arrived in Erzerum a week before. Immediately, he had established close contact with the German consulate. On February 9, 1915, Tahsin had met with Arslan who had told him the same he had said to Scheubner. As a reference he gave the name of Ahmed Ağaoğlu [or Agaeff], a leading CUP party member and ideologue, who had been a founding member of the organization in 1906.[36] The Ministry of Interior followed up on Arslan's claims and inquired with Ağaoğlu. The latter could only reply that the organization had been founded in 1906. After two years of its existence the Russian government had closed it down and he had no further information. He added that one of his former friends, a lawyer in Baku, was a member of the otherwise very large Choiski family from Elizebethpol. In case Arslan Khan was this man, he could be considered as absolutely trustworthy. There were, however, members of the family that sided with the Russians and were not trustworthy.[37] Tahsin believed Arslan's credentials and allowed him to move on to Van. Local governor Djevdet reacted precisely like the Erzerum governor before him and started his own inquiry but did not learn more than Tahsin.[38]

Now, Scheubner began developing new plans based on Arslan's information, hoping for a general Caucasian uprising.[39] According to the Vice-Consul, Arslan's proposals opened a promising avenue for the Baku project. Scheubner suggested a cavalry raid in connection with a Caucasian uprising; he himself was to become the liaison officer between the revolutionaries and the Ottoman 3rd Army's general-staff. For the new project, Scheubner requested two assistants, Paul and Karl Leverkuehn.

Being impatient, Scheubner wired that he had found a way to destroy the Baku oil industry and urged the immediate approval of his request for

33 AA-PA, Weltkrieg 11d secr./3, A 5011, Wangenheim to AA, Pera, Feb. 8, 1915 telegram 320.
34 AA-PA, Weltkrieg 11d secr./3, zu A 5011, Zimmermann to Wangenheim, Berlin, Feb. 13, 1915 telegram 279.

additionally staff. A somewhat excited Vice-Consul urged German Ambassador Hans Von Wangenheim not to wait for an incoming report but wire his consent right away.[40] Scheubner's telegram suggested recent and very dramatic developments at Erzerum. Given that Schwarz was on his way to Constantinople and would personally brief the embassy,

35 Hasan Tahsin [Uzer] was born as the son of an Ottoman officer in Saloniki in 1877. After attending school in Constantinople, he was admitted to the Ottoman administrative elite *Mülkiye* school. During his third year of studies he joined the oppositional underground "Committee of Union and Progress" as member No. 129. Soon, he began successfully organizing his classmates and founded a CUP cell in his school. The following years, Hasan Tahsin developed numerous activities, spreading CUP propaganda in the city. In 1897, Ottoman intelligence arrested Hasan Tahsin. Thus, at the age of 19, he had to leave the mülkiye and was assigned a post in a small Macedonian provincial village. He continued to serve in various Macedonian provincial positions until 1911. In 1913, Tahsin Bey became governor of Van and in 1914 of Erzerum. After Ottoman defeats and the Russian occupation of Erzerum, the government assigned Tahsin as governor of Syria in 1916. In 1918, after the Ottoman capitulation and although the CUP had fallen from power, the new government appointed him governor of Aidin. In 1919, he became a member of the Ottoman parliament for Smyrna. In 1920, however, the allies arrested Tahsin and deported him to Malta, where he wrote his memoirs. In 1921, he escaped and went to Angora where he joined the Kemalist movement. In 1924, he became deputy for Ardahan, for Erzerum in 1927, and Konia in 1933. In the aftermath of the Kurdish Sheikh Said Rebellion of 1925, Tahsin prepared a report on Muslim organizations among the Kurds. Tahsin Bey enjoyed a close friendship with the dictator Mustafa Kemal. In 1934, the latter assigned Tahsin Bey the new surname "Uzer." He died on December 3, 1939. Hayri Orhun, Celâl Kasaroğlu, Mehmet Belek, Kâzim Atakul, *Meşhur Valiler*, Ankara, Ajans-Türk Matbaacılık Sanayı, 1969 pp. 513-525; Tahsin [Uzer], *Makedonya Eşkıyalık Tarihi ve Son Osmanlı Yönetimi*, Ankara, Türk Tarih Kurumu, 1979, p. 3-23; Türkiye Büyük Millet Meclisi Vakfı, *Türk Parlamento Tarihi, I. Dönem*, vol. 3, Ankara, Türkiye Büyük Millet Meclisi Vakfı Yayınları, 1995 p. 517-518; Mehmet Bayrak, ed., *Açık-Gizli / Resmi – Gayrıresmi Kürdoloji Belgeleri*, Ankara, Özge Yayınları, 1994, p. 183-193. In his memoirs Tahsin Bey touches only briefly on his time as governor of Erzerum.

36 Başbakanlık Osmanlı Arşivi, Istanbul, *Dâhiliye Nezâreti Evrakı* (hereafter: DH), Emniyyet-î Umûmiyye Müdîriyyeti (hereafter: EUM), 2 Şube [hereafter: Şb], 5-41, Tahsin to Ministry of Interior, Erzerum, Feb. 9, 1915

Scheubner's urgency implied that Schwarz' information was already outdated.

In a follow up telegram Scheubner added that the Caucasian revolutionaries were urgently awaiting a reply. Even more importantly, strong contingents were waiting near the Russian border. Wangenheim, however, did not take the bait. He referred the matter to Berlin stressing that he had neither received any report, nor had Schwarz arrived.[41] Thus, Scheubner had failed to undermine Schwarz's standing. Soon, Wangenheim learned that the relations between consul and vice-consul had been strained for some time. Evidently, Scheubner's was trying to secure the command of future expeditions, while keeping Schwarz out of the loop.[42]

Schwarz reported on his failure to destroy the Baku oil industry. Still, he had sent out 16 agents who had twice disrupted the Batum-Baku pipeline. Little information was available on the other attacks but that was not surprising given the nature of these tasks. During the Sarikamish battle his men had blown up an important railway bridge. Plans to continue the work were, however, frustrated when Russian front lines became almost impenetrable. Schwarz complained that young Ottoman officers had obstructed his work so that he planned to continue work on Persian soil from now on. The Foreign Office, however, politely turned the offer down.[43]

---

37 DH.EUM.Kalem-i Hususi, 1-22, EUM to Ahmet Ağaoğlu, Constantinople, Feb. 17, 1915; Ahmed Ağaoğlu to EUM, Constantinople, Feb. 18, 1915. The information was swiftly telegraphed to Erzerum. EUM. 2 ŞB 5-41, Ministry to Erzerum province, Feb. 20, 1915 EUM. Ağaoğlu correctly assessed the importance of the Choiskys as the first prime minister of the Republic of Azerbajian belonged to this family. Aygül Attar, "Türk Dünyasının Bir Büyüğü: Feteli Han Hoyski," in *Askerî Tarih Bülteni 26*, (2001), 51 pp. 155-165.

38 DH.EUM. 2 Şb 5-41, Djevdet to EUM, Mar. 13, 1915, EUM to Djevdet Bey, Mar. 14, 1915.

39 AA-PA, Weltkrieg 11d secr./5, A 13936, Scheubner-Richter to Wangenheim, Erserum, Mar. 6, 1915 copy enclosure in Wangenheim to Bethmann Hollweg, Pera, Apr. 17, 1915 No. 240.

40 AA-PA, Weltkrieg 11d secr./4, A 10609, Wangenheim to AA, Pera, Mar. 24, 1915 telegram 724.

41 AA-PA, Weltkrieg 11d secr. / 5, A 12075, Wangenheim to AA, Pera, Apr. 6, 1915 telegram 827.

42 AA-PA, Weltkrieg 11d secr./5, A 14332, Wangenheim to Bethmann Hollweg, Pera, Apr. 20,1915 No. 246.

On March 19, 1915 Scheubner's report finally reached Constantinople, however, it contained no new information.[44] Most of it was based on Arslan's statements. Scheubner simply revived the known plans for an attack on Trans-Caucasia but suggested separating the operations from other German projects focusing in an area like Georgia. Meanwhile the estimated number of Muslim volunteers had dropped to 300,000 but that was still an impressive number. Nevertheless, Scheubner needed a whole Ottoman division of about 15,000 men at a time when the 3rd Army had major difficulties to man its lines. Scheubner played down the shortage of troops. He developed a grand scheme of new operations in Iran and Trans-Caucasia that would be more important than the Russian-Ottoman frontline. He believed that his somewhat surprising suggestion as the only way to destroy the Baku oil industry. Graciously, Scheubner offered to join the effort and expected Enver Pasha to bestow upon him "authority" to push through his views. In other words, Scheubner, Lieutenant of the Reserve, proposed to become commander of operations in northern Iran and western Trans-Caucasia. Some friends of his, among them Paul and Karl Leverkuehn, were to join his staff. Besides full authority, a personally hand picked staff, the only thing Scheubner needed was the final go ahead and information on the funds he could expend. Wangenheim did not even have to worry about a code name for the mission. Scheubner had shouldered this duty as well by naming the project "mountain expedition." The files do not reveal how Wangenheim felt when Scheubner asked him to pass on further reports to Liman [von Saunders] Pasha while acknowledging the receipt of the documents to Scheubner.

Wangenheim was less than enthusiastic about being turned into Scheubner's postman. The ambassador put his Vice-Consul back in place by reminding the latter that he had no right to submit "reports" on official business to third parties. Only parts of Scheubner's report were passed on to Liman while the German Foreign Office (hereafter: AA) received a copy of the whole document.

Liman had doubts about the accuracy of Arslan's information as far as numbers and weapons were concerned. He agreed, however, that an uprising would be useful. Given the bad shape the 3rd Army was in, liman refused to promise officers, troops, weapons or ammunition for the project.

---

43 AA-PA, Weltkrieg 11d secr./5, A 16649, Schwarz to Erzberger, n.p., n.d. enclosure in Erzberger to Rosenberg, Berlin, May 20, 1915.

44 AA-PA, Weltkrieg 11d secr./5, A 13113, Scheubner-Richter to Wangenheim, Erzerum, Mar. 19, 1915 No. 3 copy enclosure in Wangenheim to Bethmann Hollweg, Pera, Apr. 9, 1915 No. 220.

Scheubner had failed to convince Liman.[45] Meanwhile, Wangenheim had inquired with the embassy's military attaché and consented to the dispatch of the Leverkuehn brothers to Erzerum.[46] Other inquiries with Enver and von der Goltz pashas clarified the situation further. The ambassador learned that an uprising would fit into plans for Iran and the Ottoman government was willing to guarantee Caucasian independence. As some Ottoman troops were already operating in northwest Iran, the generals reasoned that Arslan's condition for military assistance was met as well. Thus, Scheubner was to join Ottoman forces under Halil Pasha and then join an expedition against Baku,[47] while other plans concerning Baku were given up.[48] In sum, the generals were not willing to commit additional troops. Some general political assurances had been given and demands appeared to have been met at minimal expense.

Meanwhile, Scheubner had made further plans. Now, he doubted the advisability of the Baku oil-industry's destruction. He argued the attack could jeopardize prospects for a Caucasian uprising. Accordingly, Pietschmann had given up his Baku-plans and was willing to join a Caucasian expedition under a German officer. In view of the shortage of available German officers, Scheubner knew that Pietschmann's condition strengthened his own claim for the command of the expedition. Scheubner suggested that he should serve in German uniform and would have ten German soldiers under his direct command. Once more the Leverkuehns ranged high on his wish list; particularly Paul Leverkuehn, who was

---

45 AA-PA, Weltkrieg 11d secr./5, A 13937, Liman von Sanders to Embassy, Gallipoli, Apr. 14, 1915 enclosure I copy in Wangenheim to Bethmann Hollweg, Pera, Apr. 17, 1915 No. 241.

46 AA-PA, Weltkrieg 11d secr./5, A 13936, Wangenheim to Bethmann Hollweg, Pera, Apr. 17, 1915 No. 240.

47 Halil was a young and ambitious Ottoman commander and uncle of Enver. His military qualifications were, however, somewhat controversial. General Falkenhayn considered him being useful as lieutenant of the reserves, but as a commander nothing more than an operetta figure. Wangenheim to AA, Konstantinpel, Apr. 30, 1915 A 14811 AA-PA, Weltkrieg 11d secr./5 telegram No. 1008. Bundesarchiv, Wien, Kriegsarchiv, Armee Oberkommando, Evidenzbüro Karton 3501.

   See also: Halil Kut, *İttihat ve Terakkî'den Cumhuriyet'e: Bitmeyen Savaş - Kütûlamare Kahramanı Halil Paşa'nın Anıları*, ed. by M. Taylan Sorgun, Istanbul, Yedi Gün Yayınları, 1972

48 AA-PA, Weltkrieg 11d secr./5, A 14918, Wangenheim to AA, Pera, May 1, 1915 telegram 1014.

qualified also for administrative tasks within the consular service. Scheubner did no longer see himself simply as a military commander. He informed Wangenheim that he needed instructions for political negotiations with Arslan. Ideally he would receive such instructions directly from the ambassador himself, by-passing all other officials. Clearly, Scheubner saw himself no longer as a subaltern reserve officer but as a diplomat.[49] Being attached to Halil's force was not what the ambitious German lieutenant had in mind.

Facing the harsh realities of the situation on the Ottoman eastern front, Arslan reduced his demands to a German guarantee and independence from other German projects in the Caucasus. The revised scheme was more to Wangenheim's liking, who now advised Berlin to act swiftly.[50] But it was too late, as Halil's troops had been defeated in Iran and the new expedition was put on hold.[51] By May 15, 1915, Scheubner's hopes were frustrated when he received orders to stay in Erzerum, until the new consul for Erzerum and German military liaison officer for the Caucasus, Fritz Werner Count von der Schulenburg, had reached the place.[52] Scheubner would be under his command.

Given Scheubner's low military rank, Wangenheim saw Scheubner's role only as that of a German liaison officer for the Caucasian revolutionaries and the Ottoman forces before joining the Baku expedition. The request for a sizeable group of volunteers was declined because the ambassador had doubts how the young men could be kept busy at Erzerum and, perhaps more importantly, kept watch over. The Leverkuehn brothers and a third man had to suffice as Scheubner would anyhow not be an expedition commander.[53] On June 11, 1915, the AA appointed Schulenburg as

---

49 AA-PA, Weltkrieg 11d secr./6, A 16890, Scheubner-Richter to Wangenheim, Erzerum, May 1, 1915 No. 7 inclosure I in Wangenheim to Bethmann Hollweg, Pera, May 19, 1915 No. 306.

50 AA-PA, Weltkrieg 11d secr./5, A 15206, Wangenheim an AA, Pera, May 5, 1915 telegram 1049.

51 AA-PA, Weltkrieg 11d secr./ 5, A 15753, Wangenheim to AA, Pera, May 11, 1915 telegram 1107.

52 AA-PA, Weltkrieg 11d secr./3, A 6856, Wangenheim to Bethmann Hollweg, Pera, Feb. 28, 1915 telegram 437; Weltkrieg 11 secr./5, A 15019, Nadolny to AA, Berlin, May 2, 1915 Abteilung IIIb Sektion Politik No. Pol. 1502; Weltkrieg 11d secr./5, A 16066, Wangenheim to AA, Constantinople, May 15, 1915 telegram 1139.

53 AA-PA, Weltkrieg 11d secr./6, A 16890, Wangenheim to Bethmann Hollweg, Pera, May 19, 1915 No. 306.

German consul for Erzerum. Schulenburg was to notify Scheubner that the latter's permission to call himself Vice-Consul had expired and he would be under the former's command.[54] Schulenburg left Constantinople for Erzerum on July 7, 1915 taking with him the requested political guarantees for Arslan and his organization.[55] Now, Scheubner's personal ambitions had reached a low point. But until Scheubner was replaced as vice-consul, his strong sense of independence had had some considerable impact on the local Armenian population.

II. The Armenian Genocide at Erzerum. From the Beginning of the European War to the Start of the Deportations

While the Germans were busily scheming against the Russian Caucasus, their Ottoman ally did not remain idle. At the end of August, the general secretary of the ruling Committee of Union and Progress (CUP), Midhat Şükrü [Bleda], informed the governor of Erzerum of an Ottoman plan to attack Russia by the end of August 1914.[56] By that time Talaat Bey, the Ottoman Minister of the Interior, had sent two of the most seasoned CUP executives, Bahaeddin Shakir[57] and Ömer Nadji,[58] to Erzerum. The two men headed a group of 20 trusted men. They were to organize Ottoman undercover operations against Russia, setting up the Teshkilât-ı Mahsusa ("Special Organization," hereafter: TM) in the region with local headquarters in Trebizond under Rıza Bey and Erzerum under Bahaeddin Shakir himself. Ömer Nadji moved on to Van to organize operations in Iran. He had already been active as a CUP militant in Iran before the war.[59]

By 1913, the "Special Organization" had received an elaborate administrative structure. Various departments specialized on intelligence gathering and illegal operations in those countries and areas where the Ottoman Empire had political interests. The organization consisted chiefly

54 AA-PA, Weltkrieg 11d secr./6, A 18729, Zimmermann to Wangenheim, Berlin, June 11, 1915 Ic 6710/78727 copy.

55 AA-PA, Weltkrieg 11d secr./6, A 21256, Wangenheim to Bethmann Hollweg, Pera, July 7, 1915 No. 432.

56 Osman Selim Kocahanoğlu, *İttihat-Terakki'nin Sorgulanması ve Yargılanması (1918-1919), Beşinci Şube Tahkikatı, Teşkilâtı Mahsusa, Ermeni Tehciri, Divan-ı Harb-i Örfi Muhakemâtı*, Istanbul, Temel Yayınları, [1998], p. 516.

57 An adequate study of Bahaeddin Shakir is still a desideratum. The recent publication by Çiçek provides some information but suffers from many gaps in documentation and analysis. Hikmet Çiçek, *Dr. Bahattin Şakir. İttihat ve Terakki'den Teşkilâtı Mahsusa'ya Bir Türk Jakobeni*, Istanbul, Kaynak Yayınları, 2004.

of clandestine units formed by irregulars. Kurdish and other tribesmen, various prisoners who had been pardoned and released from prisons for the organization's purpose, and other volunteers filled the ranks of the bands.[60] CUP activists, many of whom were army officers on leave from their original assignments, commanded local units. The TM and the CUP appear to have lacked their own communications network in the Erzerum area so that Bahaeddin Shakir communicated with the CUP's central committee at least in part through the governor of Erzerum.[61] The TM's tasks were broad. Marauders should destroy Russian civilian infrastructure and military installations, conduct plunder, and organize a rebellion among local Russian Muslims. The Ottoman government hoped to weaken Russian defences and prepare an Ottoman attack.

CUP and TM intelligence gathering on Russian and Ottoman Armenian communities also become increasingly important. Around the middle of August 1914, Bahaeddin Shakir and Ömer Nadji had approached prominent politicians of the Armenian Revolutionary Federation

---

58　At the time Ömer Nadji was about 36 years old. Having joined the Young Turk movement during his military education he had been persecuted by the old regime. Spending time in French exile and working for his organization in Iran, and clandestinely in the Van and Erzerum provinces, he rose within the party to the rank of a central committee member, a position he maintained after the revolution. He also gained prominence as a Turkist intellectual. In 1913 he participated in the assault of the Sublime Porte which firmly established a CUP dictatorship. Throughout his carreer he stayed close to CUP militant politics and operations in Iran. See Fethî Tevetoğlu, *Ömer Naci, Istanbul,* Istanbul, Bakanlık Kültür Müsteşarlığı, 1973. Tarık Zafer Tunaya, *Türkiye'de Siyasal Partiler,* vol. 3, Istanbul, Hürriyet Vakfı Yayınları, 1989 pp. 15, 229, 278, 425; M. Şükrü Hanioğlu, *Preparation for A Revolution. The Young Turks, 1902-1908,* New York, NY, Oxford University Press, 2001, pp. 116, 170, 208, 211-213, 216.

59　At least some of Nadji's correspondence went through the channels of the Ottoman Ministry of Interior. The central authorities informed the CUP operative on new instructions. DH, *Dâhiliye Şifre Kalemi* (Herafter: DH.ŞFR) 45-36 Minister to Van province, EUM Special No. 65 Sept. 19, 1914; Ibid. 45-46 Minister to Van Province, Spec. 71 Sept. 21, 1914. Nadji appears to have also engaged in counter-espionage. David Gaunt, *Massacres, Resistance, Protectors: Muslim-Christian Relations in Eastern Anatolia During World War 1,* Piscataway, NJ, Gorgias Press, 2006 pp. 131-32. See also: Sadık Sarısaman, "Ömer Naci Bey Müfrezesi," in *Ankara Üniversitesi Türk İnkilâp Tarihi Enstitüsü Dergisi* 8,16 (1995 [1997]), pp. 501. I m indebted to Dr. Mustafa Budak for this reference.

(Dashnaktzutiun, hereafter; ARF) at Erzerum. The ARF leaders had attended their party's 8th World Congress in Erzerum and had stayed behind as members of a committee charged with completing tasks connected with the congress. The CUP members inquired about the ARF's policy in case of war. While the ARF assured the CUP of its allegiance to the Ottoman Empire in case of a Russian attack, the Armenian politicians evaded comment when Bahaeddin Shakir and Nadji suggested that ARF members living in Russia should support an Ottoman attack on Russia or a rebellion behind Russian lines. The ARF's pledge to defend the country against aggression induced the CUP negotiators to reveal more of the CUP's plans. They detailed Ottoman war aims for a re-drawing of boundaries in the Aegean and the Balkans, as well as the creation of an "autonomous" Caucasus, dependent on the Ottoman Empire. In their response the ARF members declared that they had no authority to enter such an agreement and the negotiations ended.[62]

---

60   Arif Cemil, *I. Dünya Savaşı'nda*, pp. 27-32, 55. DH.ŞFR, 44-224 Minister to Van, Bitlis, Mosul, Erzerum, Diarbekir provinces, Sept. 12, 1915 EUM Spec. 33. After the armistice, British intelligence secured CUP correspondence detailing the role of local CUP leaders in recruiting local volunteers for the "Special Organization." On one occasion 113 criminals were released for the same purpose. Public Record Office, Kew Gardens, Foreign Office (hereafter: FO), 371/4142/83003, Webb to Curzon, Constantinople, May 19, 1919 No. 818/5032/39 (enclosure). İsmail Hacıfettahoğlu, *Sakarya Şehidi Binbaşı Hüseyin Avni Bey – Tirebolu Alparslan – Hayat_ – Eserleri*, Ankara, Atlas Yayınları, 1999, p. 23-24. Mustafa Balcıoğlu, "Teşkilatı Mahsusa Yahut Umur-u Şarkıye Dairesi," in idem, *Teşkilatı Mahsusa'dan Cumhuriyete*, Ankara 2001, p. 1-8. For the recruitment of Kurdish Alevi tribesmen by the CUP inspector of Erzerum, see Hilmi to Gül Ağa, Erzerum, Sept. 5, 1914 in Vatan Özgül, "İttihat Terakki ve Balaban Aşireti," in *Toplumsal Tarih* 16, 96 (2001) p. 38-42, here p. 42. Idem, *Dimoteka'dan Erzincan'a Bir Alevi Aşiret: Balabanlılar*, Istanbul, Pan Yayıncılık, 2005 p. 102; Taner Akçam misdated the document as Sept. 4, 1914. Taner Akçam, *Armenien und der Völkermord. Die Istanbuler Prozesse und die türkische Nationalbewegung*, Hamburg 1996, p. 56.

61   DH.ŞFR, 44-91 Minister to Erzerum Deputy Governor, Aug. 25, 1914 Special Office. In a cryptic message Midhat Shukru informed Bahaeddin Shakir that the situation had not changed and Talaat was still in Roumania. Two months later, Talaat asked Bahaeddin Shakir to proceed to Erzerum for further communications. DH.ŞFR, 47-187, Talaat to Erzerum Province, Oct. 26, 1914 EUM Spec. 77.

Bahaeddin Shakir and Nadji did not, however, give up. Now the TM organizers re-phrased their offer and approached provincial executives of the ARF. Ömer Nadji and the governor of Van, Tahsin Bey, approached Vahan Papazian, a leading ARF member and deputy for Van in the Ottoman Parliament. The move must have been coordinated with Talaat's moves in Constantinople, who approached ARF leaders in the capital. Talaat's meeting was acrimonious and according to an Armenian participant, Karekin Pastermadjian [also known as Armen Garo], threats were made.[63] In response, the ARF debated an acceleration of self-defence preparations for Armenian communities and cooperation with Russian forces in case the Ottoman government would commit massacres of Armenians.[64]

The ARF's cautionary approached seemed to be justified as anti-Armenian violence had already become a policy option for the CUP. Following the initial ARF's refusal to join an attack on Russia, Bahaeddin Shakir had improvised what might be called a "plan B." The Armenian answer that Armenians would serve the country where they were subjects and would not engage in subversive activities had not convinced the TM organizer. Bahaeddin Shakir suspected that the Armenians were helping Russia. Contacts of some local Armenians in Erzerum with the Russian consulate was proof enough for Bahaeddin Shakir. In response, he set up an improvised murder plot trying to eliminate those leading ARF members who were returning from Erzerum to Russia. The scheme, however, failed.[65] Despite all suspicions the Ottoman government knew that the Armenians were no immediate threat. On September 13, 1914, the 3rd Army had received intelligence that Russian agents had urged Ottoman

---

62 Dikran Mesrob Kaligian, "The Armenian Revolutionary Federation under Ottoman Constitutional Rule 1908-1914," Ph.D. Boston College 2003 pp. 345-347 quoting: Armenian Revolutionary Federation Archives, Watertown, MA, C 103-50 Eastern Bureau – Turkish Section Arshag Vramian to Western Bureau, Aug. 17, 1914. Ömer Nadji participated officially in the talks as the CUP's inspector for the Eastern Caucasus and Azerbaijan. Tunaya, *Siyasal Partiler*, vol. 3, p. 540.

63 Armen Garo, *Bank Ottoman. Memoirs of Armen Garo. The Armenian Ambassador to America from the Independent Republic of Armenia,* transl. by Haig T. Partizian, ed. with an introduction by Simon Vratzian, Detroit, Armenian Revolutionary Federation, 1990. The reference in Kaligian to the meeting is much less detailed. Kaligian, Ibid. p. 347 quoting Vahan Papazian, *My Memoirs* (in Armenian), vol. 2 Beirut, Hamazkain Press, 1952.

64 Kaligian, Ibid., p. 348-349.

Armenians not to rebel unless the Ottoman Empire would attack Russia.[66] Yet, this defensive Russian attitude had little impact on the shaping of Ottoman policies. The CUP and government's views had already been firmly set.[67]

To ensure control over the situation the CUP was determined to gain full control over local government. On September 14, 1915, the Ministry of Interior transferred an official of the Directorate for the Settlements of Tribes and Immigrants from Sivas to Erzerum. The central authorities did not specify the reasons for the transfer but simply ordered the provincial authorities to place the official in some public office. This way, an expert for settlement and population movements was inserted into the local administration. Whether he had further unknown assignments remains unclear.[68] Talaat was particularly concerned that leading local policemen

---

65 Arif Cemil, *I. Dünya Savaşı'nda*, pp. 46-47. See also Taner Akçam, *From Empire to Republic. Turkish Nationalism and the Armenian Genocide*, London-New York, Zed Books, 2004 p. 164. Zarevand (Zaven and Vartouhie Nalbandian), *United and Independent Turania. Aims and Designs of the Turks*. Translated from the Armenian by Vahakn N. Dadrian, Leiden, E. J. Brill, 1971 pp. 86-89 (originally published Boston 1926 in Armenian). Arthur Beylerian, *Les Grandes Puissances, l'Empire Ottoman et les Arméniens dans les archives françaises (1914 - 1918). Recueil de documents*. Préface de Jean-Baptiste Duroselle, Paris, Publ. de la Sorbonne, 1983 p. xxv (Publications de la Sorbonne, Série «Documents» - 34. The Tiflis based newspaper *Horizon* (issue 143, 1916) reported on June 29, 1916 on the advances.

66 Mehmet Nuri, Erzerum, Sept. 13, 1914 enclosure in Deputy Governor of Erzerum to 3rd Army Headquarter, Erzerum Sept. 13, 1914 in Genel Kurmay Başkanlığı, *Arşiv Belgeleriyle Ermeni Faaliyetleri 1914-1918*, 2 vols. Ankara, Genelkurmay Basım Evi, 2005 pp. 27-33. A few days later, the 3rd Army instructed all units to remove Armenians from important positions while Armenian soldiers were to be disarmed and removed from combat units. Morever local Muslim leaders were to be alerted on the situation. Civil auhorities were instructed to organize local Muslim militias. 3rd Army to all units, Sept. 19, 1914 in *Documents*, [Ankara]; Prime Ministry, Directorate General of Press and Information, n.d., Document No. 1 pp. 1-3. The book is a translation of *Askeri Tarih Belgeleri Dergisi* 81 (1982); Ottoman Supreme Army High Command, Sept. 1914 [post Sept. 24, 1914] in *Askeri Tarih Belgeleri Dergisi* 83 (1983) document 1894, pp. 7-8;.

67 DH.ŞFR, 44-43 Minister to provinces, Aug, 18, 1914 EUM.

68 DH.ŞFR, 45-5 Ministry to Erzerum Province, Sept. 14, 1914 Personnel Office Gen 13282 Spec. 36.

at Erzerum were Armenians. He had already written to Ismail Canbolat Bey at the Ministry of Interior's Directorate for Public Security on the matter proposing the removal the Armenian officials.[69] The request made sense as Talaat had ordered the surveillance of Armenian party leaders on September 6, 1914.[70] On September 28, 1915, Talaat urged provincial authorities to closely watch Armenian activities expressing concerns about possible espionage and other Armenian subversive activities in case of a war with Russia.[71] On October 10, 1914, the orders were reiterated, emphasizing that no expressions of and communications concerning Armenian nationalism should be allowed.[72]

The TM's actions against Armenians became increasingly violent as TM leaders continued recruiting powerful Kurdish tribesmen.[73] The existent Kurdish auxiliary cavalry had already come under the direct command of the 3rd Army by the middle of August.[74] Entrusting Kurdish irregulars paved the way to outrages. Soon, members of the TM began committing atrocities against Armenian villagers. Since most Armenian men in these villages had been drafted into the army, their families were at the mercy of the Kurdish guards the Ottoman government had sent to their villages. Since many of the guards were released convicts, they could hardly be expected to protect Armenian families.[75]

Following the Ottoman attack on Russian Black Sea ports, the Ottoman Empire declared a "Holy War" in November 1914 adding a religious element to the complicated situation. Armenians were Christians, like the Russians, and it was a small step for some people to identify Armenians with the enemy. On December 1, 1914, irregulars shot a priest in broad daylight. In some villages, irregulars extorted money from Armenians; in another village they killed ten Armenian peasants. At Erzerum, Schwarz

69 Arif Cemil, *I. Dünya Savaşı'nda,* p. 48.
70 DH.ŞFR, 44-200 Talaat to provinces, Sept. 6, 1914 EUM Chief Office Gen. 28 See also Uğur Ü. Üngör, "'A Reign of Terror.' CUP Rule in Diyarbekir Province, 1913-1923," MA Thesis University of Amsterdam 2005 p. 35.
71 DH.ŞFR, 45-115 Talaat to Van, Bitlis, Harput, Adana, Diarbekir, Sivas provinces, Sept. 28, 1914 EUM.
72 DH.ŞFR, 45-237, Minister to Erzerum province, Oct. 10, 1914 EUM DH.ŞFR, 45-237.
73 Özgül, *İttihat Terakki,* p. 42.
74 DH.ŞFR, 44-24 Minister to Van province, Aug. 15, 1914 Directorate of the Immigrants and Tribes Commission 1st Department.
75 AA-PA, Konstantinopel 168, J. No. zu 3610, Mordtmann, Pera, Dec. 25, 1915.

learned of these crimes from Armenian notables.[76] Armenian trust in the Ottoman police must have suffered when Talaat ordered on December 26, 1914 the removal of all remaining Armenian policemen from service.[77]

The Armenian notables' representations to Schwarz was part of a wider Armenian initiative. Following up on earlier German promises to protect Armenian rights, the Patriarchate at Constantinople kept Wangenheim informed of events. In response, the diplomat approached the Sublime Porte and urged the Ottoman authorities to take precautions against future outrages. Grand Vizier Said Halim Pasha brushed away these concerns, reiterating Ottoman suspicions and accusations against Armenians who were partly responsible for the incidents as Russian and Bulgarian Armenians had joined the Russian forces while others were suspected of having facilitated the Russian advance on Ottoman territory. Thus, although not denying such crimes, the Ottoman statesmen belittled the murder of Ottoman citizens by Ottoman troops as an understandable reaction.[78] Armen Garo was especially blamed. The latter had disobeyed the orders of his organization and joined the Armenian volunteers who fought alongside Russian troops. Meanwhile, the situation in Armenian villages deteriorated further. During the Sarikamish battle Schwarz had personally observed the plundering and massacre of Armenian civilians by Ottoman irregulars.[79] In January 1915, Armenian villages in the Tortum valley became the scene of further outrages, while two Catholic Armenian priests were arrested and kept for weeks in prison.[80] About 30,000 Armenian villagers from areas near the Russian border did not wait for further trouble and moved for their own safety behind the Russian lines.[81]

76 AA-PA, Türkei 183/36, A 389, Schwarz to Bethmann Hollweg, Erzerum, December 12, 1914 enclosure in Wangenheim to Bethmann Hollweg, Pera, December 30, 1914 No. 342.

77 DH.ŞFR, 48-166 Minister to Erzerum, Van, Bitlis provinces, Dec. 26, 1914 EUM Spec. 92, 141, 95. See also Üngör, 'A Reign of Terror,' pp. 37-38.

78 AA-PA, Konstantinopel 168, J. No. 3263, Schwarz to Wangenheim, Erzerum, Dec. 5, 1915 telegram; Türkei 183/36, A 389, Schwarz to Wangenheim, Erzerum, Dec. 5, 1914 enclosed in Wangenheim to Bethmann Hollweg, Pera, Dec. 30, 1914 No. 342. The murdered priest probably belonged to the Armenian Catholic church. See Archivio Segreto Vaticano (hereafter: ASV), Città di Vaticano, Archivio nunziatura turchia, carte Dolci, busta 9, folio 559, "The deportation of Erzerum," Aug. 1916.

79 AA-PA, Weltkrieg 11d secr./5, A 13937, Schwarz, Constantinople, Apr. 15, 1915 enclosure II in Wangenheim to Bethmann Hollweg, Pera, Apr. 17, 1915 No. 241.

On January 5, 1915, the central government ordered the provincial authorities to ascertain the people with whom Armen Garo had been in contact in the area.[82] Thus, it was probably no surprise that a brother of Armen Garo, the deputy director of the Ottoman Bank at Erzerum, was among the victims of a series of political murders. In February 1915, two soldiers shot him in the open. The local authorities did not arrest the two assassins and although their names had become known. Posseldt had shown a personal interest in the matter but in vain. Although the murder caused considerable anxiety among Armenians, calm was restored. Still, Scheubner considered the situation as being critical and believed the fear of massacres among Armenians was "not without foundation."[83] The Ministry of Interior, however, was more concerned whether indeed all Armenian police officers had been removed from service.[84] Instead of trying to restore the Armenian community's trust in the local government, the authorities launched a further strike. Again, the Armenian leadership was targeted and ten members of the local ARF, including journalists, were arrested and sent away from the city to an undisclosed location.[85]

The Armenian population's situation deteriorated further due to worsening sanitary conditions. A typhus epidemic ravaged the area. During the winter campaign it had killed many soldiers, now it spread to the civilian population. Moreover, cholera broke out in the town of Hasankale.

80 Haus-, Hof-, und Staatsarchiv (hereafter: HHStA), Vienna, PA XXXVIII 368, Kwiatkowski to Burian, Trebizond, June 12, 1915 Z.32/P. The Austro-Hungarian documents utilized in this study have been published in Artem Ohandjanian, ed., *Österreich - Armenien 1872 - 1936. Faksimilesammlung diplomatischer Aktenstücke*, 12 vols., Vienna, Ohandjanian Verlag, 1995.

81 Raymond Kévorkian, *Le génocide des arméniens*, Paris, Odile Jacob, 2006 p. 356.

82 DH.ŞFR, 49-60 Minister to Erzerum province, Jan. 5, 1915 EUM Spec. 163.

83 AA-PA, Konstantinopel 168, J. No. 3224, Scheubner Richter to Wangenheim, Erzerum, May 15, 1915 No. 9; Türkei 183/39, A 28584, Scheubner Richter Hohenlohe, Erzerum, Aug. 5, 1915 No. 23 enclosure No. 2 in Scheubner Richter to Bethmann Hollweg, Erzerum, Aug. 10, 1915; Konstantinopel 170, J. No. -, Stange, Erzerum, Aug. 23, 1915 enclosed in Liman von Sanders to Lossow, n.p. , Oct. 9, 1915 170 Military Mission J. No. 3841 M 15; AA-PA, Konstantinopel 168, J. No. -, Mordtmann, Pera, Apr. 26, 1915.

84 DH.ŞFR, 50-3 Ismail to Erzerum, Van, Bitlis provinces, Feb. 14 1915 EUM.

85 Kévorkian, Génocide, p. 356.

Other typhus cases were reported from Sivas along the army's supply lines. Thus the whole area under the command of the 3rd Army was contaminated by highly contagious and mortal diseases.[86] When in March 1915, Rafael de Nogales, a Venezuelan mercenary in the service of the Ottoman army, arrived in Erzerum; he saw freshly dug trenches along the major roads. These were used as mass graves. Dogs were feeding on the corpses. Nogales, too, learned soon about Armenian concerns about an imminent massacre.[87] The fears were aggravated by the conduct of soldiers and Kurdish irregulars who had fled from the front. They started plundering villages in the rear of the front line. The situation around the small district towns of Varto and Khinis was terrible. In February 1915, the Russian army had temporarily occupied parts of the area. This set off an exodus of the local Kurdish tribes to the west.[88] Nogales arrived at Khinis on April 12, 1915. He stayed in the house of an Armenian merchant. In the evening, the local Armenian priest visited the Venezuelan and nervously asked Nogales whether a massacre was to take place. Nogales was moved when he met with a group of Armenian men who were carrying supplies to the frontline. Gendarmes guarded these soldiers. They told him that more than half of the men had already died from hunger and cold.[89]

The Armenian men Nogales had met were Armenian soldiers who had been disarmed by the Ottoman army command. Now, the men had to serve in labor battalions. Scheubner had learned about this decision early in March 1915. The Ottoman government claimed that armed Armenians had attacked Ottoman soldiers and gendarmes in the province of Bitlis. Moreover, the Vice-Consul had learned that explosives and code books had been found in Caesarea, in central Asia Minor.[90] In reality, Ottoman

---

86 AA-PA, Türkei 183/36, A 8563, Wangenheim to Bethmann Hollweg, Pera, Mar. 3, 1915 J. No. 1532. For Ottoman concerns concerning typhus see DH.ŞFR, 50-57 Minister to provinces, Feb. 21, 1915 EUM Gen. 1030. It appears that the epidemic was particularly widespread in prisons.

87 Rafael De Nogales, *Four Years Beneath the Crescent*, Trans. By Muna Lee, New York, Scribner's Sons, 1926, pp. 43-44. In a recent publication, Mehmet Necati Kutlu discussed Nogales' memoirs. He carefully avoids mentioning the Venezuelan's accounts of anti-Armenian atrocities. Kutlu's misrepresentation of Nogales qualifies the book as a denial propaganda pamphlet. See Necati Kutlu, *Türkiye'de Bir Gezgin Şövalye Nogales Méndez*, Istanbul, Gendaş Kültür, 2000.

88 M. Şerif Fırat, *Doğu İlleri ve Varto Tarihi*, 2nd printing, Ankara, Milli Eğitim Bakanlığı, 1961, p. 110-111.

89 Nogales, *Four Years*, p. 52-54.

concerns were much more complicated and widespread. Secretly, the authorities feared a joint Kurdish and Armenian resistance and ordered provincial authorities to inquire into the matter.[91]

At Erzerum, Scheubner believed that his presence and work had prevented possible outrages. It seems that at least the local Armenian bishop shared this view and thanked Posseldt for these efforts.[92] In their statements to the Austro-Hungarian consul at Trebizond, however, an employee of the Ottoman Public Debt Administration and a Catholic Capuchin monk credited Erzerum governor, Tahsin Bey, with the maintenance of security in the city. They stated that the governor had used the services of locally influential Turks to avoid a massacre.[93] The Ottoman central authorities saw the situation totally different. They had ordered the provincial authorities to join in with the 3rd Army in frustrating any Armenian rising.[94]

In April 1915, the situation escalated. An Ottoman government campaign against Armenians was under way in the eastern provinces. After a series of attacks and massacres in Armenian villages and the murder of community leaders, the Armenian population at Van decided to resist the attempted massacre by the Ottoman authorities on April 20, 1915.[95] Scheubner learned of the defence within 24 hours and informed his superiors. Three days later, he was told that the defence had been suppressed. The Ottoman authorities maintained that as a result 400 Armenians had been killed while the survivors were fleeing to Russia. The information given by his military liaisons was, however, false.[96] Inquiring into the matter, the Germany embassy was informed at the Ministry of

---

90 AA-PA, Konstantinopel 168, J. No. 1301, Scheubner Richter to Embassy, Erzerum, Mar. 3, 1915 telegram.

91 DH.ŞFR, 50-210 Minister to Erzerum, Bitlis, Van provinces, March 9, 1915 EUM.

92 AA-PA, Konstantinopel 168, J. No. 3224, Scheubner Richter to Wangenheim, Erzerum, May 15, 1915 No. 9.

93 HHStA, PA XXXVIII 368, Kwiatkowski to Burian, Trebizond, June 12, 1915 Z.32/P.

94 DH.ŞFR, 51-15 Minister to Erzerum, Van Bitlis, Mar. 14, 1915 EUM Spec. 21.

95 AA-PA, Konstantinopel 168, J. No. 3224, Scheubner Richter to Wangenheim, Erzerum, May 15, 1915 No. 9. See also Ter Minassian, Anahide, "Van 1915," in Richard G. Hovannisian, ed., *Armenian Van / Vaspurakan*, (UCLA Armenian History and Culture Series, Historic Armenian Cities and Provinces, 1), Costa Mesa, CA 2000 p. 209-244; Nogales, *Four Years,* pp. 72-97.

Interior that the authorities would not guarantee that massacres could be avoided at Van.[97] Scheubner did not accept the authorities' stories. He secured his own information and learned about the murder of the Armenian community leaders near Van at the hands of the authorities. Armenians had not attacked the Turkish population but barricaded themselves in their own quarter. A large part of the quarter had already been destroyed.

At Erzerum, the situation deteriorated as well. In mosques, mullahs stirred up Muslim public opinion. They declared that if the local Armenians were not evicted from the city, the Russians would conquer the place. Not surprisingly, local Armenians grew more worried. Once more, the Armenian bishop implored the German vice-consulate for protection. Scheubner was willing to help and forwarded the bishop's report on the events at Van to the embassy for communication to the Armenian Patriarchate.[98] The ambassador understood that the situation in the Ottoman eastern provinces had reached a critical point. He instructed Scheubner to do his best in calming the Muslim population. Wangenheim hoped that massacres and plundering could be avoided. Scheubner was to urge the local authorities to prosecute politically suspect Armenians in accordance with the law thereby expressing his doubts about the statements of the Ottoman government. The Vice-Consul's representations should not suggest that Germany claimed a right to protect Ottoman Armenians.

---

96   AA-PA, Konstantinopel 168, J. No. 2449, Scheubner Richter to Embassy, Erzerum, April 21, 1915 telegram; Ibid, J. No. 2517 [?], Scheubner Richter to Embassy, Erzerum, April 24, 1915; Türkei 183/36, A 14223, Wangenheim informed Berlin right away but urged to keep the information secret. Wangenheim to AA, Pera, April 24, 1915 telegram 966.

97   AA-PA, Türkei 183/36, A 15061, Wangenheim to Bethmann Hollweg, Pera, April 24, 1915 No. 260.

98   Ministère des Affaires Etrangéres (hereafter: MAE), Série E, Levant, Armenie 1, Kaiané Abrahamian, Basra, n. d., enclosed in Roux to Pichon, Basra, Mar. 17, 1918 No. 60 in Beylerian, *Les grandes puissances*, p. 529-532 document No. 561; AA-PA, Konstantinopel 168, J. No. 2517, Scheubner Richter to Embassy, Erzerum, April 24, 1915 telegram; Ibid., J. No. 2540, Scheubner Richter to Embassy, Erzerum, April 26, 1915 telegram; Ibid., J. No. 2538, Scheubner Richter to Embassy, Erzerum, April 26, 1915 telegram. Mordtmann informed the Patriarch accordingly. He learned from the latter that Enver Pasha, the Minister of War and effective supreme commander of the Ottoman army, had informed the Patriarchate that the Armenians had rebelled.

In closing, Wangenheim added that the central authorities had arrested several hundred Armenians too, and repeated allegations about a widespread Armenian conspiracy.[99]

For the moment the situation remained calm at Erzerum, but the authorities stepped up their measures against Armenians. As a response to the defence of Van, the Ministry of Interior ordered on April 24, 1915, the immediate closure of Armenian political parties and the arrest of Armenians undesirables. Tahsin had to proceed carefully in order to avoid armed resistance as in Van. As a preparatory measure no travel permits were to be issued to known Armenian political activists. The provincial government also followed suit and began arrests. On April 29, 1915, Talaat gave instructions to secure documents and weapons from Armenian sources and photograph these assembled on large piles.[100] The government intended to produce some sort of excuse for his policies by putting blame on Armenians. Meanwhile, Scheubner inquired further into the events in and around Van. But to no avail. Nevertheless, he secured information on outrages against Armenians around Erzindjan organized by the local governor and the CUP deputy Halet Bey.[101] Scheubner's difficulties were in part due to Ottoman counter measures. Many of Scheubner's informants were no longer able to report. On a different level, the local authorities fed him false information. Their aim was to suggest that although a widespread Armenian movement was under way, they nevertheless maintained full control of the situation, but the attempt failed.[102] By May 4, 1915, Scheubner reported that Ottoman claims about a victory at Van were false. The struggle still continued. Ottoman troops

99 AA-PA, Konstantinopel 168, J. No. zu 2540, Wangenheim to Scheubner Richter, Pera, April 28, 1915 telegram.

100 DH.ŞFR, 52-158 Talaat to provinces, April 29, 1915 EUM Spec. 3099. Kévorkian estimated that the authorities arrested approximately 200 persons in this first round up. Again, local ARF members were specially targeted. Kévorkian, Génocide, p. 356.

101 AA-PA, Konstantinopel 168, J. No. 2616, Scheubner Richter to Embassy, Erzerum, April 30, 1915 telegram; Ibid., J. No. 2634, Scheubner Richter to Embassy, Erzerum, April 30, 1915. telegram; Türkei 183/39, A 28584, Scheubner Richter to Hohenlohe, Erzerum, Aug. 5, 1915 No. 23 enclosure No. 2 in Scheubner Richter to Bethmann Hollweg, Erzerum, Aug. 10, 1915; DH.ŞFR, 52-94, Talaat to provinces, Constantinople, April 24, 1915 in Şinasi Orel / Süreyya Yuca, *The Talât Pasha Telegrams. Historical Fact or Armenian Fiction?*, Nicosia, Rustem & Bro., 1986, p. 115-116. Minister to Erzerum province, April 24, 1915 DH.ŞFR, 52-95.

had suffered about 600 losses, dead or wounded, within a few days. At Erzerum, Ottoman police continued its searches of Armenian houses and arrested about 200 Armenians.

As ordered by the central government, the authorities claimed that they had found evidence of an Armenian conspiracy against the government. But Scheubner dismissed these claims. The number of arms found with Armenians was exaggerated. Often, the police framed Armenians once the latter had left their houses by planting evidence on the premises. This all gave rise to new fears of an imminent massacre. Scheubner took these concerns seriously. While he believed that a massacre could be avoided, he warned the embassy that the next days would be crucial.[103] Undeterred, the central government continued its campaign.

Following the ouster of Armenian police officers, Armenians who were member of political parties lost their jobs in the finance administration.[104] The arrests in Erzerum went on for several days. When Scheubner learned that 30 of the arrested were to be sent off, he feared for their lives. The German consul had evidently lost his trust in the local authorities.[105] In a private letter he stated: "Hopefully it will possible to avoid a massacre. Many

102 AA-PA, Türkei 183/36, A 15362, Wangenheim to Bethmann Hollweg, Pera, April 30, 1915 No. 266.

103 AA-PA, Konstantinopel 168, J. No. 2731, Scheubner Richter to Embassy, Erzerum, May 4, 1915 telegram. The embassy confronted Talaat with the information. The latter had to concede that the defense had not been crushed but denied the Ottoman losses. Ibid., J. No. 2793, Scheubner Richter to Embassy, Erzerum, May 8, 1915 telegram. Ibid., J. No. 3224, Scheubner Richter to Wangenheim, Erzerum, May 15, 1915 No. 9. Wangenheim for the time being accepted the Ottoman authorities' reasoning that the arrests of Armenians were necessary to contain a wide-spread Armenian conspiracy. Türkei 183/36, A 15354, Wangenheim to AA, Pera, May 6, 1915 telegram 1063; Ibid., A 15877, Wangenheim to Bethmann Hollweg, Pera, May 8, 1915 No. 286.v. Staszweski, "Zum offenen Brief an Herrn Lepsius," in *Der Neue Orient* 8 (1920) p. 13.

104 DH.ŞFR, 52-229 Talaat to Erzerum province, May 5, 1915 Ministry of Justice. DH.ŞFR, 52-249, Talaat to Erzerum, Bitlis, Van, Sivas, Kharpert, Diarbekir provinces, Constantinople, May 6, 1915. The document has been published in Türkiye Cumhuriyeti, Başbakanlık Devlet Arşivleri Genel Müdürlüğü, *Osmanlı Arşivi Daire Bakanlığı, Osmanlı Belgelerinde Ermeniler (1915 - 1920)*, Ankara, Başbakanlık Devlet Arşivleri Genel Müdürlüğü, 1994 (hereafter: OBE) p. 26 Doc. 10.

105 AA-PA, Konstantinopel 168, J. No. 2843, Scheubner Richter to Embassy, Erzerum, May 9, 1915 telegram.

have taken place. My position here is very difficult as the Armenians overrun me with requests for protection."[106] Scheubner did not believe the allegations of an imminent Armenian rebellion. Although persecutions continued and only few Ottoman troops were in the city, all the Armenians did to escape persecution was to flee. No one seemed to be intent in putting up a fight against the Ottoman police or military. Armenian villagers continued to leave their settlements close to the Russian lines either for Erzerum or Russian Trans-Caucasia.[107] In the countryside, the few isolated incidents of resistance had been insignificant. They had occurred mostly during requisitions. In some cases, Armenians had killed Turks who had demanded the delivery of girls and women. But that was self-defence. According to Scheubner, isolated incidents of sabotage and espionage were nothing extraordinary for a border region in wartime. Summing up, Scheubner attributed the relatively calm situation to a somewhat moderate Armenian policy of the local governor. Tahsin had released the majority of the arrested Armenians once it became evident that the house searches had produced no evidence of the alleged conspiracy. The governor's actions reduced the fear of the local Armenian population slightly. Therefore, Scheubner blamed the military commanders for the anti-Armenian policy who, he believed, wanted to take revenge for their defeat in the battlefield by persecuting defenceless Armenian subjects. Still, he did not anticipate any massacre unless the Ottoman army was defeated again and forced to retreat to Erzerum. In accordance with his instructions, Scheubner did not directly intervene but advised the authorities against notions of "settling accounts."[108]

---

106 AA-PA, Konstantinopel 945, J. No. 3952 [?], Scheubner Richter to Müller, Erzerum, May 8, 1915 private.

107 On January 1, the British consul at Batum estimated that well over 150,000 Christians had escaped to Russia from Persia and the Ottoman Empire. Armenian refugees from the Ottoman Empire lived under particularly desperate conditions. Every day about 350-400 people died. FO 371/2768/ 10980, "Report on activity of Armenian Refugee Relief Organizations in the Caucasus and Turkish Armenia" enclosed in Stephens to FO, Batum, Jan. 1, 1916 No. 1.

108 AA-PA, Konstantinopel 168, J. No. 3224, Scheubner Richter to Wangenheim, Erzerum, May 15, 1915 No. 9. Leverkuehn presents an account of the meeting between Scheubner and Tahsin. It is not clear whether the account is fictionalized or correct rendering of recollections Scheubner had shared with the author. Leverkuehn, *Posten,* pp. 37-38.

Scheubner's assessment of the situation was, however, incorrect. While Tahsin followed an ostensibly moderate policy in the city of Erzerum itself, he coordinated the deportation of Armenians from the southern districts of his province with the central and military authorities, as well as with the governors of Van and Bitlis provinces.[109] Moreover, it appears that Scheubner was unaware of Tahsin being a member of the TM. He enjoyed the full trust of Bahaeddin Shakir and had been transferred from Van to Erzerum specifically to become the third chief operative of the TM at Erzerum besides Bahaeddin Shakir and Hilmi Bey.[110]

On May 14, 1915, Scheubner cabled that the Armenian population of the villages on the Pasin plain was being deported to interior provinces.[111] The next day, he had found out that the deportation order had been issued by the command of the 3rd Army. The military authorities claimed that the measure was a matter of military necessity. As far as Scheubner could learn the people were sent to Mamakhatun and the Terdjan plain six to eight days away on the road to Erzindjan. Officially, the civilian authorities claimed not to be involved and refused any responsibility for what Scheubner described as a cruel expulsion. Often, the authorities informed the village notables about the deportation only six hours before the villagers were forced to leave their homes. The women used the time left hastily preparing for the journey, baking bread and boiling milk. At dawn, however, they had to abandon their work and leave things as they were at that moment. Among the 100 or so Armenian villages, three were inhabited by Catholics who were usually not identified with the majority of Apostolic Armenians. Their inhabitants, apart from six families, also had to leave. The deportation began in heavy rain and in some places while

---

109 DH.ŞFR, 52-282, Ministry to Cevdet and Abdulhalik Beys, Constantinople, May 9, 1915 EUM Spec. Register 409, in OBE, pp. 28-29 Doc. 14. Jean Naslian believed that Tahsin Bey entertained some positive feelings towards the Armenians because an Ottoman Catholic Armenian official, Hodaghian, had favorably attended to some administrative business personally important to Tahsin. During the deportations, Tahsin paid special attention to the safety of Hodaghian's family. Naslian, Jean, *Les mémoires de Mgr. Jean Naslian Eveque de Trébizonde sur les événements politico-religieux en Proche-Orient de 1914 à 1918*, vol. 1, Vienna, Impr. Méchitariste, 1955, p. 149.

110 Arif Cemil, *I. Dünya Savaşı'nda*, p. 27; Hüsameddin Ertürk, *İki Devrin Perde Arkası*, ed. by Samih Nâfiz Tansu, Istanbul, Hilmi Kitabevi, 1957 p. 111.

111 AA-PA, Konstantinopel 168, J. No. 2994, Scheubner Richter to Embassy, Erzerum, May 15, 1915 telegram; Konstantinopel 169, J. No. 3404, Scheubner Richter to Embassy, Erzerum, June 4, 1915 telegram 10.

snow was falling. Scheubner strongly refuted the alleged military necessity as mainly women and children were "herded off" leaving most of their possessions behind. Although the women could take their livestock with them, Scheubner did not think that this would be of much help to the deportees, as they were not allowed take fodder as well. Many had been forced to abandon their houses within two hours after the announcement of the deportation order. The gendarmes who were officially guarding the deported women and children beat and assaulted them. The weak and sick were abandoned, dying along the way; others were robbed. Desperate women threw their newborn babies into the Euphrates river when they could no longer provide for them. Scheubner considered all of this as hardly surprising to anyone familiar with the country. As a rule, the gendarmes treated their victims not as Ottoman citizens but as enemy civilians. Once more, Scheubner emphasized that no Armenian rising had to be expected since the men had been drafted into labor battalions.[112] On May 17, 1915, Scheubner forwarded a new appeal by the local Armenian bishop to the Armenian Patriarch by consular mail.[113] The situation of Armenians in the provincial capital became critical when news arrived that Russian troops had occupied Van and ended the siege of the Armenian quarter.[114]

Aside from the human suffering, the Vice-Consul pointed out the deportation's devastating economic consequences for the area. The

112 AA-PA, Konstantinopel 168, J. No. 2007, Scheubner Richter to Embassy, Erzerum, May 16, 1915 telegram; Konstantinopel 169, J. No. 3323, Scheubner Richter to Wangenheim, Erzerum, May 20, 1915 No. 12; Ibid., J. No. 3426, Scheubner Richter to Wangenheim, Erzerum, May 22, 1915 No. 13 (and enclosure); Konstantinopel 170, J. No. -, Stange, Erzerum, Aug. 23, 1915 enclosed in Liman von Sanders to Lossow, n.p, Oct. 9, 1915 Military Mission J. No. 3841 M 15; ASV, Archivio nunziatura turchia, carte Dolci, busta 9, folio 559, "The deportation of Erzerum," Aug. 1916. The three Catholic villages were Hintz, Ardzeti, and Tevantch.

113 AA-PA, Konstantinopel 168, J. No. 3021, Scheubner Richter to Embassy, Erzerum, May 17, 1915 telegram. Leverkuehn presents an account of the meeting. Its accuracy is, however, not beyond doubt. Leverkuehn, *Posten*, pp. 38-40.

114 AA-PA, Weltkrieg 11d secr./6, A 16397, Wangenheim to AA, Pera, May 18, 1915 telegram 1166. On inquiry from the German embassy, the Ottoman Ministry of War preferred claiming ignorance about the defeat than admitting to it. AA-PA, Weltkrieg / 118, A 16431, Wangenheim to AA, Pera, May 19, 1915 telegram 1167.

deportation caravans passed over recently prepared fields and the harvest was inevitably going to suffer tremendously. Scheubner doubted that crops that were not destroyed could be harvested, as Turkish landlords were losing their farmhands with the departing Armenian women. In addition, the consequences for the provisioning of the 3rd Army and the Ottoman war effort could not be overestimated.[115]

Meanwhile, Tahsin Bey continued to profess his opposition to the deportation orders. He informed Scheubner that while he was opposed to the deportations, he still had to obey the orders of the military. All he could do was try to mitigate the execution of the orders and protect at least the property left behind. Private sources confirmed to Scheubner that Tahsin's assurances were true and that he had cabled Constantinople urging the central government to overrule the deportation orders for the Pasin plain. However, Tahsin had failed and the central government instructed him to follow the orders of the military. Nevertheless, Scheubner came to believe that the governor had prevented the deportation of Armenians from the provincial capital.[116] On May 18, 1915, he reported again on the awful misery of the deportees. Thousands were camping in the open near Erzerum. The sights embittered the Armenian inhabitants of the city. In view of the humanitarian crisis right in front of his eyes, Scheubner urged the embassy for permission to intervene with the command of the 3rd Army on behalf of the Armenians.[117] Scheubner's dramatic description of the situation impressed even the calculating German ambassador who authorized an intervention with the 3rd Army's command. Like in his earlier instructions, the Vice-Consul was ordered to avoid giving any official character of his representation but present his move as friendly advice. The goal should be either stopping the deportations or at least mitigating them.[118]

When Scheubner visited the deportee camp, he was deeply moved by the sight. Armenian women implored him to help but the Vice-Consul could

---

115 AA-PA, Konstantinopel 169, J. No. 3323, Scheubner Richter to Wangenheim, Erzerum, May 20, 1915 No. 12.

116 AA-PA, Konstantinopel 168, J. No. 3022, Scheubner Richter to Embassy, Erzerum, May 17, 1915 telegram; Konstantinopel 169, J. No. 3323, Scheubner Richter to Wangenheim, Erzerum, May 20, 1915 No. 12.

117 AA-PA, Konstantinopel 168, J. No. 3034, Scheubner Richter to Embassy, Erzerum, May 18, 1915 telegram; ASV, Archivio nunziatura turchia, carte Dolci, busta 9, "The deportation of Erzerum," Aug. 1916, folio 559.

118 AA-PA, Konstantinopel 168, J. No. zu 3034, Wangenheim to Scheubner, Pera, May 19, 1915 telegram.

not do anything at that moment. He felt bitter about it. On his return to the city, he induced the Armenian bishop and community to organize some relief for the starving people. Since Armenians could not obtain a permit to leave the city, Scheubner went with his consular entourage to the camp some ten kilometres outside the city. At the camp he personally distributed relief to the deportees and took photos of the event. Given Scheubner's status, the provincial authorities did not stop the distribution. Hoping to extend the relief effort, local American missionaries and Scheubner sent an urgent appeal for relief funds through the embassy to William W. Peet, the treasurer of the "American Board of Commissioners for Foreign Missions" (ABCFM) at Constantinople.[119] Peet reacted quickly and wired £T250 for relief and the missionaries.[120]

Reflecting on recent developments Scheubner concluded that the Ottoman authorities were not responding to an Armenian threat. He now feared that the government intended the extermination of Armenians. The program's goal was making space for Muslim settlers who had fled from the war zone and were now housed in emptied Armenian villages. Now they took possession of these villages and in many places stole what had been left of Armenian property. Ottoman soldiers, Muslim neighbors, and refugees did not always wait for the departure of deportees before starting to plunder Armenian houses.[121]

The high degree of secrecy maintained by the Ottoman authorities gave rise to speculations about who was behind the persecutions. To his own surprise, Scheubner learned that despite his visible efforts, rumors were spreading in the city that the deportations were the result of German advice. Scheubner immediately countered the allegations. He could, not, however, make public his representations with the provincial authorities.

119 AA-PA, Konstantinopel 169, J. No. 3323, Scheubner Richter to Wangenheim, Erzerum, May 20, 1915 No. 12; Ibid., J. No. 3426, Scheubner Richter to Wangenheim, Erzerum, May 22, 1915 No. 13; Konstantinopel 168, J. No. 3519, Scheubner Richter to Embassy, Erzerum, May 24, 1915 telegram; ASV, Archivio nunziatura turchia, carte Dolci, busta 9, "The deportation of Erzerum," Aug. 1916, folio 559.
120 AA-PA, Konstantinopel 168, J. No. 3159, Wangenheim to Scheubner, Pera, May 26, 1915 telegram; Ibid., J. No. zu 3159, Wangenheim to Scheubner, Pera, May 29, 1915 telegram.
121 AA-PA, Konstantinopel 169, J. No. 3323, Scheubner Richter to Wangenheim, Erzerum, May 20, 1915 No. 12; Ibid., J. No. 3426, Scheubner Richter to Wangenheim, Erzerum, May 22, 1915 No. 13 (and enclosure).

Thus he was forced to continue working discreetly. When these steps proved to be useless, Scheubner phoned the command of the 3rd Army and prepared a visit to their headquarters. He also forwarded the copy of a letter from the priests of several Armenian villages to the Armenian bishop of Erzerum sent to the German embassy; a copy of which he made available to Tahsin.[122]

But such local efforts were by far insufficient to stop the Ottoman government. On May 23, 1915, Talaat instructed the governors of Erzerum, Bitlis, and Van that Armenians had to be deported from their provinces to the southern districts of Mosul province and the desert regions south of Urfa.[123] Following the Armenian employees in the police and finance administration, all Armenians in the Postal and Telegraph Services had to be dismissed.[124] None of these public officials were allowed to return to Constantinople.[125]

Not surprisingly, Scheubner's steps with Mahmud Kiamil Pasha, the commander of the 3rd Army, failed.[126] The General told Scheubner that the Armenian population of Erzerum would definitely be deported. Moreover, the commander made it clear that the destination of the deportations was not as Scheubner had been told so far, the plain of Terdjan, but the desert region of Deir Zor on the lower Euphrates, confirming Talaat's orders. Scheubner was shocked. He concluded that deportations on such a scale were the equivalent of a massacre as hardly half of those displaced would reach their destination alive. Only those Armenians who converted to Islam were exempted from deportations.

---

122 AA-PA, Konstantinopel 169, J. No. 3323, Scheubner Richter to Wangenheim, Erzerum, May 20, 1915 No. 12; Ibid., J. No. 3426, Scheubner Richter to Wangenheim, Erzerum, May 22, 1915 No. 13; Konstantinopel 168, J. No. 3160, Scheubner Richter to Embassy, Erzerum, May 22, 1915 telegram.

123 DH.ŞFR, 53-93, Talaat to Erzerum, Van, and Bitlis provinces, Constantinople, May 23, 1915, in Orel and Yuca, *The Talât Pasha*, pp. 118-119.

124 DH.ŞFR, 53-89, Deputy Minister of Post and Telephone to Adana, Angora, Diarbekir, Erzerum, Sivas, Van provinces, Constantinople, May 23, 1915.

125 DH.ŞFR, 53-343 Minister to Erzerum Province, June 13, 1915. EUM Spec. 23.

126 Nogales had serious reservations about the qualification of Mahmud Kiamil. "...such a poor creature as Maghmud-Kiamul Pasha, who was celebrated even among the Ottoman officers as being a nullity of nullities." Nogales, *Four Years*, p. 46.

Again, Scheubner urged his embassy for support. He warned of the economic ruin of the whole country. On the way to the army headquarters, Scheubner had visited emptied Armenian villages, a monastery, and a church, all plundered. On his return to Erzerum, Armenians had approached Scheubner once more and implored him for protection. Now, Turkish irregulars harassed Armenians even in the city. While under duress, local Armenians were forced to tear down a monument built by Russians.[127]

Understanding that his local efforts would not have the desired results, Scheubner turned again to the German embassy. He renewed his appeals to intervene with the Sublime Porte on behalf of the Armenians. In response, on May 29, 1915, the head of the embassy's Armenian desk, Johann Heinrich Mordtmann, saw Talaat to discuss the matter. The minister showed no intention to mitigate the deportation orders. Talaat maintained that the local authorities had found substantial evidence, like bombs and correspondence, implicating the Armenians at Erzerum in a conspiracy. Although Talaat had every reason to believe that Mordtmann had been briefed on the human disaster, he dared not present the deportations only as a necessary safety measure, but cynically claimed that he was securing the welfare of the deported who otherwise might be killed in their own homes. Such callous statements convinced Mordtmann that nothing could be done. Wangenheim could only inform Scheubner of Talaat's allegations.[128] Understanding the Ottoman government's determination, the ambassador went, however, one step further. Issuing further instructions, he informed the German consulates at Adana, Aleppo, Baghdad, Mosul, as well as Scheubner, that Enver planned to close a large number of Armenian newspapers, schools, and to ban all Armenian-language correspondence. More importantly, the commander had not only announced his intention "to deport all Armenian families not completely blameless," but also asked Wangenheim that Germany should not interfere with these measures. The ambassador instructed his consuls accordingly and asked them to seek only the mitigating these measures.[129] In other

---

127 AA-PA, Konstantinopel 169, J. No. 3361, Scheubner Richter to Embassy, Erzerum, June 2, 1915 telegram 1; Ibid., J. No. 3362, Scheubner Richter to Embassy, Erzerum, June 2, 1915 telegram 5. Again the accucracy of Leverkuehn's account remains doubtful. Leverkuehn, *Posten*, pp. 41-42.

128 AA-PA, Konstantinopel 168, J. No. zu 3224, Mordtmann, Pera, May 29, 1915; Ibid., J. No. zu 3224, Wangenheim to Scheubner Richter, Pera, May 30, 1915 telegram. Consul-General Johann Heinrich Mordtmann was head of the Armenian desk at the German Embassy.

words, Wangenheim had not intervened with Enver but limited himself to pre-empt possible protests from his consuls. Scheubner, however, did not give up so easily. He stressed that the allegations against Armenians were false and no bombs or anything similar had been found in Erzerum. In other words, the Vice-Consul openly disputed Talaat's honesty and thereby made it clear that he disagreed with Wangenheim's line of action.[130]

The ambassador had anticipated the coming developments correctly. The situation deteriorated further rapidly. On June 1, 1915, a massacre of Armenians in the district of Khinis had begun. Many victims were massacred in their villages or near the town. A number of Armenians were deported. Often, Kurds spared the lives of women and children by forcibly marrying some of them, or using them as cheap labor.[131] Scheubner forwarded a lengthy telegram of the Armenian bishop addressed to the Armenian Patriarchate detailing the situation. The bishop reported that in the district of Khinis all Armenian villages had been massacred. The authorities had also ordered the deportation of two Catholic Armenian villages, Norehene and Rabad. These had been exempted from deportation so far. Moreover, the governor had ordered the deportation of 160 of the wealthiest Armenian notables from Erzerum to Mosul as retaliation for the events in Van. More deportations from the city were expected. Like Scheubner, the bishop was certain that the deportations were nothing but another form of massacre.[132]

The embassy could only view the communication of such detailed information through the consular wire as another, little veiled, urgent appeal by Scheubner. But it was again in vain as the response from the embassy was once more negative. Wangenheim made it absolutely clear that he declined further interventions on behalf of Armenians. In plain language, the ambassador ordered Scheubner to refrain from making representations to the military authorities.[133] Besides, Wangenheim did not forward the bishop's appeal in its original form to the Armenian Patriarchate. He argued that such assistance would compromise the

129 AA-PA, Konstantinopel 168, J. No. 3300, Wangenheim to Büge, Rössler, Hesse, Scheubner Richter, Holstein, Pera, May 31, 1915 telegram.

130 AA-PA, Konstantinopel 169, J. No. 3358, Scheubner Richter to Embassy, Erzerum, June 2, 1915 telegram 6; Ibid., J. No. 3373, Scheubner Richter to Embassy, Erzerum, June 2, 1915 telegram 7.

131 Naslian, *Les mémoires*, p. 151. Nogales gives May 19, 1915 as the date of the massacre, Nogales, *Four Years,* p. 53. Kévorkian, *Génocide*, pp. 368-371. Also see appendix 1 to this article.

German embassy in the eyes of the Ottoman government. Returning to a classic of Ottoman propaganda, the ambassador informed Scheubner that the former deputy Pastermadjian had joined the Russian forces. In view of the events at Van and the actions of the former deputy, Wangenheim argued that the Armenians had brought their own fate upon themselves. He instructed Scheubner to inform local Armenian circles that according to law the German embassy had no right to act as an intermediary between Ottoman citizens and their government.[134] Obviously, Wangenheim was somewhat irritated by Scheubner's insistence and support for a cause that the embassy had given up on. Moreover, German officers in Constantinople, notably Fritz Bronsart von Schellendorf, Enver's right hand, vehemently opposed Scheubner's actions and pushed for a change.[135]

---

132 AA-PA, Konstantinopel 169, J. No. 3404, Scheubner Richter to Embassy, Erzerum, June 4, 1915 telegram 10. In fall of 1915, Scheubner Richter traveled with a group of Turkish irregular cavalry to Mosul. Along the way he found the information of the bishop confirmed as he saw the destroyed villages. Türkei 183/39, A 33278, Neurath to Bethmann Hollweg, Pera, Nov. 9, 1915 No. 660. The Armenian bishop of Erzerum had sent a written appeal to Scheubner, outlying the justification for the deportation of the Ottoman authorities and disproving these point by point. The Catholic Armenian bishop sent likewise assurances of loyalty on behalf of his community to the German Vice-Consul and pleaded for the life of the threatened people. Ibid., A 28584, Armenian Apostolic Bishop to Scheubner Richter, Erzerum, June 4, 1915 enclosed in Scheubner Richter to Bethmann Hollweg, Erzerum, Aug. 10, 1915; Ibid., Melchisedechian to Scheubner Richter, Erzerum, June 8, 1915. The Catholic Armenian village Khotchodour at a greater distance from Erzerum was deported as well. ASV, Archivio nunziatura turchia, carte Dolci, busta 9, "The deportation of Erzerum," Aug. 1916, folio 559.

133 AA-PA, Konstantinopel 169, J. No. auf 3358, Wangenheim to Scheubner Richter, Pera, June 3, 1916 telegram.

134 AA-PA, Konstantinopel 169, J. No. zu 3404, Wangenheim to Scheubner Richter, Pera, June 4, 1916 telegram. Nevertheless, Wangenheim was willing and did make the substance of the bishop's telegram available to the Patriarchate. See also Ibid, J. No. zu 3426, Wangenheim to Scheubner Richter, Pera, June 6, 1915.

135 HHStA, PA XII 463, Kwiatkowski to Czernin, Samsun, May 26, 1917 No. 21/ P. See also Bronsart's marginal notes to Scheubner's report No. 12. AA-PA, Konstantinopel 169, J. No. 3323, Scheubner Richter to Wangenheim, Erzerum, May 20, 1915 No. 12.

The Deportations at Erzerum.

The first Armenians ordered to leave the city, on June 15, 1915, were not local notables but poor families. One day before the deportation, Talaat sent fresh orders to Erzerum, Bitlis, Diarbekir, and Harpoot provinces. The minister confirmed that the provincial authorities had reported an earlier massacre of 500 Armenian deportees between Erzerum and Erzindjan. Now Talaat ordered the protection of the deportees.[136] At first glance, Scheubner's efforts appeared to have had some impact. However, the near future would show if Talaat's orders were simply issued as material for excuse making or not.

Once more, local Armenian clergy asked Scheubner to intervene on behalf of their community. Informing them of the embassy's order, Scheubner declined any official steps. But he still tried influencing the local authorities with an eye to mitigate the order's execution. The Vice-Consul anticipated that bands of irregulars would rob and murder the deportees. Since he could not accompany the deportees himself nor send his own staff with them, all he could do was to ask the governor to provide protection for the Armenians on the road.[137] Clearly, Scheubner's compliance with Wangenheim's order had quickly reached its limits. Quite soon, Scheubner had confirmation that his concerns had been justified. News reached Erzerum that the villagers, who had been sent off first, had become victims of Kurds and irregulars. The majority of men and women had been slaughtered while some women were abducted. Carefully avoiding any direct accusation, Scheubner reported that the authorities were either unable or unwilling to protect the Armenians. Implying that a new situation had arisen, the Vice-Consul demanded fresh instructions from the embassy for immediate steps to prevent further slaughter.[138] In his response, Wangenheim allowed Scheubner to make some cautious representations with the governor. Reiterating his earlier orders, these representations had to be done in a "friendly form," reminding the official of the negative effect on the Ottoman image such "incidents" would

---

136 DH.ŞFR, 54-9, Talaat to Diarbekir, Mamuret-ul-Aziz, Bitlis provinces, Constantinople, June 14, 1915 EUM Spec. 20, in OBE, p. 44 (doc. 35); DH.ŞFR, 54-10, Talaat to Erzerum province, Constantinople, June 14, 1915 EUM Spec. 25, in OBE, p. 43 (doc. 34).

137 AA-PA, Konstantinopel 169, J. No. 3555, Scheubner Richter to Embassy, Erzerum, June 10, 1915 telegram 18; Ibid., J. No. 3556, Scheubner Richter to Embassy, Erzerum, June 10, 1915 telegram 19.

138 AA-PA, Konstantinopel 169, J. No. 3741, Scheubner Richter to Embassy, Erzerum, June 16, 1915 telegram 33.

produce abroad. At a future peace conference, the Ottoman position would suffer. The reference to diplomatic complications was a manoeuvre to justify the German initiative. The ambassador added that he would make representations with the central authorities in the same direction.[139]

When Scheubner confronted the governor with information about the massacres, the latter admitted these and expressed his regret. Tahsin promised to do his best to prevent similar occurrences in future. The governor told Scheubner that Mahmud Kiamil had insisted on the immediate execution of the deportation orders. Tahsin maintained that he had informed the General that the roads were unsafe. The latter, however, had refused to provide escorts for the deportees. Major Von Staszweski of the German corps of engineers who served as a member of the German military mission with the Ottoman 3rd Army recalled a meeting with Tahsin and Mahmud Kiamil concerning the deportations. When the General learned that Tahsin had given Armenians some time to organize their affairs, he reprimanded the governor reminding him that Muslims at Van had not been given any time.[140] Ottoman military correspondence shows that Mahmud Kiamil was indeed a driving force behind the deportations. On June 19, 1915, the General requested from the Ottoman Ministry of War the authorization for the wholesale deportation of the Armenian population from the provinces of Erzerum, Trebizond, Van, Bitlis, Kharpert, Diarbekir and Sivas to areas in Aleppo and Mosul provinces.[141] Kiamil's determination is further confirmed by a decree that any Muslim who would protect an Armenian should be hanged in front of his house and his house be destroyed. Officials and military personnel would be court-martialled for this crime.[142] In sum, Tahsin accepted only a "formal" responsibility for the atrocities as the real power in the province rested with Mahmud Kiamil. All Scheubner could do was to see to it that the General would learn of the consular representations.[143]

On June 16, 1915, the first group of notables and their families, together with about 500 persons, left Erzerum. They were sent through the Dersim mountains to Kharpert and then on to Urfa. The provincial authorities

---

139 AA-PA, Konstantinopel 169, J. No. zu 3741, Wangenheim to Scheubner Richter, Pera, June 21, 1915 telegram 12.

140 Staszweski, Zum offenen Brief, p. 13.

141 Mahmud Kiamil to Ministry of War, June 19, 1915, in Genel Kurmay Başkanlığı, *Ermeni Faaliyetleri,* pp. 187-188.

142 Kocahanoğlu, *İttihat-Terakki'nin Sorgulanması,* p. 520.

143 AA-PA, Konstantinopel 169, J. No. 3822, Scheubner Richter to Embassy, Erzerum, June 22, 1915 telegram 42.

gave the Armenians an escort of one officer and 15 gendarmes. According to official sources, 14 men of the group were killed on the road. Scheubner, however, found out that the official figure was false and almost all men had been murdered.[144] The group had been attacked by Bahaeddin Shakir's irregulars and Dersim Kurds.[145] Survivors from the group later reported not only on the series of extortions they had been subjected to, but also were able to identify the names of prominent killers and the locations of the crimes. Like in other areas, TM leaders coordinated and directed the attacks of Kurds on the deportees.[146]

Scheubner was able to obtain more information on the situation along the major roads from a member of his own staff. On June 18, 1915, a group of foreigners led by the Austrian geographer Victor Pietschmann left Erzerum accompanied by Scheubner's assistant, Carl Schlimme. At the governor's request, an Armenian family and the sister of the Armenian bishop accompanied them. At Baiburt, the local authorities demanded from Pietschmann and Schlimme to give up all Armenians in their group. As they refused, the authorities took away their drivers and they had to carry on without them. When Schlimme tried to inform Scheubner about the incident, the local telegraph office declined accepting his telegrams. While arguing with the clerk, an attempt was made to abduct the Armenians, although they were under Austrian and German protection. Pietschmann and Schlimme threatened to shoot the attackers and together with the Armenians in their company they made their way out of Baiburt. On the way to Erzindjan, they passed numerous checkpoints manned by irregulars. One group of irregulars numbered 400 men and was lead by a

---

144 AA-PA, Konstantinopel 169, J. No. 3718, Scheubner Richter to Embassy, Erzerum, June 18, 1915 telegram 37; Türkei 183/39, A 28584, Scheubner Richter to Hohenlohe, Erzerum, Aug. 5, 1915 No. 23 enclosure No. 2 in Scheubner Richter to Bethmann Hollweg, Erzerum, Aug. 10, 1915; Konstantinopel 170, J. No. -, Stange, Erzerum, Aug. 23, 1915 enclosed in Liman von Sanders to Lossow, n.p, Oct. 9, 1915 Military Mission J. No. 3841 M 15. Ida Stapleton, "Incidents during the deportation of Armenians from Erzroom, Turkey, in June and July, 1915, known personally to Dr. Ida S. Stapleton (Mrs. Robert)," in James L. Barton (compiler), "*Turkish Atrocities*": *Statements of American Missionaries on the Destruction of Christian Communities in Ottoman Turkey, 1915-1917*, Gomidas Institute, Ann Arbor, MI 1998, p. 23.
145 Kocahanoğlu, *İttihat-Terakki'nin Sorgulanması*, p. 521.
146 Kévorkian, Génocide, pp. 360-361. For further information on the role of Kurdish tribes, see Kaiser, *A Scene*, pp. 162-165.

French speaking Ottoman officer. Thus it seems safe to assume that the officer was a graduate of a military college and probably a CUP member. The German consul at Trebizond, Heinrich Bergfeld, concluded that the CUP had formed these bands. When gendarmes, who accompanied the German group, refused to go any further, they suggested massacring the Armenians in the party. Upon arrival in Erzindjan, the local authorities arrested the Armenians without giving any reason. Later the officials claimed that the Armenians had carried weapons, despite the fact that a search of the arrested in the presence of Schlimme had produced no weapons at all.[147]

On June 19 and 20, 1915, a second group of notables, altogether about 300 families or about 3,000 persons, left Erzerum in the direction of Baiburt. Scheubner reported that his representations had met with some success. An escort of 100 gendarmes had been given to that caravan. At Baiburt, the men were separated from the group. Despite all efforts, Scheubner could not secure any information on the men's fate and he suspected that all had been murdered. The surviving women and children reached Erzindjan without further incidents.[148] On the day of the deportations, Mahmud Kiamil Pasha had cabled a request for the wholesale deportation of the Armenians of Erzerum, Trebizond, Van, Bitlis, Kharpert, Diarbekir and Sivas provinces to the Ottoman Ministry of War: "...I hereby request the relocation of the Armenians living in the cities mentioned above to Aleppo and Mosul, and help for immediate issuing of the due orders to be given by the army to the governors, and their approval for the task." The wording of the secret communication obscures the fact

147 AA-PA, Türkei 183/39, A 28584, Schlimme, Erzerum, August 5, 1915 enclosure No. 2 to Scheubner to Bethmann Hollweg, Erzerum, Aug. 10, 1915; Konstantinopel 169, J. No. 4030, Bergfeld to Embassy, Trebizond, July 2, 1915 telegram 9; Türkei 183/37, A 22559, Bergfeld to Bethmann Hollweg, Trebizond, July 9, 1915 No. 35.

148 AA-PA, Konstantinopel 169, J. No. 3818, Scheubner Richter to Embassy, Erzerum, June 21, 1915 telegram 39; Türkei 183/39, A 28584, Scheubner Richter to Hohenlohe, Erzerum, Aug. 5, 1915 No. 23 enclosed in Scheubner Richter to Bethmann Hollweg, Erzerum, Aug. 10, 1915 J. No. 598. Without presenting further evidence, Leverkuehn claims that Tahsin had threatened Scheubner, but thereafter consented to the dispatch of the gendarmes. Leverkuehn, *Posten,* pp. 43-45. Based on Armenian survivor accounts, Kévorkian gives considerably higher numbers: 1300 families who were later joined by 370 more, a total of about 10,000 persons. Scheubner's other information was, however, confirmed, Kévorkian, *Génocide,* p. 362

that deportations were well under way and Kiamil had anyhow been giving orders to civil authorities. It appears that in view of Scheubner's representations the commander felt it necessary to obtain additional support from Enver, thus taking precautions against being held responsible at a future date.[149] He might have been aware of the Entente's May 24, 1915 announcement to hold anyone implicated in Armenian atrocities personally responsible.[150]

It took a few days until Scheubner learned about atrocities during the deportations. On June 23, 1915, Garabed Hadji Oghlu Georgian, a 55 years old Armenian peasant, came to the consulate. He had been deported from the village Irdazur. Being shot through his left hand, he had barely survived and escaped massacre in the area of Mamakhatun. Before the deportation, he had supplied the consulate with eggs and other farm produce. The inhabitants of 13 villages on the Pasin and Erzerum plains, about 9,000-10,000 people, had left their homes in a caravan of 600-700 carts.[151] They had arrived safely at Mamakhatun and the Euphrates Bridge nearby. At Mamakhatun, the local kaimakam (district governor) together with ten gendarmes and 20 irregulars joined them. After passing the bridge, the caravan came to mountainous terrain. At a narrow passage, people in hiding began firing upon them. The kaimakam ordered the caravan to retreat but now Kurds again attacked the caravan. The irregulars offered armed resistance to the attackers, while the gendarmes fled. Due to the efforts of the irregulars, about 100 carts and the majority of the deportees were saved. After having collected the survivors, the kaimakam proposed a different route and received £T200 from the Armenians. However, when the deportees made a stop at the Euphrates, Kurds attacked once more. Some Armenians escaped by reaching the opposite river bank, while Kurdish snipers killed many, while others drowned or died from their wounds. The survivors made their way to a village, where they spent the night in an Armenian church. The next morning, irregulars appeared and began shooting the Armenians. A series of murders and other outrages followed over the next days in which Kurdish villagers, Muslim refugees,

---

149 Mahmud Kiamil to Ministry of War, June 19, 1915 in Genel Kurmay Başkanlığı, *Ermeni Faaliyetleri*, p. 187.

150 For the text of the declaration, see Beylerian, *Les Grandes Puissances*, p. 29.

151 The witness named specifically the village Padishvan from the Pasin plain, and the villages Oumoudoun, Shipek, Kizilkilise, Erginis, Chamshkavank, Kirsinkeuy, and Irzadour. AA-PA, Türkei 183/39, A 28584, "Statement by Garabed Hadji Oghlu Georgian," Erzerum, n.d., enclosed in Scheubner Richter to Bethmann Hollweg, Erzerum, Aug. 10, 1915 J. No. 598.

and camel drivers joined in. They abducted many women, while the men were killed right away. Garabed was left lying wounded on the ground, supposed to be dead. He managed to reach the Kurdish village of Khom. Here the inhabitants treated him well. After two days, he clandestinely reached Erzerum and the consulate.[152]

On June 26, 1915, Talaat made it clear to the provincial authorities that delays in the deportations were unacceptable.[153] The third group of notables left Erzerum the same day. This caravan consisted of about 300 families. The group reached Erzindjan without being attacked on the road. Tahsin had told Scheubner that these three groups would probably remain either in Kharpert, Erzindjan, or Baiburt until the roads were safe. The governor refused to accept any responsibility for the deportation beyond these places.[154] In Erzerum itself, Scheubner thought that the deportations were conducted in "perfect order" and he did his best to reassure the Armenians with an eye to avoid local Armenian resistance.[155] By now, he knew that Mahmud Kiamil had ordered the deportation of all Armenians from the city. Scheubner repeated his earlier assessment that the order was based on "racial hatred" and not military necessity. Mahmud Kiamil had told him that after the war the "Armenian Question" would no longer exist. Once more, the Vice-Consul emphasized the deportations' negative effects on the war effort, as most of the craftsmen working for the military and all drivers were Armenians.[156]

---

152 Ibid.
153 DH.ŞFR, 54-156, Minister to Erzerum province, Constantinople, June 26, 1915 EUM Special Office No. 4578, in OBE, p. 51 (doc. 46).
154 AA-PA, Konstantinopel 169, J. No. 3921, Scheubner Richter to Embassy, Erzerum, June 26, 1915 telegram 46; Türkei 183/39, A 28584, Scheubner Richter to Hohenlohe, Erzerum, Aug. 5, 1915 No. 23 enclosure No. 2 in Scheubner Richter to Bethmann Hollweg, Erzerum, Aug. 10, 1915 J. No. 598. Kévorkian gives for this group as well considerably higher numbers, namely about 500 families with a total of 7,000 to 8,000 persons. The difference in numbers could result from an inclusion of Armenian deportees that did not originate from Erzerum city. Kévorkian, Génocide, p. 364.
155 AA-PA, Konstantinopel 169, J. No. 3921, Scheubner Richter to Embassy, Erzerum, June 26, 1915 telegram 46.
156 AA-PA, Konstantinopel 169, J. No. 3922, Scheubner Richter to Embassy, Erzerum, June 26, 1915 telegram 47; Konstantinopel 170, J. No. -, Stange, Erzerum, Aug. 23, 1915 enclosed in Liman von Sanders to Lossow, n.p, Oct. 9, 1915 Military Mission J. No. 3841 M 15.

By June 30, 1915, Ottoman officials confirmed that about 3,000 Armenians had been murdered during the first part of deportations. The number was, however, far too low. Scheubner ascertained that Kurdish and Turkish irregulars had slaughtered about 10-20,000 victims.[157] He suspected that the director of the Erzerum police, Khulussi Bey, who had returned recently from Mamakhatun, was mainly responsible for the organization of the massacres.[158] According to private sources and information obtained from Tahsin, complete anarchy reigned on the deportation route near Terdjan. The German officer August Stange, who had fought before with the TM on the Russian front near the Black Sea, stated that the massacres were not only condoned by the military, but that military units actually took part in the atrocities. Unable to deny the facts, Tahsin continued his excuse-making. Again he claimed that he did not have enough forces to stop the carnage.[159] Soon, more disturbing news arrived from Baiburt, Erzindjan, and Terdjan. The massacre of Armenians had recommenced there. At the same time, the infamous Khulussi Bey left Erzerum for the sites of the atrocities. Scheubner concluded that the local authorities were involved in the massacres while the CUP promoted the killings. The Vice-Consul informed the embassy that the CUP acted as a kind of second local government, operating in the dark. Scheubner continued collecting information on Khulussi and the local ÇUP. He learned that the former had been in Terdjan and Erzindjan for five months before returning to Erzerum. Armenian and Turkish sources confirmed earlier news that Khulussi had been the chief organizer of the massacres in those places. Scheubner, Posseldt, and Stange identified Khulussi, Mahmud Kiamil, Bahaeddin Shakir, the local deputy Seyfullah Effendi, Hilmi Bey, and two others as being responsible for outrages against Armenians in the Erzerum district. Moreover, the Vice-Consul suspected

---

157 AA-PA, Konstantinopel 96, J. No. 4024, Scheubner Richter to Embassy, Erzerum, June 30, 1915 telegram 50; Türkei 183/39, A 28584, Scheubner Richter to Hohenlohe, Erzerum, Aug. 5, 1915 No. 23 enclosure No. 2 in Scheubner Richter to Bethmann Hollweg, Erzerum, Aug. 10, 1915 J. No. 598.

158 AA-PA, Konstantinopel 96, J. No. 5132, Scheubner Richter to Embassy, Erzerum, July 1, 1915 telegram 55.

159 AA-PA, Konstantinopel 169, J. No. 5293 [?], Scheubner Richter to Embassy, Erzerum, July 6, 1915 telegram 60; Konstantinopel 170, J. No. -, Stange, Erzerum, Aug. 23, 1915 enclosed in Liman von Sanders to Lossow, n. p., Oct. 9, 1915 Military Mission J. No. 3841 M 15.

that Khulussi and Seyfullah engaged in blackmailing Armenians in order to extort money for themselves.[160]

Despite all this information, Scheubner still tried to influence Tahsin. He urged the governor to implement some mitigating measures. He succeeded in securing oxcarts for poor families until Erzindjan and beyond. Moreover, the governor allowed sick people, families without male members, and single women to remain behind in Erzerum.[161] At the same time, the Sublime Porte had exempted Armenian craftsmen who were needed for the Ottoman war effort from deportation.[162] However, this exemption did not last long. The military authorities revoked it and the craftsmen and their families were sent off with a fourth large caravan from the city. They reached Erzindjan rather safely. By July 15, 1915, almost no Armenian men remained in Erzerum. At that time, the few Armenian men left were mostly physicians and pharmacists and those too sick to move.[163] Meanwhile, Scheubner accompanied Tahsin on a visit to Erzindjan where they saw Armenian deportees from Erzerum camped nearby.[164]

160 AA-PA, Konstantinopel 169, J. No. 4148 [?], Scheubner Richter to Embassy, Erzerum, July 7, 1915 telegram 63; Ibid., J. No. 4354 [?], Scheubner Richter to Wangenheim, Erzerum, July 9, 1915 No. 20; Konstantinopel 170, J. No. 4674 [?], Scheubner Richter to Wangenheim, Erzerum, July 28, 1915 No. 21; Ibid., J. No. -, Stange, Erzerum, Aug. 23, 1915 enclosed in Liman von Sanders to Lossow, n. p., Oct. 9, 1915 Military Mission J. No. 3841 M 15; Konstantinopel 168, J. No. -, Mordtmann, Pera, Apr. 26, 1915. Kévorkian gives a slightly different composition of this CUP group. According to Armenian sources, the group managed the lists of deportees. Based on an Armenian survivor account, Kévorkian assumes that a local assembly of CUP members and Muslim notables discussed the deportations already before April 25, 1915. Based on this account Kévorkian deems it probable that such meetings took place in all provinces. Kévorkian, Génocide, pp. 356-357. This conclusion is, however, speculative given the limited information provided.

161 Ibid.

162 AA-PA, Konstantinopel 96, J. No. 5166, Scheubner Richter to Embassy, Erzerum, July 1, 1915 telegram 54.

163 Talaat officially informed Mahmud Kiamil Pasha on the deportation of all Armenians and the dispatch of new military informants. DH.ŞFR, 54/a-10 Talaat to Commander of 3. Army, July 15, 1915 Ministry of Interior Central Office Spec. 55.

164 AA-PA, Konstantinopel 943, J. No. 5476, Scheubner informed the embassy about his departure for Erzindjian on July 11, 1915. Scheubner to Embassy, Erzerum, July 11, 1915 telegram 64.

Scheubner's repeated representation had alerted the Ministry of Interior who inquired with Tahsin about the complaints.[165] The Vice-Consul used the opportunity to inquire into their situation. Later, the deportees were sent further south by way of the Kemah gorge, a notorious location for massacres. While Scheubner was in Erzindjan, Mahmud Kiamil Pasha ordered the immediate deportation of remaining Armenians in the town. Scheubner had no doubt that they were sent to certain death. Near Ashkale and Baiburt, the group was plundered while military authorities shot several of the physicians and pharmacists.[166] On his return, Scheubner was upset about Mahmud Kiamil's actions. Tahsin was upset as well, but for other reasons. He had been informed that individuals were taking advantage of the deportation and enriching themselves. In a telegram to Sabit Bey, the governor of Harpoot, he wrote: "Everywhere I am saying that whatever we did, we have not done it to fill the pockets of some persons with money."[167] The next day, Tahsin reported to Constantinople receiving a reply the following day. The Ministry of Interior emphasized that it was absolutely necessary to punish those responsible for the misdeeds. Further reports were ordered on such evens and the punishment of the perpetrators.[168] Another concern of the Ministry of Interior was that the massive deportations interfered with the transport of supplies for the 3rd Army.[169]

---

165 DH.ŞFR, 54-293, Talaat to Erzerum Province, July 5, 1915 Kalem-i Mahsus No. 33.

166 AA-PA, Türkei 183/39, A 28584, Scheubner Richter to Hohenlohe, Erzerum, Aug. 5, 1915 No. 23 enclosure No. 2 in Scheubner Richter to Bethmann Hollweg, Erzerum, Aug. 10, 1915 J. No. 598. Scheubner's assessment of Tahsin Bey's more moderate attitudes towards the Armenians as well as Mahmud Kiamil's taking advantage of Scheubner's and the governor's absence from the city was confirmed by the Armenian Catholic witnesses. ASV, Archivio nunziatura turchia, carte Dolci, busta 9, "The deportation of Erzerum," Aug. 1916, folio 559. Among the killed Armenian physicians were Baghdasar and Misak Baghdasarian and a certain Ghazaros of Erzeroum. Les persécutions contre les médecins arméniens pendant la guerre générale en Turquie, Constantinople, Union des médecins arméniens, 1919 pp. 27, 29.

167 FO 371/6500/E3557 Tahsin to Sabit, [Erzerum], July 16, 1915 No. - translation.

168 DH.ŞFR, 54/ A-37, Minister to Erzerum Province, July 17, 1915 EUM Spec. 4725.

169 DH.ŞFR, 54/A-50, Minister to Erzerum Province, July 17, 1915 EUM Spec 40.

On July 28, 1915, Tahsin detailed the excesses committed by Special Organizaton members and attached gendarmerie officers in Erzerum. They had taken over Armenian property, were abusing Armenian girls, and committing atrocities along the roads to Harpoot. The roads were littered with corpses of women and children who could not be buried.[170] In an undated telegram, Bahaeddin inquired with his CUP colleague Reshneli Nazım at Harpoot whether the Armenians in his region were indeed killed or simply deported.[171] An army commander later claimed that all decisions for massacres and atrocities were coordinated by Bahaeddin Shakir, but it appears that the General was eager to whitewash the army.[172]

Scheubner's continued reports on the massacre of Armenians must have created some problems for the Ottoman central government. On June 31, 1915, Mahmud Kiamil informed Enver Pasha that he had taken all precautions for a safe deportation. However, the information could not have been more misleading. Throughout July, the extent of the carnage along the Erzindjan road became increasingly known at Erzerum. In a communication to Constantinople, Fuat Ziya Bey, the inspector of the 3rd Army's lines of communication, blamed massacres in the region of the Kop mountain on deserters and Kurds.[173] German eyewitnesses, however, saw the situation differently. Large-scale massacres had taken place at the Kemah gorge near Erzindjan and close to Baiburt. The victims had been mainly Armenians deported from Trebizond and Erzindjan. According to trustworthy informants, among them Schlimme, the atrocities at Kemah had been the work of Ottoman troops and gendarmes. It was evident that assassins had killed most men coming from Trebizond. The surviving women and children were in desperate need. Many were half naked, carrying grass, which was their only form of nutrition. When the women begged Schlimme for some money, gendarmes started beating them and pushed them ahead towards the gorge of Kemah. On his way from Erzindjan to Trebizond, Schlimme encountered more Armenian women

---

170 Tahsin, July 28, 1915 in Kocahanoğlu, *İttihat-Terakki'nin Sorgulanması*, p. 518.
171 Ibid.
172 Ibid., p. 522.
173 Cemalettin Taşkıran, "1915 Ermeni Tehciri Sırasında Osmanlı Devleti'nin Aldığı Tedbirlerine Bir Bakış," in Genel Kurmay Başkanlığı, *Beşinci Askerî Tarih Semineri Bildirileri*, I, Ankara, Genel Kurmay Basımevi, 1996, pp. 139-140. See also Yücel Aktar, "Enver ve Cemal Paşalarla Osmanlı Valileri, İmzalı Belgeler, Soykırım Tezlerini Çürütüyor," in *Yeni Türkiye* 7, 37 (2001) p. 326.

and children on the road whom the gendarmes treated "like animals." In a village, the gendarmes denied even water to the deported women and children. On July 1, 1915, close to Trebizond, Schlimme met a caravan of Armenian notables. Returning to Erzerum, Schlimme had to travel the same road. On the first part of his journey, he saw the naked bodies of more than 20 murdered Armenian men. Seeing more corpses further down the road, he learned from local inhabitants that most of the deported Armenian men had been killed near Gumushkhane. Accompanying gendarmes were said to have raped and killed many women. After passing through Baiburt once more, Schlimme met Armenian acquaintances who had been recently sent off from Erzerum. They stated that their group had fared comparably well so far.[174]

Scheubner was certain that Ottoman irregulars were killing with the consent of the Ottoman authorities. He had ascertained that the roads were generally safe for all with the exception for Armenians.[175] When the Ottoman 3rd Army moved its headquarters to Erzerum, Mahmud Kiamil openly asserted his authority over the city. Not surprisingly, the local CUP leaders supported the order. They told Scheubner that the real motives of the government were to exterminate the Armenian population. The Vice-Consul asserted that the common Muslim citizens suffered from the economic consequences of the deportations and did not approve the ruthless anti-Armenian policy. Almost all military and civilian officials, however, approved of it. Scheubner understood that the combination of massacres, deprivations during the march to the desert, and finally the desert climate would bring about the projected goal of the Ottoman authorities.[176] By August 5, 1915, Scheubner reported that no Armenian remained in his consular district. The Armenian communities in the city of Erzerum and the surrounding districts had ceased to exist. Despite the massacres of the deportees, the Vice-Consul thought that Armenians in his

174 AA-PA, Konstantinopel 170, J. No. 4415 [?], Scheubner Richter to Embassy, Erzerum, July 27, 1915 telegram 65; Türkei 183/39, A 28584, Scheubner Richter to Hohenlohe, Erzerum, Aug. 5, 1915 No. 23 enclosure in Scheubner Richter to Bethmann Hollweg, Erzerum, Aug. 10, 1915 J. No. 598; Ibid., Schlimme, Erzerum, August 5, 1915 enclosure 2; Konstantinopel 170, J. No. -, Stange, Erzerum, Aug. 23, 1915 enclosed in Liman von Sanders to Lossow, n. p., Oct. 9, 1915 Military Mission J. No. 3841 M 15.

175 AA-PA, Konstantinopel 170, J. No. 4416 [?], Scheubner Richter to Embassy, Erzerum, July 27, 1915 telegram 66.

176 AA-PA, Konstantinopel 170, J. No. 4674 [?], Scheubner Richter to Wangenheim, Erzerum, July 28, 1915 No. 21.

area had fared well in comparison to others. Far more extensive atrocities had been committed in neighboring provinces. Scheubner had learned that almost no Armenian men had survived the deportations in the Trebizond province. The plain of Khinis, however, had been the scene of large-scale massacres. To Scheubner, the deportations were nothing but a form of total extermination of the victims, plunder and destruction. On a different level, it was an attempt to terminate all Armenian cultural and political aspirations. The economic weakening of the survivors was destroying the material basis for an independent Armenian cultural existence. The Vice-Consul reported that many Turkish landlords and businessmen had asked him why Germany had induced the Ottoman government to commit such atrocities. Everyone understood that the new "system for the solution of the Armenian Question" differed radically from earlier massacres during the 1890s. A Muslim notable explained to Scheubner that during the earlier massacres the "fight" had been between men. Now, innocent women and children were murdered – contrary to Islamic law. The notable stressed that the atrocities were not the result of an enraged popular crowd but were systematic murders, committed on the order of the government and the CUP. The man added that rumors were about that Germany had urged the deportations in order to settle Armenians along the German owned Baghdad Railway.[177] Refuting Ottoman propaganda claims, Scheubner stressed that the Armenians had not offered any resistance against the massacres perpetrated by Kurds and Ottoman irregulars. The latter had already committed atrocities against Russian Muslims in Trans-Caucasia during the winter campaign.[178]

When Scheubner's successor, Schulenburg, arrived in Erzerum, he followed a cautious policy trying his best not to antagonize the local civilian and military authorities. No doubt, he had received instructions to this

177 These rumors triggered a nervous response among German diplomats. For the next six months, the German Foreign Office expended considerable efforts to secure an official Ottoman denial. Despite some Ottoman opposition German pressure generated some results. On December 15, 1915, Talaat sent a telegram to all local authorities, informing them that these allegations were baseless. The minister stated that no foreign government had been involved in the government's decision. DH.ŞFR, 59-19, Talaat to all provinces and districts, Constantinople, Dec. 16, 1915 EUM Gen. 757.

178 AA-PA, Türkei 183/39, A 28584, Scheubner Richter to Hohenlohe, Erzerum, Aug. 5, 1915 No. 23 enclosure 2 in Scheubner Richter to Bethmann Hollweg, Erzerum, Aug. 10, 1915 J. No. 598.

effect. More important was perhaps that he took over his assignment at Erzerum after the last deportation caravan had left the province. Only few Armenians had remained behind, all of them under special protection. The Austro-Hungarian consul at Trebizond, Ernst Kwiatkowski, noticed that Schulenburg, as well as Bergfeld, both downplayed the massacres of Armenians. But being confronted with the traces of atrocities, like decomposing corpses of slaughtered women and children at Shabinkarahisar, Schulenburg comprehended the real situation and changed his attitudes and reporting.[179]

Saving a Few.

During the last weeks of his tenure as Vice-Consul at Erzerum, Scheubner did all he could to save at least some of those who had appealed to him for help. He put up a determined resistance against all Ottoman attempts at deporting these last members of the Armenian population at Erzerum. After his departure, Schulenburg continued the struggle. The German officials could only protect a couple of dozen Armenians. These were either members of a foreign organization or could expect protection on account of their special relations to the German consulate.

In June 1915, a small group of Armenian Catholic sisters and Mechitarist monks had asked Scheubner for protection. The latter had asked the embassy to inform the Armenian Catholic Patriarch, Monsignore Paul Terzian, that he should considered the immediate departure from Erzerum of all Catholic Armenian sisters as imperative. Scheubner promised organizing safe conduct for them and loaning them the necessary funds. The return of Pietschmann to Constantinople provided a good opportunity for the evacuation of the sisters and Mechitarists.[180] Soon, however, Scheubner realized that the evacuation was impossible. Although the Austro-Hungarian embassy had agreed that the Armenians could accompany Pietschmann, Scheubner deemed the roads as too unsafe for any Armenian to travel, even under the protection of allied officers and soldiers.[181]

179 HHStA, PA XII 463, Kwiatkowski to Burian, Trebizond, Dec. 12, 1915 No. 84 P; Ibid., Kwiatkowski to Czernin, Samsun, May 26, 1917 No. 21/P. AA-Weltkrieg 11d secr./12, A 13891, Schulenburg, Kerasund, Apr. 28 1916 No. 23a enclosure in Nadolny to AA, Berlin, April 25, 1916 No. Pol. 7689 secret.
180 AA-PA, Konstantinopel 169, J. No. 3592, Scheubner Richter to Embassy, Erzerum, June 12, 1915 telegram 28; Ibid., J. No. 3641, Scheubner Richter to Embassy, Erzerum, June 14, 1915 telegram 30.

The Ottoman central authorities, for their part, had authorized the Catholics' transfer to Sivas, but the matter remained unresolved when Scheubner handed over his post to Schulenburg.[182] The latter had considerably more confidence in the Ottoman authorities. He considered sending the sisters and the Mechitarists with a Turkish escort to Constantinople. Given Schulenburg's attitudes the Mechitarists did not dare inform the new consul when they learned that their assassination on the road had been planned. Instead they secretly sent a letter to the Austro-Hungarian consul at Trebizond, but this official shared Schulenburg's assessment. Nevertheless, he asked the Austro-Hungarian embassy to show some interest in the matter with the Ottoman government.[183] Unlike its consul, the Austro-Hungarian embassy had little confidence in the Ottoman authorities. On September 25, 1915, an Austro-Hungarian diplomat approached Mordtmann and requested assistance in the matter of the Armenian Catholics as no Austro-Hungarian consulate existed in Erzerum. The Austro-Hungarian embassy wanted to know if the people were still alive and could be evacuated to Constantinople.[184] The Catholic sisters had remained in Erzerum all summer when in September their funds were finally exhausted. Now, they appealed through the German consulate to their congregation for permission to leave Erzerum.[185] In response, the German embassy inquired about the safety of the Mechitarists and Catholic sisters and requested information on a route for their evacuation.[186] Schulenburg responded that both the sisters and the Mechitarists not only wanted to leave the city, but that the command of the 3rd Army insisted on their removal for "security reasons," implying that the few isolated Catholics posed a threat to the army. On October 6, 1915,

---

181 AA- PA, Konstantinopel 169, J. No. zu 3641, Wangenheim to Scheubner Richter, Pera, June 16, 1915 telegram 9; Ibid., J. No. 3717, Scheubner Richter to Embassy, Erzerum, June 18, 1915 telegram 35.

182 DH.ŞFR, 54-321, Talaat to Erzerum province, July 6, 1915 Special 35; DH.ŞFR, 55-161, Minister [Talaat] to Erzerum province, Aug. 23, 1915 Special 48.

183 HHStA, PA XXXVIII 464, Amrig to [?], enclosed in Kwiatkowski, Erzerum, Aug. 31, 1915 Kwiatkowski to Burian, Trebizond, Sept. 24, 1915 Z.63/P.

184 AA-PA, Konstantinopel 97, J. No. 8288, Lechanofsky to Mordtmann, Constantinople, Sept. 25, 1919.

185 AA-PA, Konstantinopel 97, J. No. 8174, Schulenburg to Embassy, Erzerum, Sept. 29, 1915 telegram 98.

186 AA-PA, Konstantinopel 97, J. No. 8154, Hohenlohe to Schulenburg, Pera, Sept. 30, 1915 telegram 55.

the Ministry of Interior informed the provincial authorities that the planned transfer of the five Mechitarists had met with approval. But now, the Army Headquarters wanted to send them to Aleppo.[187] Schulenburg urged the embassy to secure permission for the trip to Constantinople.[188] The embassy informed the sisters' congregation but the latter had no funds to meet the expenses of the sisters' journey and asked the embassy to cover the costs.[189] Schulenburg calculated that the sisters needed at least £T100 to come to the capital.[190] With winter approaching, the matter became increasingly pressing.[191] The Austro-Hungarian embassy continued its own efforts as well.[192]

Finally, on October 16, 1915, the Ministry of Interior gave permission for the sisters and the Mechitarists to come to Constantinople.[193] Consequently, Schulenburg advanced £T50 to the sisters.[194] The Mechitarists and the sisters left Erzerum on November 22, 1915. Schulenburg had issued a German passport for one of them.[195] At Constantinople, some members of the group submitted a substantial report to Monsignore Angelo Maria Dolci, the Apostolic Delegate to Constantinople, on the events at Erzerum and the observations they had

---

187 DH.ŞFR, 56-310, Talaat to Erzerum Province, Oct. 6, 1915 EUM.

188 AA-PA, Konstantinopel 97, J. No. 8288, Schulenburg to Embassy, Erzerum, Oct. 3, 1915 telegram 104.

189 AA-PA, Konstantinopel 97, J. No. 8171, Neurath to Superior of the Congregation of the Immaculate Conception, Pera, Oct. 1, 1915; Ibid., J. No. zu 8171, Neurath to Superior of the Congregation of the Immaculate Conception, Pera, Oct. 1, 1915; Ibid., J. No. zu 8171, Neurath to Schulenburg, Pera, Oct. 4, 1915 telegram 59.

190 AA-PA, Konstantinopel 97, J. No. 8483, Schulenburg to Embassy, Erzerum, Oct. 7, 1915 telegram 107; Ibid., J. No. 8483, Neurath to Superior of the Congregation of the Immaculate Conception, Pera, Oct. 11, 1915.

191 AA-PA, Konstantinopel 98, J. No. 9122, Schulenburg to Embassy, Erzerum, Oct. 23, 1915 telegram 121; Ibid., Mordtmann, Pera, Oct. 23, 1915.

192 AA-PA, Konstantinopel 98, J. No. zu 9122, Leschanofsky to Mordtmann, Pera, Oct. 28, 1915; Ibid., Neurath to Schulenburg, Pera, Oct. 28, 1915 telegram 85.

193 DH.ŞFR, 57-33, Talaat to Tahsin, Constantinople, Oct. 16, 1915, in Yuca and Orel, *The Talât Pasha*, p. 124.

194 AA-PA, Konstantinopel 98, J. No. 9506, Schulenburg to Embassy, Erzerum, Nov. 3, 1915 telegram 128.

195 AA-PA, Konstantinopel 98, J. No. 11493, Schulenburg to Embassy, Erzerum, Nov. 21, 1915 No. 846; Ibid., J. No. 10229, Schulenburg to Embassy, Erzerum, Nov. 22, 1915 Ibid. telegram 142.

made on their way to Constantinople.[196] On December 20, 1915, Dolci reported to the Holy See on the deportation of Catholic Armenians. All 3,000 Armenians of the Erzerum diocese had been deported. The former and present bishops were now at Agn and Erzindjan. No news was available about the fate of 40 to 50 priests. The greater part of the community members had been killed. Those still alive were located at Kharpert, Urfa, and Deir Zor.[197]

Blinding the German Vice-Consulate

The second small group of protégés consisted of Armenians working or having worked for consulates or being otherwise connected with foreign institutions. With progressing deportations from the city, the Ottoman authorities increased efforts to deport this small group as well. On June 20, 1915, the Ottoman authorities ordered Persian Armenians who lived in Erzerum to be ready to leave the city within eight days. The local Persian Consul General tried to secure a three weeks' delay so that the Persian Armenians could settle their business affairs. The Persian ambassador intervened with Talaat as well and but could only secure an extension of eight days.[198] At the same time, the Ottoman authorities ordered the deportation of the American missionary station's personnel.[199]

Around the middle of June, Scheubner discussed with Tahsin whether the landlord of the German consulate, Sarkis Solighian, would be allowed to stay in Erzerum or might travel to a city of his choice and eventually to Germany. Solighian was a former professor of German language at the Armenian Sanasarian School and a valuable informant of the vice-consulate.[200] He also worked as an interpreter for Scheubner, recording eyewitness statements of Armenian victims. Tahsin conceded that Solighian would be allowed to stay until the roads were safe. In an effort to strengthen Solighian's position, Scheubner made him the official

196 ASV, Archivio nunziatura turchia, carte Dolci, busta 9, "The deportation of Erzerum," Aug. 1916, folio 559. See also, Naslian, *Les mémoires*, pp. 157-160, 168-169.

197 Archivio della sacra congregazione degli affari ecclesiastici straordinari, Città di Vaticano, Austria 463, (12687), Dolci to Gasparri, Constantinople, Dec. 20, 1915 No. 121.

198 AA-PA, Konstantinopel 169, J. No. 3918, Scheubner Richter to Embassy, Erzerum, June 21, 1915 telegram 43; Ibid., Mordtmann, Constantinople, June 29, 1915.

199 AA-PA, Konstantinopel 96, J. No. 5139 Scheubner Richter to Embassy, Erzerum, July 1, 1915 telegram 54.

administrator of the consular building. After all, Solighian had been the de
facto administrator. Tahsin did not oppose the measure. He also agreed to
Scheubner's proposal of keeping Solighian in Erzerum until a suitable
travel opportunity would offer itself, when the general deportation of the
Armenian population was announced. On June 29, 1915, Khulussi Bey
visited the consulate and inquired if Scheubner would consent to the
immediate deportation of Solighian. Scheubner replied that the governor
had allowed Solighian to stay. Following Khulussi's visit, Scheubner went
to the house of the vice-consulate's former honorary interpreter, Elfasian.
The house was located close to a police station. While the driver was
waiting outside in the official consular carriage, a policeman turned up.
Although the police knew that Elfasian did not have a special permit to stay
in Erzerum, the policeman demanded such a document from Elfasian. As
the latter could not present the requested permit, he was ordered to leave
immediately. Scheubner objected to the arbitrary measure and felt
personally insulted, since the order was given in his presence. The next
morning, July 1, 1915, Scheubner went to Tahsin's office where he learned
that both Solighian and Elfasian had been arrested. The Vice-Consul
protested to the governor who was already informed of the arrests. Now,
Tahsin suggested releasing the two if Scheubner would agree to their
deportation by July 3, 1915. Scheubner agreed to the proposal. However,
instead of releasing the two men, the authorities sent them to Ilidja, 16
kilometers west of the city. Scheubner reported the arrests to the German
embassy and went to Ilidja inquiring about the safety of the arrested.
Scheubner labeled the trip officially as a private recreation activity.
Interned Armenians often disappeared without trace while in custody.
Scheubner's visit was a step to prevent this. The action seemed to be
prudent since the governor had personally told the Vice-Consul that he
could not guarantee the safety of the two Armenians as long as Scheubner
would not agree to their deportation. This was nothing less than an attempt
at blackmail on the part of the Ottoman authorities. Tahsin was upset at
Scheubner's attempt to protect the two men. In retaliation, Tahsin took

200 Solighian (or Soghkian) was born in Kharpert in 1854. After the successful
  completion of his education at Erzerum's Sanasarian School, he went with a
  grant to Germany where he studied at the University of Jena. On his return
  to Erzerum he joined the teaching staff of the Sanasarian School and became
  one of the first three principals. He taught German, religion, and music. He
  married in 1912. The couple had three sons. Hratch A. Tarbassian, *Erzurum
  (Garin): It's Armenian History and Traditions*, English trans. by Nigol
  Schahgaldian, n. p., Garin Compatriotic Union, 1975, p. 110.

Scheubner's visit as a pretext for not releasing the prisoners. Moreover, the governor assumed that their release would leave "a bad impression" on the local Muslim population. In other words, he put the blame for the continued arrest of Solighian and Elfasian on Scheubner. Unofficially, the authorities accused Solighian of having been a member of the ARF. Scheubner did not believe the accusations and protested against the behavior and insinuations of the Ottoman official in written form. At length, he detailed the actions taken by Tahsin and the series of agreements the latter had broken. Reminding Tahsin of the Ottoman-German alliance and the negative impression the officials' action would leave with the Germans, Scheubner once more urged the release of the two Armenians. In a further letter, the Vice-Consul insisted on a prompt answer from Tahsin, making it clear that the governor must not treat the issue in a dilatory manner. Tahsin, however, remained adamant on his condition to release Solighian only when the latter would leave Erzerum immediately for Urfa. Moreover, the governor demanded from Scheubner the release from duty of a certain Garabed, one of the Vice-Consul's Armenian servants. The latter had to be deported as well. Scheubner was appalled by the measures against his staff. He concluded that the local authorities pursued two objects. First, they wanted to demonstrate to the public that the German Vice-Consul was incapable of protecting those Armenians connected with him. Secondly, the authorities attempted to cut off the vice-consulate from independent sources of information. When Scheubner confronted Tahsin with his conclusions, the latter denied these. The governor told the Vice-Consul that Khulussi Bey had informed him that Scheubner would resist any attempts on the part of the local authorities to arrest Solighian. Thus the arrest was made in broad daylight on a main street of the city. Scheubner made it clear that the allegations were untrue and accused the police chief of lying. Tahsin retorted with another accusation against the Vice-Consul. Now, he asserted that Scheubner had freed the two arrested from an Ottoman prison. The Vice-Consul rejected the allegation. Scheubner made it clear that the assertions were untrue and once more accused the police chief of lying. Scheubner urged the embassy for support and further instructions regarding the protection of the threatened persons.[201]

Although Scheubner had fulfilled Tahsin's demand that he would not hinder Solighian's departure, the man was still kept in prison by July 2, 1915. Meanwhile, Scheubner doubted that Tahsin Bey was still in charge of the local situation since he could not even honor his own promises. Given the damage for German prestige brought about by Solighian's arrest and the behavior of Tahsin, the Vice-Consul strengthened his appeals to the German embassy for intervention in Constantinople once more.[202] Wangenheim, however, advised the Vice-Consul that the German diplomatic service had no right to interfere with the arrest and deportation of the three Armenians in question since the latter were not privileged officials. Nevertheless, the embassy had appealed to the Sublime Porte and had obtained a promise that the central government would contact the provincial authorities in the matter.[203] Scheubner personally guaranteed that the Ottoman police had no evidence against Solighian and Elfasian. He strongly emphasized that the Ottoman authorities in Erzerum simply desired to publicly expose the powerlessness of the Germans to protect Armenians.[204] For the time being, Wangenheim could only reassure Scheubner that the embassy was working on the case and that the Ottoman government was inquiring into the matter.[205] The Ottoman provincial authorities carefully avoided giving Scheubner any written statement concerning the matter. Thus they maintained the deniability for their actions as far as possible. Along these lines, Tahsin proposed a deal to Scheubner on July 5, 1915. After the governor had refused to release Solighian and Elfasian from prison, he suggested releasing them from prison if Scheubner would not oppose their deportation, this time scheduled for July 8, 1915. Scheubner replied that the German embassy was taking steps to postpone the deportation of Solighian and Elfasian.

---

201 AA-PA, Konstantinopel 96, J. No. 5124, Scheubner Richter to Embassy, Erzerum, June 30, 1915 telegram 48; Ibid., J. No. 5131, Scheubner Richter to Embassy, Erzerum, June 30, 1915 telegram 52; Scheubner Richter to Embassy, Erzerum, July 7, 1915 J. No. 5333. Konstantinopel 96 telegram 62; Ibid., J. No. 5758, Scheubner Richter to Tahsin Bey, Erzerum, July 3, 1915 copy enclosures 1 and 2 in Scheubner Richter to Wangenheim, Erzerum, July 8, 1915 No. 19; Türkei 183/39, A 28584, "Statement by Garabed Hadji Oghlu Georgian," Erzerum, n. d., enclosed in Scheubner Richter to Bethmann Hollweg, Erzerum, Aug. 10, 1915.

202 AA-PA, Konstantinopel 96, J. No. 5132, Scheubner Richter to Embassy, Erzerum, July 1, 1915 telegram 55; Ibid., J. No. 5150, Scheubner Richter to Embassy, Erzerum, July 2, 1915 telegram 57; Ibid., J. No. 5213, Scheubner Richter to Embassy, Erzerum, July 3, 1915 telegram 58.

203 AA-PA, Konstantinopel 96, J. No. 5132, Wangenheim to Scheubner Richter, Pera, July 3, 1915 telegram 20.

204 AA-PA, Konstantinopel 96, J. No. 5274, Scheubner Richter to Embassy, Erzerum, July 6, 1915 telegram 59.

205 AA-PA, Konstantinopel 96, J. No. zu 5213/5274, Wangenheim to Scheubner Richter, Pera, July 6, 1915 telegram 21.

Thus, Scheubner argued that he could not give his decision until he had received further instructions from Constantinople. Tahsin, however, insisted. Being pressed for an answer, Scheubner openly declined his consent to the deportation of the two Armenians. Now, the local authorities acted swiftly and sent off both Armenians to Baiburt, the known massacre area, on July 6, 1915. Trying to save face, Tahsin made excuses for his behavior and disregard for the German ally's appeals by putting the blame on the military who allegedly had ordered the deportation.[206] Scheubner was not too impressed by the show. Tahsin's allegation did not account for his constant communications with the Ministry of Interior on the matter which he was hiding from Scheubner. In fact, the Ministry had asked for his assessment whether the two Armenians could remain in Erzerum.[207] Scheubner urged the embassy to secure permission for the return of both deportees to Erzerum. In Constantinople, Mordtmann made repeated representations with the Ottoman Ministry of Interior but the officials evaded him. On July 13, 1915, seven days after the deportation of Solighian and Elfasian, the Ministry informed Mordtmann that according to information received from Erzerum the three Armenians had to be deported from the city.[208] The Ministry had cabled the authorities accordingly.[209] In the end, Wangenheim could only express his regrets to Scheubner.[210]

Despite all setbacks, Scheubner's insistence brought about some positive results for Solighian, Elfasian, and the latter's wife. They were kept under guard for their protection at Baiburt. Scheubner hoped that on his request they would be transferred to Erzindjan later on. Moreover, Mahmud Kiamil had promised Scheubner that the three would be allowed to stay there. In case of need they would be moved to Aleppo and not to Urfa. Both Tahsin and Mahmud Kiamil were at pains to assure Scheubner that

---

206 AA-PA, Konstantinopel 96, J. No. 5332, Scheubner Richter to Embassy, Erzerum, July 6, 1915 telegram 61; Ibid., J. No. 5758, Scheubner Richter to Wangenheim, Erzerum, July 8, 1915 No. 19.

207 DH.ŞFR, 54-369, Talaat to Erzerum province, July 9, 1915 Special No. 37.

208 AA-PA, Konstantinopel 96, J. No. zu 5213, Mordtmann, Pera, July 5, 1915; Ibid., J. No. zu 5274, Mordtmann, Pera, July 6, 1915; Ibid., J. No. zu 5333, Mordtmann, Pera, July 8, 1915; Ibid., J. No. 5758, Scheubner Richter to Wangenheim, Erzerum, July 8, 1915 J. No. 5758 No. 19; Ibid., J. No. zu 5333, Mordtmann, Pera, July 13, 1915.

209 DHŞFR, 54-435, Talaat to Erzerum province, July 13, 1915 Special No. 35.

210 AA-PA, Konstantinopel 96, J. No. zu 5333, Wangenheim to Scheubner Richter, Pera, July 14, 1915 telegram 22.

the whole affair was solely the result of mismanagement by the executing police officers. Both officials claimed that they had not intended antagonizing the German consulate and apologized for the affair. Moreover, they declared that the responsible police officers would be punished. Their real attitudes were, however, different. These became obvious when they refused to allow the three Armenians to return to Erzerum.[211] Their families stayed in Erzindjan until February 1916, when the military authorities ordered their removal to Sivas. Schulenburg arranged their journey and they arrived safely.[212] The Elfasian family stayed in Erzindjan until late spring 1916 when they tried to move to Constantinople.[213]

Scheubner's fight for his protégés and his insistence secured the stay of a few other Armenians in the consulate. The Ottoman authorities did not touch these Armenians and left them alone until shortly before the fall of the city. Karl Werth was in charge of the administration of the consulate when Schulenburg was not in the city. On February 9, 1916, he cabled from Erzerum that the military authorities had ordered the deportation of all Armenian women and children who were still under the protection of the German consulate. Werth asked the embassy for intervention, as deportation under those conditions meant certain death. Even wealthy Muslim families had frozen to death on the road to Erzindjan.[214] On February 12, 1916, Werth was forced to evacuate the consulate altogether and travelled with his staff and the few Armenians left to Erzindjan.[215] Schulenburg approved of Werth's action and criticized Mahmud Kiamil's attitudes sharply. He thought that the General had developed xenophobia against anyone non-Turkish and this had almost reached pathological forms. Schulenburg ridiculed the General's order that there was a grave national danger to Turkey if Russian troops had come into contact with the

---

211 AA-PA, Konstantinopel 170, J. No. 6438, Scheubner Richter to Wangenheim, Erzerum, Aug. 4, 1915 No. 22.

212 AA-PA, Konstantinopel 101, J. No. 2324 / II 5934, Schulenburg to Embassy, Erzindjan, Feb. 25, 1916 telegram 23; Konstantinopel 99, J. No. 2464, Schulenburg to Embassy, Feb. 29, 1916 telegram 29.

213 AA-PA, Konstantinopel 101, J. No. 4447, Werth to Embassy, Sivas, Apr. 21, 1916 telegram 53.

214 AA-PA, Konstantinopel J. No. 532, Werth to Embassy, Feb. 9, 1916 telegram 15.

215 AA-PA, Der Weltkrieg 89, A 6123, Schulenburg to Metternich, Erzindjan, Feb. 17, 1916 (copy) enclosed in Metternich to Bethmann Hollweg, Pera, Mar. 3, 1916 No. 103.

Armenian cook of the German consulate. On the advice of German officers and the Ottoman military, Schulenburg ordered the further withdrawal of the whole consulate to Sivas.[216]

In April 1916, Schulenburg did his best to secure the safety and future of one of the Armenian girls in the German consulate. Avnik Chilingirian was the daughter of a wealthy Armenian notable. Her father had managed to place her under Scheubner's protection, when he was deported to Surudj. Schulenburg had hoped to send her to Germany, where she could stay with his elderly mother. However, the plan had failed and he inquired with his friend, the councillor of the German embassy, Constantin von Neurath, whether the latter would take a personal interest in her welfare.[217] After some deliberations, the embassy arranged a place for the girl to stay at the Armenian Patriarchate.[218] The other Armenian women and children remained under Werth's protection and moved with the offices from Erzindjan on to Sivas. It took Werth almost a year to find safe accommodation for them. However, he could count on the support of his superiors, as the women and children had to be protected to avoid damage to German prestige and future accusations.[219]

Despite all setbacks and failures, in the case of Solighian, the German efforts were successful. He and his family stayed in Sivas until the end of the war. Later, they moved to Constantinople and Rochester, NY. In the U.S., Solighian continued his teaching career and became a speaker for the Armenian General Benevolent Union. He died in 1937.[220]

The Goals of the Ottoman Central Government

In his communications to Constantinople, Scheubner reported on the deportations and atrocities usually in connection with the overall military situation. He made it clear that the acts of the local civilian and military authorities had negative consequences for the Ottoman war effort. Moreover, he, like his successor Schulenburg, dismissed accusations against Armenians and claims of military necessity when even the last remaining women and children were deported. Obviously, Ottoman propaganda did

216 Neurath forwarding Schulenburg's report of Mar. 23, 1916 sent from Erzindjan. AA-PA, Deutsche Konsulate Türkei, No. 57, Erserum Bd. 1, Ic 4608, Neurath to Bethmann Hollweg, Pera, Apr. 12, 1916 No. 4010.

217 AA-PA, Konstantinopel 100, J. No. 4014 / II 5859, Schulenburg to Embassy, Erzindjan, Apr. 8, 1916 telegram 9; Ibid., J. No. 4828, Schulenburg to Neurath, Erzindjan, Apr. 16, 1916 private.

218 AA-PA, Konstantinopel 100, J. No. II 5859, Neurath to Schulenburg, Pera, June 28, 1916 private.

not convince the two military officers. Nevertheless, the continued allegations and lies had some impact on the Vice-Consuls. They did not fully comprehend what the Ottoman government tried to achieve with the extermination of the Armenians.

The Ottoman central authorities followed a systematic policy of ethnic cleansing and massacre. Contrary to Tahsin's assurances, the civilian authorities played a critical part in this regard. At Constantinople, the Ministry of Interior closely supervised the deportations in the Erzerum province. The central government constantly gave detailed orders to the local authorities concerning various aspects of the process. On June 12,

---

219 AA-PA, Deutsche Konsulate, No. 57 Türkei, Erserum Bd. 2, Ic 4444, Bergfeld to Bethmann Hollweg, Sivas, Apr. 16, 1917 No. 25. Such concerns were well founded. The efforts of the German officials at Erzerum to save the few remaining Armenians soon became the center of rumors. These rumors reached the British government and were later included in the well-known British Parliamentary blue book published in 1916. Here, Scheubner's inability to intervene officially on behalf of Armenians was presented as support for the Ottoman anti-Armenian campaign. Moreover, German officers were accused of participating in the plunder of Armenian property. Scheubner and Schlimme were presented as rapists. According to one allegation, Scheubner was believed to have publicly abducted Miss Tchilingirian. "German officers at Erzerum helped the Turks to organize the deportation and also took their share of the booty. Almost every one of them had kidnapped Armenian girls. An officer called Schapner [Scheubner, H. K.], for instance took with him four girls; another called Karl [i.e. Carl Schlimme, H. K.], two girls; and so on – there was a long list of names which the reporter could not remember." James Bryce, Arnold Toynbee, eds., *The Treatment of Armenians in the Ottoman Empire, 1915-1916. Documents Presented to Viscount Grey of Fallodon by Viscount Bryce. Uncensored Edition,* ed. and intro. Ara Sarafian, Gomidas Institute, Princeton, NJ 2000, Doc. 56 p. 266. Mr. Safrastian attributes Scheubner's statement that he could not intervene to Edgar Anders who at that time was interned in Russia. Safrastian also recorded the accusation involving the fate of Miss Tchilingarian: "One Captain Schapner (?) is said to have forced Miss Tchilingarian, a handsome girl, to follow him. On her resisting and crying, she was dragged about in the streets and roughly handled. This worthy German also carried off Mrs. Sarafian, a young woman educated in Switzerland. Another German lieutenant Karl (?) [i.e. Karl Schlimme, H. K.], dragged five women to his rooms, and so on" Ibid., pp. 268-269, Doc. 57. See also Ibid., p. 266, Doc. 56.

220 Tarbassian, *Erzerum,* p. 110.

1915, Ali Munif Bey, the deputy Minister of the Interior, requested precise information on the location of the deported Armenian villages and their agricultural potential. Secondly, he requested official estimates of the capacity of these places for the settlement of Muslims.[221] On June 22, 1915, Ali Munif Bey instructed the provincial authorities at Erzerum that Armenian schools could be used for the use of Muslim settlers. The value of the real estate had to be entered in a special register.[222] The same day, the Ministry of Interior demanded precise data on the number of Armenians who had converted to Islam.[223] On June 24, 1915, Ali Munif Bey reiterated his demand for precise information on the number and location of the emptied villages and those that were to be emptied. Moreover, the ministry wanted information on the number of deportees and the deportation routes they were sent along.[224] On July 20, 1915, the Ministry of Interior addressed all Ottoman provincial and district administrations with a circular telegram. The central authorities demanded a map, detailing the administrative organization of the provinces and districts down to the village level. Moreover, two sorts of statistics had to be prepared, showing the demographic situation before and after the deportations.[225] At the same time, Talaat was worried about the number of Armenians who had converted to Islam and the attitudes of the local officials.[226] On July 24, 1915, the Ministry of Interior requested the number of deported Armenians up to that day, of those Armenians who had still remained at their places of residence, and of those who were in the

---

221 DH.ŞFR, 54-15, Ali Münif to Adana, Aleppo, Erzerum, Bitlis, Van, Diarbekir provinces, Marash district, Constantinople, June 14, 1915 İskân-i Aşâyir ve Muhâcirîn Müdîriyyeti (hereafter: IAMM). Later in his life, Ali Munif Bey would adamantly down play his role in the genocide and deny any responsibility. Ali Münif [Yeğena], *Ali Münif Bey'in Hâtıralar*, edited by Taha Toros, Istanbul, İsis Yayınları, 1996. For a discussion of these memoirs see Hilmar Kaiser, "Dall'impero alla republicca: le continuità del negazionismo turco," *in* Marcell Flores, ed., *Storia, verità, giustizia. I crimini del XX secolo*, Milano, Bruno Mondadori, 2001, pp. 89-113.

222 DH.ŞFR, 54-101, Ali Münif to Adana, Aleppo, Marash abandoned property commissions, Adana, Erzerum, Bitlis, Diarbekir, Aleppo, Broussa provinces, Marash, Cesarea, Karesi districts, June, 22, 1915 IAMM 316.

223 DH.ŞFR, 54-100, Minister to the governors of Van, Trabzon, Erzerum, Bitlis, Kharpoot, Diarbekir, Sivas provinces and Djanik province, June 22, 1915 EUM Spec. 4531.

224 DH.ŞFR, 54-137, Ali Münif to Adana, Erzerum, Bitlis, and Van provinces, Constantinople, June 24, 1915 IAMM.

course of their deportation.[227] By July 28, 1915, the Ottoman Ministry of War and Ministry of Interior had learned of rumors that Ottoman officials had taken money from Armenians. Now, the ministries inquired into the veracity of these reports.[228]

On August, 4, 1915, the Ministry of Interior decreed that Catholic Armenians had been exempted and that the number of those remaining was to be reported.[229] The same day, the local authorities learned that Protestant Armenians had also been exempted from deportations, and that precise information on the number of remaining Protestants was needed at Constantinople.[230] Given the progress of deportations, the exemption could hardly have mattered. The Ministry of Interior continued asking for updates on the state of deportations. On August 25, 1915, it again requested figures for deported Armenians and their current location. Moreover, data was needed on the remaining Protestant and Catholic Armenians and their numbers in proportion to the Muslim population.[231]

---

225 DH.ŞFR, 54/A-51, Ministry of Interior to all provinces and districts, Constantinople, July 20, 1915 EUM Gen. 397. The local authorities were, however, unable to meet the deadline for delivering the material. Thus, Talaat had to renew his instructions in September. DH.ŞFR, 55/A-115, Talaat to all provinces and districts, Constantinople, Sept. 7, 1915 EUM Spec. 533.

226 DH.ŞFR, 54/A-49, Talaat to Adana, Aleppo, Bitlis, Diarbekir, Erzerum, Kharpert, Mosul, Sivas, Trebizond, Van provinces, Djanik, Eskishehir, Kutahia, Marash, Mersin, Nighde Urfa, Zor districts, Constantinople, July 20, 1915 EUM Spec. 4752.

227 DH.ŞFR, 54/A-100, Ministry of Interior to Adana, Aleppo, Bitlis, Diarbekir, Erzerum, Kharpert, Sivas, Trebizond, Van provinces, Djanik, Marash, Urfa districts, Constantinople, July 24, 1915 EUM Gen. 400.

228 DH.ŞFR, 54/A-146, Talaat to Adana, Aleppo, Angora, Bursa, Bitlis, Diarbekir, Erzerum, Kharpert, Sivas, Trebizond provinces, Djanik Marash districts, Constantinople, July 28, 1915.

229 DH.ŞFR, 54/A-252, Talaat to Adana, Aleppo, Angora, Bitlis, Diarbekir, Erzerum, Kharpert, Sivas, Trebizond, Van provinces, Djanik, Marash, Urfa districts, Constantinople, August 4, 1915 EUM Spec. 423, in OBE p. 72 (doc. 76).

230 DH.ŞFR, 55-20, Minister to Adana, Bitlis, Diarbekir, Erzerum, Konia, Kharpert, Sivas, Trebizond, Van provinces, Afion, Djanik, Eskishehir, Izmit, Karesi, Marash, Nigde, Urfa districts, Constantinople, August 14, 1915 EUM Special Dept. No. 5028, in OBE p. 78 (doc. 83).

231 DH.ŞFR, 55-208 Ministry of Interior to provinces and districts, Constantinople, Aug. 25, 1915 EUM Spec. 5260 .

On August 28, 1915, Talaat asked provincial authorities to submit reports and photos documenting an Armenian uprising against the government and the Muslim population.[232] On August 29, 1915, at the height of the general deportations the Ministry of Interior once again stressed the official motives for its actions and cautioned the provincial authorities to follow their orders properly. Some exceptions from deportations such as Protestants and Catholics had to be respected.[233] At Erzerum such exceptions were of little importance. Following the fall of Erzerum in February 1916 and despite the ensuing military and administrative chaos, Talaat insisted on receiving information on those Armenians who might not have been deported so far.[234]

Hidden from the eyes of the German consulate at Erzerum, the Ottoman central government followed a program of ethnic engineering throughout the empire. The whole population had been classified into various categories. The goal was to create an ethnic Turkish dominance. Non-Turkish groups that the CUP believed it could absorb into the Turkish population like Kurds and other Muslim peoples were subjected to an assimilation program. Those populations that posed unmanageable obstacles to the CUP had to disappear, either by expulsion or murder. The quick execution was so important that the Ottoman government even risked undermining its own excuses concerning the Armenian massacres. It was hardly a credible policy to insist on the one hand on an Armenian threat to national security and the existence of widespread Armenian rebellion in the eastern provinces, while on the other hand, the same administration initiating a comprehensive settlement program in exactly the same areas. The real object of the Ottoman government was not simply to dispose of the Armenians during wartime. The authorities wanted to create new realities. The establishment of a dominant Muslim, preferably Turkish, peasantry would produce new demographic realities that a future peace conference could hardly change.[235]

---

232 DH.ŞFR, 55-150, Ministry to Adana, Aidin, Aleppo, Angora, Bitlis, Broussa, Diarbekir, Erzerum, Kharpert, Sivas, Trebizond, Van provinces, Afion, Cesarea, Djanik, Izmid, Marash, Urfa districts, Constantinople, Aug. 22, 1915 EUM Spec. 5204.

233 DH.ŞFR, 55-292, Minister to Erzerum and other provinces, Constantinople, August 29, 1915 EUM, in OBE, p. 87 (doc. 99).

234 DH.ŞFR, 63-50, Talaat to Erzerum, Bitlis provinces, Apr. 19, 1916 EUM Spec. 561, in OBE, p. 136 (doc.172).

The Confiscation of Armenian Property

Since the Armenian population's deportation was not a temporary measure, the Ottoman government confiscated by far the major part of Armenian property during the initial weeks of the genocide. The bankrupt government needed Armenians' wealth for financing its demographic program and also the war effort. In Erzerum, however, the expropriation of Armenian property did not proceed as smoothly as it had been hoped for. Once more, it was Scheubner who created serious problems for the Ottoman authorities. Scheubner had been alarmed by the news of imminent deportation of 160 rich notables and their families. Most of these notables were merchants of substance. They owed banks in Constantinople about £T100,000. After the plundering of Armenian villages, the merchants had already suffered heavy losses and the banks' claims were considered endangered. Even under normal circumstances, the merchants would have been unable to take with them more than a small part of their movable property. Thus they were forced to leave behind substantial assets. One of their business partners, Pierre Balladour, the director of the local branch of the Imperial Ottoman Bank, acted swiftly. His main concern was to protect the interests of his bank. He had developed a plan and convinced the governor to support it. Balladour suggested the formation of a mixed commission, consisting of two Armenians, one Turk, and one Greek. The commission would take into safekeeping the property and goods of deported merchants. It would not, however, accept any responsibility for deposits' security. The assets would be used as securities for the claims of the various banks against the deported Armenians.[236] The Ottoman Bank at Constantinople quickly approved

---

235 Research on the Muslim settlement program in connection with the Armenian Genocide is still scarce. For first results see Fikret Adanır, Hilmar Kaiser, "Migration, Deportation, and Nation-Building: the Case of the Ottoman Empire," in René Leboutte, ed., *Migrations and Migrants in Historical Perspective. Permanencies and Innovations*, Bruxelles, Peter Lang Verlag, 2000, p. 273-292; Fuat Dündar, *İttihat ve Terakki'nin Müslümanları İskân Politikası (1913-1918)*, Istanbul, İletişim Yayınları, 2001; Idem, "İttihat ve Terakki'nin Etnisite Araştırmaları," in *Toplumsal Tarih* 16, 91 (2001) p. 43-50. See also: Nesim Şeker, "Demographic Engineering in the Late Ottoman Empire and Armenians," in *Middle Eastern Studies* 43, 3 (2007), pp. 461-474.

236 AA-PA, Konstantinopel 169, J. No. 3425, Scheubner Richter to Embassy, Erzerum, June 4, 1915 telegram 11; Ibid., J. No. 3414, Scheubner Richter to Embassy, Erzerum, June 4, 1915 telegram 12.

Balladour's proposal and sanctioned his actions.[237] Accordingly, the Armenian merchants brought bales containing wool and cotton cloth, silk, leather, etc. and received receipts for their deposits.[238] Having obtained his superiors' authorization Balladour suggested that the German consulate, in other words Scheubner Richter personally, should participate in the registration and custody of the assets. But Scheubner declined the request with Wangenheim's approval.[239] The Armenian Apostolic and Catholic churches became the main storage space for the deposits. The ABCFM mission at Erzerum was a third place that accepted valuables for safekeeping. Several rich merchants entrusted their life insurance policies to the missionaries. Evidently, they had little trust in the authorities' promises about their safety.[240] Two other proposals by Balladour were of more immediate importance for the Armenian deportees. First, he tried to secure the bank's intervention with the central authorities on behalf of his local Armenian bank staff and, secondly, he proposed paying out hard currency to a limited circle of Armenian customers in order to provide them with ready cash for the road. The bank declined Balladour's request in the case of his local employees and advised him to continue local efforts. This response was certainly of little consolation for the branch manager as he had already exhausted his own influence. The central branch's reply to Balladour's second suggestion was more positive and the manager was authorized to pay out a total of up to £T3,000 with a maximum of £T50 per family. The Armenians had to provide securities, preferably jewelry and the like, that were not liable to requisition by the authorities.[241]

Tahsin's support for Balladour's plans was to remain only temporary. Since he had not received specific orders in regard to the deportees'

237 AA-PA, Konstantinopel 169, J. No. zu 3414, Wangenheim to Scheubner Richter, Pera, June 5, 1915 telegram.

238 MAE, Nouvelle Série 951, Ottoman Bank, n. p., Feb. 15, 1917 enclosed in Ottoman Bank to Briand, Paris, Feb. 20, 1917 A 39 f-3.

239 AA-PA, Konstantinopel 945, J. No. 4396, Scheubner Richter to Embassy, Erzerum, June 6, 1915 telegram 14; J. No. zu 4396, Wangenheim to Scheubner Richter, Pera, June 8, 1915 telegram 13.

240 Library of Congress, Morgenthau Papers, Reel 7/718, Heizer to Morgenthau, Trebizond, Sept. 25, 1915. United States – National Archives (hereafter: US-NA), Washington, D.C., Record Group 59, 867.5064/6, Heizer to Morgenthau, Trebizond, Oct. 16, 1915. Most of the documents from the US-NA and Library of Congress have been published in Ara Sarafian, compiler, *United States Official Records on the Armenian Genocide 1915-1917*, Princeton, NJ and London, Gomidas Institute, 2004.

property, he supported Balladour. The Ottoman Bank's decision became known in Erzerum just in time. On June 6, 1915, Tahsin Bey had inquired with the central government concerning the procedures to be followed in regard to Armenian property and sent a telegram to Talaat. The response was cabled on June 9, 1915. The Ministry of Interior informed the governor that all confiscated Armenian possessions should be auctioned off. Moreover, a secret manual had already been sent out. The Ministry's "Directorate for the Settlement Tribes and Immigrants" had been charged with the supervision and organization of the confiscations. According to the instruction, special "Liquidation Commissions" were to be formed that should register all Armenian property. These transferred Armenian properties to the state or individual Muslim settlers and businessmen. This way, the government hoped to create a new Turkish business elite and expand Muslim rural settlement.[242]

The commissions did not, however, confiscate the deposits with the Ottoman Bank and the U.S. mission, since the manual had been promulgated after the handover of the goods and valuables. On August 5, 1915, Scheubner forwarded a list of claims German banks in Constantinople had against Armenian debtors resulting from credits. Merchandise and assets that Armenian merchants had handed over for safekeeping to the Ottoman Bank were stored in a local Armenian church near the bank's offices. A German officer had estimated the value of the deposits at £T150,000. Scheubner was sure that at least a part of the German banks' claims had been secured and possibly also a part of the balance belonging to Armenians. All other Armenian property in the city had been seized by the Ottoman government or been taken over by individuals.[243]

---

241 AA-PA, Konstantinopel 945, J. No. 4396, Ottoman Bank to Embassy, Constantinople, June 7, 1915; J. No. zu 4396, Wangenheim to Scheubner Richter, Pera, June 8, 1915 telegram 13. Having been deported from Erzerum to Kharpert Shushanig Dikranian was able to retrieve £T50 through the local branch of the Ottoman Bank, which seems to be in line with the instructions send to Balladour. Kévorkian, *Génocide*, p. 362.

242 DH.ŞFR, 53-303, Ministry of Interior to Tahsin Bey, Constantinople, June 9, 1915, in Yuca and Orel, *The Talât Pasha*, p. 119. For more information on the confiscation of Armenian property see Hilmar Kaiser, *1915-1916 Ermeni Soykırım Sırasaında Ermeni Mülkleri, Osmanlı Hukuku ve Milliyet Politikaları*, in Erik Jan Zürcher, ed., *İmparatorluktan Cumhuriyet'e Türkiye'de Etnik Çatışma, Istanbul, İletişim Yayınları*, 2005 pp. 123-156.

Later in August 1915, the military authorities removed the seals of the Ottoman Bank from the depot and sealed the church again, this time affixing government seals. Balladour appealed to his superiors in Constantinople where his representations resulted in an inquiry of the central government. German acting Ambassador Hohenlohe instructed Scheubner to support Balladour and stress that the Armenian assets had been secured with the consent of the governor and before the formation of the Liquidation Commission. Consequently, the depot belonged to the Ottoman Bank, which was fully responsible for the assets. Hohenlohe emphasized that no legal basis existed for the seizure of the property until a new law had been passed.[244]

On September 26, 1915, with the passing of the provisional law on so-called "abandoned property" the situation concerning the depot changed fundamentally. Within in two weeks, the central government instructed the local authorities to provide an inventory of the remaining Armenian property.[245] When the German Orientbank forwarded a list of its claims of about £T9,000 against Armenians in Erzerum, the response from the embassy was disquieting.[246] Neurath cautioned the bank, informing it that he was not sure whether Schulenburg would still be able to protect the interests of the bank.[247] About the same time, the Ottoman military in Erzerum began requisitioning goods from the Ottoman Bank's depot at the Armenian church. Under the supervision of Balladour and Schulenburg, the military first took about 6,200 kilograms of leather and 750 kilograms of furs.[248] In the following months, the Ottoman Bank accepted further requisitions by the military, but resisted attempts on the part of the liquidation commission to seize the depot altogether. The bank

243 AA-PA, Konstantinopel 170, J. No. 6652, Scheubner Richter to Wangenheim, Erzerum, Aug. 5, 1915 No. 26; Ibid., J. No. -, Stange, Erzerum, Aug. 23, 1915 enclosed in Liman von Sanders to Lossow, n. p., Oct. 9, 1915 Military Mission J. No. 3841 M 15.

244 AA-PA, Konstantinopel 96, J. No. zu 6652, Hohenlohe to Scheubner Richter, Pera, Sept. 3, 1915 telegram 33.

245 DH.ŞFR, 56-325, Said, Revenue Office, Secretariat to Erzerum Revenue Directorate, Oct. 7, 1915, No. 12.

246 AA-PA, Konstantinopel 97, J. No. 8263, Orientbank to Embassy, Constantinople, Oct. 2, 1915.

247 AA-PA, Konstantinopel 97, J. No. zu 8263, Neurath to Orientbank, Pera, Oct. 8, 1915.

248 AA-PA, Konstantinopel 97, J. No. 8291, Schulenburg to Embassy, Erzerum, Oct. 10, 1915 telegram 101.

feared that the commission would auction off all assets despite the fact that under the current circumstances the goods would fetch only a fraction of their real value. Therefore, the bank anticipated heavy losses in case of a confiscation by the commission. As an alternative, the bank suggested to sell the goods itself at a favorable moment. In the ensuing conflict between the commission and the bank, the latter assumed that the goods had been pawned to the bank. The commission, however, argued that the goods had to be used for covering all claims against the proprietors. While Balladour was willing to defend his position in court, he had serious doubts that he would win the case. The main problem was that although the bank had made an inventory of all goods, it had not received an official certificate detailing its rights in regard to the assets. As a possible solution, Schulenburg suggested that the bank itself might bid for the goods at the action thereby trying to minimize losses. For the time being, however, Balladour could not do little more than proposing joint action by his own, the German, and Austro-Hungarian banks and asked for further instructions from his superiors.[249]

Cooperation between the banks was a difficult matter. The Ottoman Bank and the Orientbank had not yet come to an agreement that stipulated that it would represent the latter's claims against Armenian debtors. So far, Schulenburg had supported Balladour since the consul had assumed that the Ottoman bank would act on behalf of the Orientbank like it did for other German claimants. In the absence of an agreement between the banks, however, Schulenburg would be forced to share the commission's position that the Armenian property in the depots had to be used to cover all claims.[250] While the two banks and the Ottoman authorities argued over the Armenian property, a Russian advance on Erzerum rendered the dispute pointless. At the end of January 1916, both the governor and army commander Mahmud Kiamil ordered the local bank to hand over the keys to the churches and evacuate the city for Erzindjian.[251]

On February 26, 1916, Russian troops routed the Ottoman 3rd Army once more and occupied Erzerum. The fall of Erzerum, however, did not mean the end of the struggle for the property. It seems that only some of the parties involved in the case had changed. In this situation, the Ottoman

249 AA-PA, Konstantinopel 98, J. No. 10516, Schulenburg to Embassy, Erzerum, Nov. 3, 1915 No. 788.

250 AA-PA, Konstantinopel 98, J. No. 10397, Schulenburg to Embassy, Erzerum, Nov. 26, 1915 telegram 145.

251 AA-PA, Konstantinopel 945, J. No. B 1223, Werth to Embassy, Erzerum, Jan 31, 1915 telegram 8.

Bank profited from being an international institution with branches and offices in the Ottoman Empire, western Europe, and Russia. The staff of the Ottoman Bank's Erzerum branch left the city two days before the Russian conquest. The bank's building burned down when the surrounding quarter went up in fire. In the ruins, Russian troops found four safes and opened them. Shortly afterwards, Mr. Algardi, a representative of the Ottoman Bank, went to Erzerum but the authorities refused him access to the relevant papers. In May 1916, however, Algardi ascertained that a considerable part of Armenian property was still in the depots in Erzerum. With the assistance of the French diplomatic service, the bank secured permission for Algardi to return to Erzerum and prepare an inventory of the depots. Algardi learned that an estimated 2,000 of the originally 6,000 bales of merchandise had been left when the Russians occupied the city. The Russian army transferred a part of the bales to an army depot. Later, nearly 370 bales were handed over to people who claimed these as their property upon presenting some evidence. However, due to abuses the return of the merchandise had been suspended.

At the same time, the Russian army began requisitioning goods it could use for its war effort. When Algardi gained access to the various depots, he registered 2,465 packages in the Armenian church and 712 in the Russian army depot. A large number of the bales and packages had been damaged and their contents had partly deteriorated. Algardi feared that everything would be lost if the goods remained in the damaged church building. Thus he proposed selling everything at a public auction. The proceeds would then be transferred to the Ottoman Bank for safekeeping until the end of the war. Then, Armenian proprietors would receive their share of the proceeds upon presentation of the original receipts they had obtained in 1915. The Russian military authorities neither accepted Algardi's proposals nor did they officially recognize his inventory. Later, the military authorities refuted the claims of the bank to the property, as the owners were unquestionably Armenians. Moreover, the Russian authorities announced that after another requisition the remaining goods would be sold and the proceeds kept with the Russian civilian authorities.[252]

Concerns for the rights of the proprietors were only officially at the core of the discussions between the Russian authorities and the Ottoman Bank. Both parties knew very well that few, if any, of the merchants had escaped massacre. Thus, obtaining control of the merchandise amounted to gaining

---

252 MAE, Nouvelle Série 951, Ottoman Bank, n. p., Feb. 15, 1917 enclosed in
  Ottoman Bank to Briand, Paris, Feb. 20, 1917 A 39 f-3.

full possession of it. In its correspondence, the Ottoman Bank revealed its intention to seize the assets. Declaring that it would only surrender the merchandise to its owner if the latter could furnish original receipts was nothing but a show of bad faith. Clearly the bank was afraid that some of the owners might have survived and would claim their property. While survival would have been one major achievement, protecting documents from theft and maintaining them intact would have been another matter. Thus, insisting on the presentation of original receipts would have served as further security for the bank in its desire to profit from the owner's personal disaster. The bank's precautions against potential abuse also appears questionable as it had earlier refused accepting any responsibility for the protection of the merchandise. Recourse to legal action on the part of the owner would have been unlikely as impoverished survivors could hardly afford lengthy legal disputes in court. The strategies of the Russian authorities and the Ottoman Bank show that it was not only the Ottoman government which did all it could to profit from thinly veiled theft of Armenian property.

III. The Road to Mosul

The arrival of Schulenburg relieved Scheubner of his numerous consular duties. For the rest of his stay in the city Scheubner concentrated on preparing the raid into Persia. He left Erzerum on September 25, 1915 as part of a detachment headed by Ömer Nadji and himself.[253] The combined detachment numbered about 650 men. Scheubner had at his disposal about 100 infantry, 30 mounted irregulars, and one piece of mountain artillery. Ömer Nadji's unit was considerably larger, about 500 men according to German military reports. The irregulars joining the expedition were "cowards" and used to "plunder and theft."[254] It is not

---

253 AA-PA, Weltkrieg 11d.secr./7, A 28370, Hohenlohe to AA, Pera, Sept. 29, 1915 telegram 2208. The telegram was intended for German military intelligence.

254 AA-PA, Weltkrieg 11d secr. /8, A 29930, Wangenheim to AA, Pera, Oct. 16, 1915 telegram 2370. The ambassador forwarded military attachés Von Lossow's report to the German Supreme Army Command. Türkei Weltkrieg 11d secr./9, A 37451, Schulenburg, Erserum, Nov. 28, 1915 No. 6 copy enclosure in Nadolny to AA, Berlin, Dec. 27, 1915 Sektion Politik No. Pol. 4961. For only slightly different figures see: Sarısaman, *Ömer Naci Bey*, p. 503. See also: İsrafil Kurtcephe, "Birinci Dünya Savaşında Bir Süryani Ayaklanması," in *OTAM* 4 (1993) p. 292.

entirely clear whether Scheubner knew that the expeditionary force formed part of the Ottoman "Special Organization."[255]

After the Russian occupation of Van, Nadji had transferred to Erzerum.[256] His presence at Erzerum had been a matter of importance to the CUP's central committee which had to authorize his stay there.[257] According to Aziz Samih [İlter] who served at the time as an officer at the 3rd Army's general staff, Nadji spent his time in Erzerum showering the CUP and Ottoman central high command with requests to allow him an independent raid into Iran unless he was not busy with drinking and feasting. He asked for only 100 men. When he failed to succeed, he entered an agreement with Scheubner whose activities were watched with some suspicion by the 3rd Army. Following repeated inquiries the officer's at the 3rd Army's general staff understood that Scheubner had been planning some operations behind the Russian lines and was active with German propaganda in Iran for which he had considerable funds at his disposal. The German's importance rose even higher when Enver Pasha ordered the 3rd Army to support Scheubner.[258]

Finally, Nadji and Scheubner came to an agreement for a joint raid into Iran. Originally the main purpose of the expedition had been to bring Scheubner and Nadji safely to their Persian destinations. Military command was to be assumed by Veli, an older captain. Scheubner, however, had rejected this arrangement, being afraid of becoming fully dependent on the captain and Nadji. In the end, Scheubner received his

---

255 Kurtcephe, *Süryani Ayaklanması*, p. 292.

256 For some time following the Russian occupation of Van the Ottoman authorities appear to have had lost track of Nadji. DH.ŞFR, 54-69 Talaat to Van governor Djevdet Bey, June 19, 1915 Special Office No. 27.

257 DH.ŞFR, 55-28 Talaat to Erzerum governor Tahsin Bey, Aug. 16, 1915 Special Office. Interestingly, the telegrams concerning Nadji's moves were all directed to the provincial governor personally. As these governors were trusted party members, it appears that at least part of the CUP communications went through the Ottoman Ministry of Interior's channels.

258 Aziz Samih [İlter], *Birinci Dünya Savaş'ında Kafkas Cephesi Hatıraları*, ed. by Zekeriya Türkmen and Elmas Çelik, 2nd ed. Ankara, Genelkurmay Askerî Tarih ve Stratejik Başkanlığı Yayınları, 2007 p. 53. İlter was rather critical about independent German efforts in Iran. Flavoring his criticism with contemporary gossip, he claimed that German officer had been engaging in intimate contact with Iranian girls. İlter's claim that the officers had "married" the girls appears more concession to Muslim public opinion than reality. Ibid., p. 54

own small detachment, but had no authority over Nadji's soldiers.[259] Scheubner's first task was to establish a base in Persia for communication with the Caucasus.

Knowing little on Nadji's policies and role within the CUP's strategy, Scheubner assumed the TM leader had opposed the persecution of Armenians. This was important in Scheubner's view as he believed that despite the almost complete annihilation of the Ottoman Armenian communities, cooperation with the ARF was still possible and would be a valuable source of support for the Trans-Caucasian campaign. Evidently, Nadji had not shared information on the unsuccessful earlier negotiations with the ARF. Thus, Scheubner's failure to convince his superiors, when he argued that the CUP's anti-Armenian policy would be detrimental to the envisioned campaign in the Trans-Caucasus, seemed to have been of consequence. While supporting Scheubner's ideas in principle, Zimmermann thought it advisable to caution Scheubner that his endeavor was unlikely to succeed.[260] Scheubner did not give up, using his influence with Ömer Nadji against other Young Turks in the detachment during the raid whenever Armenians were concerned.[261]

The journey to Bitlis and Mosul often turned into a nightmarish experience. All Armenian villages along the route had been destroyed. Scheubner had not seen any Armenian men alive. While the government tried to hide the atrocities from the Germans by removing Armenian corpses along their way, the latter had still seen burnt and decomposing corpses of men, women, and children everywhere. These victims often bore bayonet wounds, indicating that the murderers had been regular Ottoman troops. Kurds stated that all Armenians had been killed. Most likely referring to Mush, Scheubner informed the embassy that he himself had detected only cases of Armenian self-defence but no rebellion. Moreover,

---

259 AA-PA, Weltkrieg 11d secr./10, A 3899, Schulenburg to Stellvertretenden Generalstab Abt. IIIb Pol., Trapezunt, Jan. 11, 1916 No. 8 copy enclosure in Nadolny to AA, Berlin, Feb. 10, 1916 No. Pol. 5736. Leverkuehn's account of the arrangement differs somewhat from these reports and most likely represents Scheubner's views. Leverkuehn, *Posten,* pp. 56-57.

260 AA-PA, Türkei 183/39, zu A 28584, Zimmermann to Wangenheim, Berlin, Oct. 20, 1915 No. 782. AA-PA, Konstantinopel 171, J. No. 6175, Neurath to Erzerum, Pera, Oct. 28, 1915.

261 AA-PA, Weltkrieg 11d.secr./ 10, A 3899, Scheubner to Schulenburg, Mosul, Dec. 7, 1915 copy enclosure in Schulenburg to Stellvertretenden Generalstab Abt. IIIb Pol., Trapezunt, Jan. 11, 1916 No. 8 copy enclosure in Nadolny to AA, Berlin, Feb. 10, 1916 No. Pol. 5736 secret.

Turkish officers were spreading rumors that Germans were behind the extermination of Armenians. The scenes of horror would not change when he continued on to Mosul.[262]

In Mush, Scheubner learned the detachment's advance to Persia via Van was out of question. Russian troops had advanced beyond Van and were now threatening to cut off the units' route to Bitlis. Ottoman counter attacks under the TM leader Yakub Djemil had failed. While the Russians did not march further on Bitlis at that time, they still posed a serious threat that made local officials nervous.[263]

The detachment reached Bitlis on October 10, 1915. As supplies for the troops were not ready, the detachment planned to stay for some days. Scheubner's confidence in the unit's reliability had been profoundly shaken. He reported that based on his experiences on the march to Bitlis, he considered outrages against the local population particularly in Persia as inevitable as long as he had no greater authority over the whole unit or obtained full command. Avoiding any direct reference to Armenians, there could be no doubt that the slaughter of Armenians lay at the foundation of his call for greater authority. Being himself a lieutenant, some Ottoman officers openly questioned his authority due to their higher rank. Similarly, he tried to boost his standing by trying to obtain the title of Vice-Consul once again.[264] Scheubner argued that giving up his consular title would harm his political prestige vis-à-vis Ottoman officials. Moreover, he trusted that the title would increase his ability to counter CUP political moves in Persia, once the detachment got there. After all, he stated, his assignment was both, a political and military one.[265] The AA, however, did not share his analysis and turned down the request. Moreover, Neurath advised Scheubner to desist from bringing up the matter once more.[266] Obtaining

---

262 AA-PA, Konstantinopel 171, J. No. 6401, Holstein to Embassy, Mosul, Nov. 6, 1915 telegram 62. The information was forwarded verbatim to the AA. Türkei 183/39, A 33278, Neurath to Bethmann Hollweg, Pera, Nov. 9, 1915 No. 660. Türkei 183/45, A 33457, Scheubner-Richter to Bethmann Hollweg, München, Dec. 4, 1916 Tgb.Z. 243. HHStA PA XII 463 Kwiatkowski to Czernin, Samsun, May 26, 1917 No. 21/ P.

263 AA-PA, Weltkrieg 11d secr./ 10, A 3899, Scheubner to Schulenburg, Mosul, December 7, 1915 copy enclosure in Schulenburg to Stellvertretenden Generalstab Abt. IIIb Pol., Trapezunt, January 11, 1916 No. 8 copy enclosure in Nadolny to AA, Berlin, Feb. 10, 1916 No. Pol. 5736 secret.

264 AA-PA, Weltkrieg 11d secr./.8, A 30144, Wangenheim to AA, Pera, Oct. 16, 1915 telegram 2383; Konstantinopel 944, J. No. 9654, Scheubner to Wangenheim, Near Bitlis, Oct. 14, 1915 No. 1.

again the title of Vice-Consul was, however, not the only promotion Scheubner sought as he had also applied for military promotion using the same arguments.[267] Scheubner had not, however, told the full story behind his request. He felt the need to have additional authority because he feared further Armenian massacres, this time committed by members of the detachment. One of the CUP officers in the detachment, Dr. Fuad, had been an organizer of massacres in Trebizond province, but it is not certain that Scheubner knew that Fuad was a leading TM member in the area.[268]

In Bitlis Scheubner witnessed the shocking fate of Armenian women and children; 500 of them were kept prisoner in an Armenian church; others were in Turkish houses.[269] Instructions from the embassy provided Scheubner with an opportunity to make inquiries into the situation. A German missionary, Sister Martha Kleist, had been at Bitlis but been without communications for some time. Scheubner learned from the two remaining American missionaries, Miss Myrtle O. Shane and Miss Grisell M. MacLaren, that Kleist had died. The Americans gave him the personal effects of the deceased which he later delivered.[270] The missionaries later wrote about Scheubner:

> "These officers listened with interest to the story of what had taken place in Bitlis. They sent food to the women kept in prison in a starving condition, and later they gathered up children and brought

265 AA-PA, Konstantinopel 944, J. No. 8760 Scheubner to Embassy, Bitlis, Oct. 12, 1915 telegram 3; Ibid. J. No. 9654 , Scheubner to Wangenheim, Near Bitlis, Nov. 14, 1915 No. 1.

266 AA-PA, Konstantinopel 944, J. No. ad 9654, Neurath to Holstein, Pera, Nov. 10, 1915 telegram 73

267 AA-PA, Weltkrieg 11d secr./8, A 30530, Nadolny to AA, Berlin, Oct 20, 1915 Sektion Politik No. Pol.3869.

268 Arif Cemil, *I. Dünya Savaşı'nda*, p. 45; Ertürk, *İki Devrin*, p. 111. Leverkuehn describes Fuat as Nadji's right hand man and an ardent, even fanatic, nationalist. Leverkuehn, *Posten*, pp. 65-66. It is likely that Fuad is identical with Fuad Sabıt, director of the Special Organization's India, Egypt, Afghanistan and Arabia Department; see Erdal Eydoğan, *İttihat ve Terakki'nin Doğu Politikası 1908-1918*, Istanbul, Ötüken, 2005 p. 75, 77.

269 AA-PA, Türkei 183/39, A 33278, Neurath to Bethmann Hollweg, Pera, Nov. 9, 1915 No. 660. Leverkuehn, *Posten*, pp. 65-68. For further information see: Kévorkian, *Génocide*, pp. 416-420.

270 Grace H. Knapp, *The Tragedy of Bitlis. Being Mainly the Narratives of Grisell M. McLaren*, New York, Fleming H. Revell, 1919, p. 130. Republication: London, Sterndale Classics, 2002 p. 87

them to the American ladies. Because of their evident sympathy for the Armenians they incurred the suspicion of the government and were constantly shadowed by spies."[271]

Scheubner and Leverkuehn did not hide their views from the missionaries. Leverkuehn made a point in expressing his indignation: "As officers we are compelled to shut our eyes to these things, but as men the alliance with these people is unbearable."[272] Communicating was a difficult as the local authorities had sent a doctor to monitor the visit. While Scheubner and the Leverkuehn brothers out-smarted the spy; they could not directly help the missionaries when these asked for protection of the Armenians still in their care. [273]

Scheubner informed the embassy about a festive reception by the local authorities and population,[274] but he did not tell the full story. At a dinner the CUP members drank alcohol and got into an elated mood. Now they expressed themselves frankly, making mocking remarks about Scheubner's support for Armenians. The German seized the chance and brought up the issue of the Armenians in the missionaries' care. The provincial governor consented to see one of the missionary ladies. Miss Shane was called upon and with Scheubner interpreting for her she asked for permission to keep all Armenians they in their care or to move with them to Kharput. The governor responded that the central government's orders were precise and could not be changed. All Armenian women had to leave Bitlis while the Armenian children would be sent to government schools throughout the country. For the time being, however, the Armenians would be allowed to stay with the missionaries as they were assisting the mission in medical work that benefited the Ottoman army. The response was a favor to Scheubner who had used all his influence over Ömer Nadji to obtain this concession.[275]

From now on, the Leverkuehns concealed, like Scheubner, a gun under their uniform. They had seen and heard enough to be concerned about

271 Knapp, *Tragedy of Bitlis*, p. 132. Republication, p. 88.
272 Myrtle O. Shane, "Statement of observations while in Bitlis and on the road between Bitlis and Harput – May 1915 to December 1915," April 20, 1918, in Barton, *Turkish Atrocities*, p. 18. The missionary ladies remained a concern of the U.S. embassy at Constantinople. On November 6, 1915, Talaat inquired into their health following an embassy request. Talaat to Bitlis Province, Nov. 6, 1915 EUM Spec. 57 DH.ŞFR, 57-306.
273 Leverkuehn, *Posten*, pp. 64-65.
274 AA-PA, Weltkrieg 11d secr./8, A 30741, Neurath to AA, Pera, Oct. 23, 1915 telegram 2451.

their personal security.[276] On their onward journey at Siirt, the detachment met Halil Bey's expeditionary force on its march to the Mesopotamian front. Again, the German could observe the attitude of an Ottoman commander towards Armenians. When Leverkuehn watched Halil's entourage he saw several bathtubs among the military equipment. He concluded that Halil had taken some Armenian women into personal entourage.[277]

Meanwhile, Scheubner's expedition faced new problems. While his superiors like Schulenburg had anyhow doubted the chances for success, the Ottoman 3rd Army hoped that the raid might divert some Russian forces away from its main front line.[278] Many of the expeditions' problems were homemade. Scheubner noticed that he was fed false information either deliberately or because of the officials' ignorance. Equally disappointing for Scheubner was that supplies for his detachment were hard to come by, both in Bitlis and Siirt. When supplies were available, his detachment was discriminated against. Nadji for his part could draw on the funds and supplies of the CUP, although transfers were not always as smoothly as Nadji might have hoped.[279] In response Scheubner decided to gather his own intelligence and took pre-cautions to secure independent supplies. Soon after leaving Siirt, he separated from his unit and went ahead of the detachment to Mosul in order to secure supplies.[280] He arrived in Mosul on November 1, 1915 but faced a new challenge. The Armenian Genocide was again catching up with him. [281]

---

275 AA-PA, Konstantinopel 374 J. No. 11183, Scheubner Richter to Consulate Mosul, Mosul, Nov. 6, 1915 enclosure in Holstein to Embassy, Mosul, Nov. 9, 1915 J. No. 815. Later, Leverkühn incorrectly claimed that Shane had obtained permission to take 100 Armenians to Diarbekir. Leverkuehn, *Posten*, p. 67.

276 Leverkuehn, *Posten*, pp. 67-68.

277 Leverkuehn, *Posten*, pp. 72-73.

278 AA-PA, Weltkrieg 11d secr./8, A 31462, Neurath to AA, Pera, Oct. 30, 1915 telegram 2500.

279 DH.ŞFR, 57-40 Talaat to Bitlis province EUM Oct. 13, 1915; DH.ŞFR, 57-129 Talaat to Bitlis province, Oct. 22, 1915 EUM Spec. 53; DH.ŞFR, 57-262 Talaat to Bitlis province, Nov. 1915 EUM Spec. 56.

280 AA-PA, Weltkrieg 11d secr./10, A 3899, Scheubner to Schulenburg, Mosul, Dec. 7, 1915 copy enclosure in Schulenburg to Stellvertretenden Generalstab Abt. IIIb Pol., Trapezunt, Jan. 11, 1916 No. 8 copy enclosure in Nadolny to AA, Berlin, Feb. 10, 1916 No. Pol. 5736.

Halil Bey and his staff reached Mosul on November 3, 1915. The Ottoman officers believed that it was the time to massacre the Armenians of Mosul. After all, they had Christian soldiers of their unit and massacred Christians all along their route. One of Halil's officers announced the plan to German Consul Walter Holstein and tried to intimidate the latter by stating that any help for Armenians would be contrary to Turkish-German friendship. The Consul's conception of friendship was, however, a different one. He cabled to Constantinople urging the embassy to secure orders for Halil to abstain from his plan. Halil's troops were to reach Mosul within one or two days. The embassy approached Foreign Minister Halil Bey. Military Attaché Otto von Lossow was to approach Enver. The attaché, however, did not want to discuss with Enver what he thought to be purely civilian affair. Instead he passed the issue on to von der Goltz Pasha.[282] The embassy's immediate representation to the Foreign Ministry had some preliminary success. The minister had promised to ask Enver to prohibit action against Armenians in Mosul. For the time being things appeared to have settled down; but not for long.[283]

The Defense of Hazik

One episode during Scheubner's Iranian raid gained wider importance. Hazik (Idil) was a village located on the road from Cizre to Midiat. Nearby, Christians were holding out against Ottoman gendarmes. In 1919, the affair became prominent in debates on German complicity in the Armenian Genocide when Johannes Lepsius claimed that Scheubner had prevented the massacre of these Christians. Recently, Vahakn Dadrian asserted that the affair was proof of Goltz' involvement in the killing of Armenians. Hazik was, however, not an Armenian village but a Syrian Christian one.[284]

The resistance of the Chaldean and Syrian Orthodox Christians in the Tur Abdin Mountains east of Mardin had begun in July 1915. After a series of massacres ordered by the governor of Diarbekir, Reshid Bey, they made this last stand for survival. German Consul Holstein had repeatedly reported on the actions of Reshid, who was known as the "butcher of

---

281 AA-PA, Weltkrieg 11d secr./8, A 31782, Neurath to AA, Pera, Nov. 2, 1915 telegram 2537.

282 AA-PA, Konstantinopel 171, J. No. 6350, Holstein to Embassy, Mosul, Nov. 4, 1915 telegram 60. Türkei 183/45, A 33457, Scheubner-Richter to Bethmann Hollweg, München, Dec. 4, 1916 Tgb. Z. 243.

283 AA-PA, Konstantinopel 171, J. No. ad 6350, Neurath to Holstein, Pera, Nov. 5, 1915 telegram 69.

Diarbekir." He saw the defense as being justified as the people were simply fighting for their lives.[285] On July 23, 1915, Mahmud Kiamil reported shortly on the resistance and on August 4, 1915 a local commander gave some additional details on the fighting in the area, indicating that the besieged Christians had not given up and were still holding out.[286]

The matter became more complicated on October 29, 1915, when Ömer Nadji announced to move with his troops against the besieged. Halil Bey supported the expedition as the troops had no other pressing assignments at the moment. Soon, however, requests for reinforcements showed that the presumably easy task was in reality much more complicated as it had seemed before. Nadji had to negotiate with defenders.[287]

On November 4, 1915, on having learned that Goltz had supposedly ordered the Ottoman 4th Army to move against these Christians, Holstein warned the embassy and proposed an alternative solution to Goltz.[288] The consul argued that the people were not and should not be treated as rebels.

---

284 Johannes Lepsius, ed., *Deutschland und Armenien, 1914 - 1918. Sammlung diplomatischer Aktenstücke*, Potsdam, Tempel-Verlag, 1919 Reprint: with an introduction by Tessa Hoffmann and an epilogue by M. Rainer Lepsius, Bremen, Donat & Temmen Verlag, 1986 pp. lviii-lix. Dadrian, *German Responsibility*, pp. 57-58. Contrary to all available evidence, Dadrian recently reiterated his claim that the village in question was not Hazik but an "unnamed village is described as being in the vicinity of Hesak." Moreover, he advances the false allegation that Scheubner Richter was "involved in the operation." Through his selective use of sources Dadrian misleads his readers. He creates a false impression about the historic record thereby re-affirming this author's earlier finding that Dadrian's statements cannot be taken at face value. Vahakn N. Dadrian, "The Armenian Question and the Wartime Fate of the Armenians as Documented by the Officials of the Ottoman Empire's World War I Allies: Germany and Austria-Hungary," in *International Journal of Middle East Studies*, 34 (2002), p. 68 note 56.

285 AA-PA, Konstantinopel 170, J. No. 4429, Holtstein to Embassy, Mosul, July 28, 1915 telegram 18.

286 Mahmud Kiamil July 23, 1915 Askeri Tarih Belgeleri Dergisi 85 (1985) Document No. 2012, p. 81-82, Süleyman Faik to 3rd Army High Command, Aug. 4, 1915 in Ibid., Document No. 2013, p. 85.

287 Gaunt, *Massacres, Resistance*, pp. 282-283, 450-464. Gaunt reproduced relevant documentation from the Turkish military archives in facsimile, transliteration, and translation.

288 AA-PA, Konstantinopel 171, J. No. 6381, Holstein to Embassy, Mosul, Nov. 4, 1915 telegram 60.

They had escaped massacre and were now trying to save their lives. Warning against a wholesale slaughter, Holstein suggested negotiations with the besieged. The defenders at Hazik were willing to give up against security of life and property. Holstein had already persuaded the governor of Mosul to open negotiations but Haidar could not officially get involved as the village was not within his jurisdiction.[289] Holstein stressed that the defenders could trust Ottoman officials. Thus the participation of a German officer or consular official and a local Syrian bishop from Mosul was crucial. While having offered his own services, Holstein added that Scheubner was ready for the task as his troops were about to be sent to the scene. Moreover, the consul knew that Haidar was willing to join the effort.

At the embassy, Neurath contacted Lossow. The military attaché should bring up the issue with the Ministry of War as military orders were needed. Two days later, on November 6, 1915, Goltz informed Holstein that Enver wished for a peaceful solution. He demanded that the defenders at Hazik put down their arms immediately. Importantly, Enver rejected the idea of German involvement in the matter. The governor of Diarbekir and the 4th Army had been instructed accordingly. It appears that Goltz had taken up the issue right away and used his influence with Enver. Goltz also intervened with Talaat to obtain orders for the governor.[290]

The next day, on November 7, 1915, the embassy updated Holstein. Goltz had provided detailed information. Quite some time ago the Ottoman Supreme High Command had ordered the Ottoman 4th Army to restore peace and quiet in the area around Midiat. The order could not, however, be executed as troops were lacking. Now, Goltz believed that the matter rested with him as the incoming commander of the Mesopotamian front. Halil had offered one of his regiments but then he had convinced Nadji to offer both, his own and Scheubner's unit, for the task.[291] Goltz

289 AA-PA, Weltkrieg 11d secr./10, A 3899, Scheubner to Schulenburg, Mosul, Dec. 7, 1915 copy enclosure in Schulenburg to Stellvertretenden Generalstab Abt. IIIb Pol., Trapezunt, Jan. 11, 1916 No. 8 copy enclosure in Nadolny to AA, Berlin, Feb. 10, 1916 No. Pol. 5736.

290 AA-PA, Konstantinopel 171, J. No. ad 6488, Neurath to Holstein, Pera, Nov. 6, 1915 telegram 76.

291 AA-PA, Weltkrieg 11d secr./9, A 37451, Schulenburg, Erserum, Nov. 28, 1915 No. 6 copy enclosure in Nadolny to AA, Berlin, Dec. 27, 1915 Sektion Politik No. Pol. 4961. Weltkrieg 11d secr./10, A 3899, Scheubner to Schulenburg, Mosul, Dec. 7, 1915 copy enclosure in Schulenburg to Stellvertretenden Generalstab Abt. IIIb Pol., Trapezunt, Jan. 11, 1916 No. 8 copy enclosure in Nadolny to AA, Berlin, Feb. 10, 1916 No. Pol. 5736.

did not want to slow down the movement of other troops to Baghdad and asked Nadji to go ahead. Nadji had reported that the rebels were at an inaccessible spot in the mountains but Goltz did not know the position of Nadji's detachment. The General supported a peaceful solution and encouraged negotiations. Following Holstein's proposal, Goltz suggested that the consul and the governor Haidar should coordinate with Nadji. Even the participation of a Syrian bishop in the negotiations appeared as advisable. In line with Enver's orders, Scheubner was to be left out as no German officer should be involved.

For clarification, Goltz requested a copy of the embassy's instructions for consuls and a briefing on the AA's and the embassy's policy in regard to the Armenian question.[292] Neurath gave the General a broad overview of the ongoing extermination of Armenians and Ottoman propaganda strategies. While the embassy used usual official rhetoric on alleged Armenian misconduct, the memorandum was a condemnation of the Ottoman ally. It emphasized that Ottoman authorities were massacring Armenians and other Christians. Given the context of the time, it was a warning for Goltz to be cautious. The embassy also denounced Ottoman attempts to put the blame for the slaughter on Germany. Goltz must have understood what was going on and what he was going to get into.[293] On November 8, 1915, Lossow informed Holstein that Goltz had changed directives. Now Nadji's detachment was to protect local Muslims, while troops under Scheubner's command had to stay out. The troops should wait for a larger contingent. Lossow added that he and Goltz had confused Nadji Bey with an officer of the same name they knew. Thus Goltz had rather limited trust in the CUP executive. While not risking a public embarrassment for Nadji by a recall, Goltz changed the assignment and obtained a similar result.[294]

It seems, however, that Goltz's assessments were based on incomplete information. In fact, he was not in command. In an order to 3rd Army, Enver had made absolutely clear that it was Mahmud Kiamil who was in

---

292 AA-PA, Konstantinopel 171, J. No. zu 6381, Lossow to Embassy, Constantinople, Nov. 6, 1915 Military-attaché No. 59; Ibid. J. No. ad 6381, Neurath to Holstein, Pera, Nov. 7, 1915 telegram 71.

293 AA-PA, Türkei 175a/36, A 33704, Neurath to Bethmann Hollweg, Pera, Nov. 12, 1915 No. 669.

294 AA-PA, Konstantinopel 171, J. No. ad 6381, Neurath to Holstein, Constantinople, Nov. 8, 1915 telegram 72. Leverkuehn's account emphasized Scheubner's role, suggesting that the officer had been the key figure in the affair, while after all he simply followed the orders of his superiors. in p. 83.

charge. The latter was to coordinate the movement of troops. Enver reserved also for himself the final word in any decision to be taken. Apparently, Goltz was not notified of Enver's telegraphic correspondence or his decisions.[295]

In Mosul, Holstein's initiative had turned out to be rather successful. When he discussed the matter Haidar, the governor, told him that he had to stay out of internal Ottoman affairs. Holstein thought that Haidar had come increasingly under the influence of Halil and his people. It seems that Holstein had not received his instructions to the same effect. The governor for his part had his own agenda. He asked Holstein to secure Goltz's help in obtaining orders from the Ministry of Interior. The governor hoped for orders instructing him to join Nadji's mission. Such authorization was necessary as Midiat was under Reshid Bey's jurisdiction. Given the ministry's misgivings about German interference Haidar asked for discretion, and indeed a copy of Holstein's telegram was passed on to Goltz.[296] The next day, Holstein had good news. Haidar informed him that a number of the defenders had put down their weapons. Negotiations with others were under way and a satisfactory result seemed likely.[297] Meanwhile, the AA instructed the embassy to obtain a peaceful solution.[298] For Nadji, however, negotiations were unacceptable and he attacked both with his own and Scheubner's Ottoman soldiers. But the force proved to be insufficient for the task and was repelled. Nadji's force lost 15 men killed and 26 gravely wounded. Now reinforcements were needed. By the time of the skirmish, Goltz' staff had reached nearby Nisibin. One of the German staff officers assessed Ottoman forces at six battalions with four pieces artillery. But the Ottoman defeat caused anxiety among local Kurds, who feared that the defenders might take revenge for the massacre of Armenians as some survivors had made it to Hazik. For the time being, however, negotiations were under way.[299] Nadji had prevailed

295 Gaunt, *Massacres, Resistance*, pp. 286, 290-291,462-463.474-477, 482-483.

296 AA-PA, Konstantinopel 171, J. No. 6488, Holstein to Embassy, Mosul, Nov. 10, 1915 telegram 63.

297 AA-PA, Türkei 175a/36, A 34101, Neurath to AA, Pera, Nov. 24, 1915 telegram 2774.

298 AA-PA, Türkei 175a/36, zu A 34101/33704, Zimmermann to Metternich, Berlin, Dec. 1, 1915 No. 922.

299 Hans von Kiesling, *Orientfahrten. Zwischen Ägeis und Zagros. Erlebtes und Erschautes aus schwerer Zeit*, Leipzig, Dieterich'sche Verlagsbuchhandlung, 1921 pp. 67-68, 128. For a detailed account of the fight for Hazik see: Gaunt, *Massacres, Resistance*, pp. 288-290.

over the more radical CUP activist Dr. Fuad and captain Veli. He obtained a compromise: the defenders gave up six rifles as a token of their surrender and were allowed to remain where they were. Thus no further troop despatches were needed. Nadji even obtained two pieces of artillery from the 4th Army units for his Persian campaign.[300] On February 14, 1916 Metternich reported that the "problems" between the Syrian Christians and the Ottoman authorities had been resolved. Goltz's influence had contributed to the positive outcome. [301]

Meanwhile Scheubner had ordered all Germans under his command to proceed to Mosul. Officially, he was not willing to get involved in the internal affair. He explained to his German superiors that he tried to avoid being compromised and endanger his Persian venture. Scheubner also claimed that Goltz had accepted his decision. The statement was in line with Scheubner's self-esteem but factually it was not exactly true.[302] Scheubner had been bluntly reminded of his dependence on his superiors' directives when Schulenburg ordered him to rejoin his unit which he had left behind.[303]

The Hazik defence was not an Armenian self-defence. The Ottoman authorities dealt with such desperate Armenian acts ruthlessly. Thus Goltz's actions throw some light on his attitude towards Ottoman Christians in general. His attitude towards Armenians can be better understood by taking a look at Goltz's and his staff's journey from Constantinople to Mosul.

Colmar Von Der Goltz

Goltz's assignment to the Persian and Mesopotamian fronts brought an end to a long lingering conflict between him and Liman von Sanders, the

300 AA-PA, Weltkrieg 11d secr./10, A 3899, Scheubner to Schulenburg, Mosul, Dec. 7, 1915 copy enclosure in Schulenburg to Stellvertretenden Generalstab Abt. IIIb Pol., Trapezunt, Jan. 11, 1916 No. 8 copy enclosure in Nadolny to AA, Berlin, Feb. 10, 1916 No. Pol. 5736.

301 AA-PA, Türkei 175a/37, A 4515, Metternich an Bethmann Hollweg, Pera, Feb. 14, 1916 No. 66.

302 AA-PA, Weltkrieg 11d secr./10, A 3899, Scheubner to Schulenburg, Mosul, Dec. 7, 1915 copy enclosure in Schulenburg to Stellvertretenden Generalstab Abt. IIIb Pol., Trapezunt, Jan. 11, 1916 No. 8 copy enclosure in Nadolny to AA, Berlin, Feb. 10, 1916 No. Pol. 5736.

303 AA-PA, Weltkrieg 11d secr./9, A 37451, Schulenburg, Erserum, Nov. 28, 1915 No. 6 copy enclosure in Nadolny to AA, Berlin, Dec. 27, 1915 Sektion Politik No. Pol. 4961.

commander of the Dardanelles front who was at least formally still the head of the German Military Mission. Liman was not Goltz's only problem. Enver, who officially pretended to hold Goltz in the highest esteem, regarded Goltz in reality as "too soft" and "too old." Thus the General's despatch was a welcome opportunity to remove the General from Constantinople, without causing an embarrassment.[304]

At Constantinople, Goltz had hardly been directly exposed to the extermination of the Armenians.[305] This was now to change. He and his staff were to come face to face with deported, dying, and massacred Armenians.

Some of the officers recorded their observations in written accounts or with photos. On November 15, 1915, Goltz left Constantinople for Baghdad.[306] He took with him the officers of the German-Persian Military Mission and some additional staff. The group was divided into several separate units. Hans von Kiesling was part of the third party leaving Constantinople catching up with Goltz at Aleppo.[307] On his way south, Kiesling saw the Armenian deportations. He described the misery, saw the dying at the roadside and observed how valuable personal and other items belonging to Armenians were sold at a pittance. Decomposing corpses littered the scene. Kiesling noted that solidarity among Armenians had partly broken down. Competition for a piece of bread meant the survival of fittest.[308] Other officers took photos of the deported Armenians. Being unaware of Ottoman counter-measures, one officer had his films developed by the best photo studio in Aleppo. All films, however, were destroyed as the studio worked with Ottoman intelligence.[309]

Near the Mamure railhead in the Amanus mountains the Ottoman authorities had concentrated some 60,000 Armenian deportees who were on their way to the Syrian desert. The situation in the transit camp was atrocious; many deportees were exhausted or sick. Sanitary conditions were

---

304 AA-PA, Persien 24/1, A 29020, Wangenheim to AA, Pera, Oct. 6, 1915 telegram 2289; Türkei 139/36, A 22906, Treutler to AA, Pless, Aug. 1, 1915 telegram 251.

305 He is believed to have accepted the Ottoman deportation law of May 27, 1915. Evidence on this instance is, however, still very weak. See Deutsch-Armenische Korrespondenz (1918) No. 2, p. 1.

306 AA-PA, Persien 24/2, A 33114, Metternich to AA, Pera, Nov. 15, 1915 telegram 2677.

307 Hans von Kiesling, *Mit Feldmarschall von der Goltz Pascha in Mesopotamien und Persien,* Leipzig, Dieterich'sche Verlagsbuchhandlung, 1922, p. 22.

308 Kiesling, *Orientfahrten,* pp. 6-7.

awful while relief was hardly available. Thus the Ottoman authorities tried to hide this appalling sight from Goltz. Gendarmes with fixed bayonets swept through the camp, wounding and killing the terrorized victims. In the ensuing chaos families got separated, babies and old people were abandoned. But the authorities had obtained their goal. The camp disappeared and Goltz would not see it.[310]

East of the Amanus mountains, the authorities could not hide the huge concentration camp near Katma railway station. Here, Goltz stopped and watched the inferno. An Armenian survivor recalled the visit: "We heard it rumored that the idol of Turkey, the German, von der Goltz, would come to Katma for a visit. The priest and several others planned to see him and ask for mercy and some Arabian tents. The pasha did not approach the camp. From a distance of two miles, where he stopped his automobile, he viewed the camp through his field-glasses. The priest and his company could not approach him. Through his interpreter, the pasha sent word, telling the people not to come close with their typhus germs. Through the interpreter again, the people put their petition before the pasha. He told them that when he is in Aleppo, he would see that those tents they asked for would be sent to them. He went, but no tents arrived. Instead, there came an edict from him ordering those who could walk to get ready to leave the camp. Those unable to leave would be shot, to end their sufferings in that concentration camp."[311]

Goltz was by no means indifferent to the fate of the deportees. In a letter to his wife he recorded his impressions. He described the deportations as a terrible human tragedy. Despite all Ottoman efforts, he had seen enough along the road. But Goltz was not willing to admit who was responsible for

---

309 Rafael de Nogales, *Four Years Beneath*, pp. 180-181. A considerable number of photos did, however, escape destruction and were preserved in the collection of Armen T. Wegner in the Wegner papers, Deutsches Literaturarchiv, Marbach am Neckar. Wegner himself was member of Goltz's mission. See Martin Tamcke, *Armin T. Wegner und die Armenier. Anspruch und Wirklichkeit eines Augenzeugen*, Hamburg, Lit-Verlag, 1996 (Studien zur Orientalischen Kirchengeschichte, vol. 2).

310 Elizabeth Webb, The Exiling of the Armenians, enclosure in Elizabeth Webb to Barton, Oberlin, Oh., Nov. 14, 1917 Harvard University, Houghton Library, Cambridge, MA, American Board of Commissioners for Foreign Missions, Central Turkey Mission reel 672.

311 Khoren K. Davidson, *Odysee of an Armenian of Zeitoun*, with a Foreword by Aram Saroyan, New York, Vantage Press, 1985, p. 82.

the mass murder. Instead he put the blame on Britain, claiming that the killings were a consequence of the war which Britain had caused.[312]

After Katma, Goltz spent the next few days in Aleppo. Here his visit brought a conflict between two leading German community members out into the open. Martha Koch, the wife of a prominent German businessman, had known Goltz for years. Lately she had been in touch with Goltz during her service as a nurse in German-occupied Belgium where Goltz had headed the occupation administration.[313] Koch spoke Arabic fluently and enjoyed a reputation as an art collector, who also advised foreign collectors and museums for their purchases. She commanded considerable influence in the city both with the business community and Ottoman officials. At times, she was the only person who could organize transport for German officers.[314] Learning that the General was coming to Aleppo, Koch tried to land a coup.

She invited Goltz to stay in her house where she regularly entertained German military personnel. The invitation was an affront to German Consul Walter Rössler who saw his prestige threatened.[315] Thus he complained that Koch would be upsetting the Ottoman ally and requested instructions for Goltz to decline Koch's invitation.[316] The General followed suit and took quarters with Ahmet Bey, a prominent Arab notable.[317] Unfortunately, Goltz' luggage had been delivered to Koch's house, who refused its surrender. Following a determined intervention by German officers, she reluctantly gave up. Her insistence brought her the strong dislike of Friedrich Kress von Kressenstein, a German officer commanding Ottoman troops under Djemal Pasha, who found her

---

312 Goltz to his wife, Aleppo, 22.11.1915, in Colmar Frhr. von der Goltz, Denkwürdigkeiten, edited by Friedrich Frhr. von der Goltz and Wolfgang Foerster, Berlin, Mittler & Sohn, 1929, p. 428.

313 Sven Hedin, *Bagdad, Babylon, Nineve,* Leipzig, Brockhaus, 1918, p. 14.

314 His, Wilhelm, *Die Front der Ärzte,* 2nd. Ed. Leipzig, Velhagen & Klasing, 1931 pp. 153-154; H. G. Merkel, "Von der wolhynischen Front nach Bagdad (Winter 1915/16)," in *Mitteilungen des Bundes der Asienkämpfer* 13,9 (1931), p. 99.

315 Nogales described the salon of Ms. Koch "was an oasis of refinement in that city". Nogales, *Four Years,* p. 163.

316 AA-PA, Aleppo Pkt. 2 Bd. 3, J. No. 2595 Sekr., Rössler to Embassy, Aleppo, Nov. 9, 1915, telegram 159.

317 HHStA, Aleppo–Konsulatsarchiv Karton 2 (1911-1916), Dandini to Pallavicini, Aleppo, Nov. 27, 1915, No. 21.

"terribly disagreeable."[318] Nevertheless, Kress soon cooperated with Koch in saving Armenians. [319]

Koch also worked for a German propaganda network set up by Max Freiherr von Oppenheim.[320] She was in charge of distributing propaganda materials in the Aleppo region. Not surprisingly, her close relations with German officers and propaganda work brought her a reputation of being a German spy.[321] After the British occupation of Aleppo, Dr. Faradjalian, an Armenian Catholic at Aleppo, accused her of having obtained antiquities robbed from an Armenian church at Mardin. He claimed that thanks to her military connection Koch had obtained goods worth about £T1,000,000 for sale after the war, and had a fortune of £T3,000,000.[322]

Being a supporter of the CUP or profiting from the Armenian Genocide was, however, not on Koch's mind. In reality she was an ardent supporter of persecuted Armenians. In July 1915, she had appealed to Wangenheim, pleading for the lives of two Armenian parliamentary deputies, Zohrab and Vartkes. Denying her real motives, Koch pre-empted potential criticism of her mixing with German policies. But that was exactly what she did. Indeed, her appeal was a cover letter for a petition of Sahag II, Catholicos

318 Germanisches Nationalmuseum, Nürnberg, Kress Archiv, Abt. d, Reihe D, II. Akten, A. Allgemeine Familienangelegenheiten und einzelne Familienmitglieder, No. 166 Erinnerungen an den Weltkrieg 1914/1918, Bd. 7 Tagebuch 22.09.1915 - 11.12.1915, entries Nov. 20, 1915 and Nov. 23, 1915.

319 The fight between Koch and Rössler, however, continued well into 1917. Only the visit of Wilhelm His, a leading German physician, brought about a change in their relations and invitations were exchanged again. His, *Die Front*, pp. 220-221.

320 Aram Andonian, *Documents officiels concernant les massacres arméniens*, Paris, Imprimerie Turabian, 1920, p. 58. Given Koch's record of supporting Armenians, it appears likely that Andonian invented the story of Koch's conversion thus accommodating the rumours about her anti-Armenian activities and the known facts proving the contrary.

321 H. V. F. Winstone, *The Diaries of Parker Pasha*, London, Quartet Books, 1983, p. 99.

322 FO 371/3657/512/6160, Dr. Faradj Allah, Aleppo, Nov. 29, 1918 copy enclosure in Younghusband to Director of Military Intelligence, G.H.Q. Dec. 13, 1918 copy enclosure in Director of Military Intelligence to FO, Jan 10, 1919 B.I/1675; FO 371/4172/1270/24597, E. MacRury, Miscellaneous Political Notes, Aleppo, Dec. 12, 1918 copy enclosure in Military Intelligence to FO, Feb. 12, 1919 M.I.1.a. 63490. See also FO 608/244/8183, Webb to Balfour, Constantinople, April 7, 1919 No. 481/1315.

of Cilicia, who also tried to save the two men.[323] Her move followed unsuccessful representations by Rössler, suggesting that the effort was well coordinated, despite the differences between Koch and the consul.[324] Koch was a determined opponent of the CUP. German officers knew her views and General Gerold von Gleich believed that she was taking quite some risks.[325] Gleich probably did not know that Koch had been hiding an Armenian in the basement of her house. Kress helped her to save the man who was wanted by the authorities.[326] A month later, Koch scored an important, albeit temporary, victory in her efforts to save Armenians. On December 21, 1915, at a breakfast in honor of Djemal Pasha the issue of Armenian orphans in Aleppo was laid before the commander. Besides Koch, Djemal, and Kress, Föllner, the director of the Baghdad Railway construction company at Aleppo, and Busse, a high ranking naval officer, were also present.[327] They showed the General the indescribable misery of the orphans. Having flattered the vain Djemal, pointing how popular he was in German journals, Djemal authorized relief for orphans on the part of the local Germans.[328] In sum, at Aleppo, Goltz was right in the center of local German resistance to the genocide.

After leaving Aleppo, Goltz reached the Euphrates bridge at Djerablus. Again local authorities emptied a makeshift concentration camp. They forced the sick and dying people out of sight, using whips liberally. When Goltz arrived, all Armenians had disappeared. Later, a number of Germans visited the site and detected human remains partly devoured by vultures at less visible spots.[329] Further east, Kiesling wandered through the destroyed

---

323 AA-PA, Konstantinopel 169, J. No. 4314, Sahag II an Wangenheim, Aleppo, July 11, 1915 enclosure in Koch to Wangenheim, Aleppo, July 11, 1915.

324 The initiative was first discussed in Kaiser, *Germany and the Armenian Genocide*, pp. 127-142 and Idem, *Germany and the Armenian Genocide*, Part II, p. 137.

325 HStA Stuttgart, M 660/010 Nachlass Gerold von Gleich Heft No. 157 p. 83. Aram Andonian reports that Koch had originally hated Armenians but changed her attitudes when confronted with their sufferings. Aram Andonian, *Documents officiels*, p. 59.

326 "Die Wüstenschwester" in *Orient-Rundschau* 20,3 (1938) p. 30.

327 Friedrich Freiherr Von Kress von Kressenstein, *Mit den Türken zum Suezkanal*, Berlin, Vorhut-Verlag Otto Schlegel, 1938 pp. 135-136. MA-Freiburg, Reichsmarine 40/504, War Diaries Commander Busse, December 16, 1915 – February 22, 1916 folio 56-57.

328 Raith, "Deutschtum in Persien" in *Mitteilungen des Bundes der Asienkämpfer* 11 (1929) p. 108. For further detals see Kaiser, *At the Crossroads*, p. 54.

Armenian village of Tell Ermen.[330] Near Nisibin his horse suddenly made a huge jump to the side. Kiesling saw numerous white spots in the grass. These were naked and mutilated male and female corpses which were only a few days old. The air was filled with a terrible stench.[331]

Goltz reached Mosul on November 30, 1915.[332] Here he learned that orders had been given to remove all Armenians from the city towards the Euphrates. The matter of killing the local Armenians was again on the agenda. Goltz ordered the governor to call off the deportation and cabled the central authorities. When he did not receive a satisfactory answer for four weeks, he requested his immediate recall from his command. Finally, Enver conceded but reminded Goltz that he had no right to interfere in internal Ottoman affairs. But, Goltz had saved many lives for the time being.[333] His energetic intervention was confirmed to the British authorities in spring 1918 by Boutros Abed, the Patriarchal Archdeacon of the Chaldean Catholic Church in Egypt. He reported that the Chaldean Patriarch at Mosul had asked Goltz to save four Chaldeans and Syrian Orthodox men who had been condemned to death and to spare 50 other Chaldeans from Baghdad from further deportation. Goltz intervened accordingly.[334]

Goltz' willingness to assist Ottoman Christians was not a new development that had emerged after his departure from Constantinople. Nor was it purely humanitarian. Goltz had understood that the extermination of the Christian communities created serious problems for the war effort. Being entrusted with operations in Iran as well, he took with him the Nestorian bishop Simon Kelaita. The cleric had been living in Germany and was to act as a go-between in Iran. The AA supported the plan and Goltz took Kelaita under his personal protection. The bishop reached Mosul safely, where he joined Scheubner's men. His mission did not, however, succeed.[335]

In his recent discussion of Goltz's policies concerning Mosul and the 6th army's area of control, Krethlow argued that Golt's motive were only

329 Martin Niepage, *Ein Wort and die berufenen Vertreter des deutschen Volkes. Eindrücke eines deutschen Oberlehrers aus der Türkei*, Berlin, privately published, p n.d. (1916) p. 10.

330 Kiesling, *Orientfahrten*, p. 62.

331 Ibid., p. 63.

332 Kiesling, *Mit Feldmarschall*, p. 43

333 Raith, *Deutschtum*, pp. 108-109.

334 FO 371/3400/40423/100453, Boutros Abed to Marini, Cairo, Mar. 20, 1918 copy enclosure in Clayton to FO, Jerusalem, May 19, 1918 J/13837/B.

marginally influenced by humanitarian consideration or the idea to make a stand for the Armenians. Instead, the author believes that the General was primarily interested in the extension or assertion of his own authority.[336] Military commanders could, however, interfere in civilian matters only on grounds of military necessity. Thus, Krethlow confuses the form of Goltz's orders with their intended effect. From in 1915, up to this death in 1916, Goltz worked for the survival of persecuted Christians within his area of command. His decisions, however, did not take place in a vacuum. Enver's consent to let the Syrian Christians survive was much easier to obtain than a similar decision for the Armenians of Mosul. Here, Goltz had to use all his personal authority. The disparity in Enver's policies towards the Syrians near Hazik and the Armenians at Mosul suggests that the Ottoman military authorities made a clear distinction between Syrians and Armenians. This distinction casts doubts on Scheubner's assertion that the Ottoman authorities tried to implicate him in the Armenian Genocide. These doubts appear to be further sustained by Enver's order that Scheubner should not mix in the affair. After all, it had been Scheubner who developed the idea of an Ottoman intrigue. He was the one person who profited from the story. Understanding that his absence from his unit at Cizre had met with disapproval from his superiors, Scheubner was pressed to present the affair in as positive a light as possible. His claim that his early arrival at Mosul had frustrated the CUP was intended to deflect criticism of his personal conduct.[337] By the time he submitted his claims, he had received information from Goltz and Holstein on the issue. Goltz knew that Enver had objected to Scheubner's participation near Hazik. But in his usual manner Scheubner tried to present himself and his actions as being at the center of events. The final decision on his role in the affair had,

---

335 AA-PA, Türkei 175a/36, A 35397, Goltz to AA, Mossul, Dec. 7, 1915 telegram; Persien 17/2, A 10713, Metternich to Bethmann Hollweg, Pera, Apr. 21, 1916 No. 182. Leverkuehn misrepresents Kelaita's role as being simply an interpreter. Leverkuehn, *Posten*, pp. 103, 106.

336 Krethlow, *Von Der Goltz*, p. 72 see also p. 77.

337 "Es ist gewissen Kreisen - zu denen Nadschi übrigens nicht gehört - nicht gelungen, mich in ein Unternehmen hineinzuziehen, das leicht zu einer starken Kompromittierung des deutschen Ansehens in dieser Gegend hätte führen können." AA-PA, Weltkrieg 11d secr./10, A 3899, Scheubner to Schulenburg, Mosul, Dec. 7, 1915 copy enclosure in Schulenburg to Stellvertretenden Generalstab Abt. IIIb Pol., Trapezunt, Jan. 11, 1916 No. 8 copy enclosure in Nadolny to AA, Berlin, Feb. 10, 1916 No. Pol. 5736. See also Leverkuehn, *Posten*, pp. 101-102.

however, been taken in Constantinople. Scheubner was receiving orders and was not a commander acting on his own discretion.

The Iranian Raid

From Mosul Scheubner reported that he had secured support from Kurdish tribes for the Iranian raid. The 8th Army had given him orders to depart for Revanduz on December 8, 1915.[338] Once again, Scheubner sought to enhance his standing and authority and suggested a new scheme. Halil had offered him a battalion for the advance into Iran. Scheubner was tempted to take this opportunity. His superior Schulenburg, however, understood that this proposal was way beyond the authority of the persons involved. Consequently, Scheubner was instructed to obtain the consent of Goltz.[339] As Goltz needed forces on the Mesopotamian front, he was less than excited about the plan and dismissed it. Even worse for Scheubner's ambitions was that on November 29, 1915 Goltz put Nadji's and Scheubner's contingents under Haidar's command and ordered them to move against Sautshbulaq. After the capture of the city, Scheubner was once more to be placed under Schulenburg's authority. Unable to voice open criticism, Scheubner used his version of the Hazik affair to question Haidar's command. He doubted that he now had enough authority with Haidar to prevent persecutions of Christians. On the other hand, Scheubner still maintained that he was the military and political leader of the expedition.[340]

---

338 AA-PA, Weltkrieg 11d secr./9, A 35888, Lossow, Pera, Dec. 11, 1915 telegram enclosure in Nadolny to AA, Berlin, Dec. 11, 1915 No. Pol. 4722.

339 AA-PA, Weltkrieg 11d secr./9, A 37451, Schulenburg, Erserum, Nov. 28, 1915 No. 6 copy enclosure in Nadolny to AA, Berlin, Dec. 27, 1915 Sektion Politik No. Pol.4961.

340 AA-PA, Weltkrieg 11d secr./10, A 3899, Schulenburg to Stellvertretenden Generalstab Abt. IIIb Pol., Trapezunt, Jan. 11, 1916 No. 8 copy enclosure in Nadolny to AA, Berlin, Feb. 10, 1916 No. Pol. 5736. Taner Akçam recently wrote that Scheubner had been a "German consul in Erzurum, who served in Halil Paşa 's army, relates that he received orders to attack and "punish" some Armenian villages. Protesting that this was an "internal Turkish affair," the consul refused to carry out the orders and transferred them to a Turkish officer. Idem, *A Shameful Act. The Armenian Genocide and the Question of Turkish Responsibility*, transl. by Paul Bessemer, New York, NY, Metropolitan Books, 2006 p. 173. The author confuses the chain of events as Scheubner was never assigned to any military command during his tenure in the consular service.

Considering the original plan, the expedition had achieved little, and problems increased with the expedition to the Caucasus. Arslan had left Erzerum, catching up with Scheubner in Bitlis. By then, he had changed his mind and did not want to get to the Caucasus as soon as possible. Instead, he wished to travel westward to meet some members of his clan for which he needed a substantial subsidy of £T800.[341] Given these delays, Scheubner had sent an emissary to the Caucasus. Meanwhile, Arslan did his best to minimize his dependence on Scheubner and established good relations with Turkish officers. Trying to play both sides against each other, Arslan traded information with Scheubner on the CUP members' plans. At least, incoming news from Baku appeared to be encouraging. Apparently, an uprising was prepared but ammunition and weapons were missing and, equally important, the population expected a Turkish invasion. Scheubner's and the German AA's doubts about Arslan grew. Some information suggested that Caucasian revolutionary was a fraud and the embassy ordered a close surveillance. Despite these serious doubts, the Caucasian project was based mostly upon his information about a rebellion in the eastern Caucasus. Scheubner, however, did not share the suspicions of Arslan being a Russian spy. Instead, he assumed that the latter was delaying the expedition's departure for the Caucasus because of Pan-Turkish influences. His superior Schulenburg was less concerned about Turkish aspirations as long as the rebellion took place. Still, he agreed that Arslan's new pro Pan-Turkist attitudes might harm German interests in the future.[342]

---

341 AA-PA, Weltkrieg 11d secr./9, A 37451, Schulenburg, Erserum, Nov. 28, 1915 No. 6 copy enclosure in Nadolny to AA, Berlin, Dec. 27, 1915 Sektion Politik No. Pol. 4961.

342 AA-PA, Weltkrieg 11d secr./9, A 37578, Metternich to AA, Pera, Dec. 30, 1915 telegram 3064; Weltkrieg 11d secr./10, A 3899, Schulenburg to Stellvertretenden Generalstab Abt. IIIb Pol., Trapezunt, Jan. 11, 1916 No. 8 copy enclosure in Nadolny to AA, Berlin, Feb. 10, 1916 No. Pol. 5736.; Weltkrieg 11d secr./11, A 5153, Schulenburg to Stellvertretenden Generalstab Abt. III b Pol., Trapezunt, Jan. 27, 1916 No. 12 enclosure in Nadolny to AA, Berlin, Feb. 24, 1916 No. Pol. 5973; Weltkrieg 11d secr./ 13, A 18573, Scheubner to Schulenburg, Bukan, February 25,1916 No. 19 J. No. 36 Confidential report of the expedition commander No. 3 copy enclosure in Schulenburg to stellv. Generalstab Abteilung Politik, Samsun, June 25, 1916 No. 28 copy enclosure in Hülsen to AA, Berlin, July 13, 1916 No. Pol. 8542.

In the coming months, relations with Arslan further deteriorated as his promises were not realized. In the end, Scheubner believed that Arslan was a coward. Finally, Haidar had Arslan put under arrest. In response, Arslan demanded German protection and alerted the German embassy which instructed Holstein to look into the matter.[343] The consul learned that while Arslan was officially suspected to be a spy, personal reasons were more likely the true cause for the arrest.[344] It seems that Scheubner had little knowledge of an ongoing investigation. Mahmud Choisky, another member of Arslan's clan and whom Arslan had wished to meet before going to Iran, had changed sides and escaped to Russian. This triggered inquiries into Arslan's conduct but the suspicions were not substantiated.[345]

By now the Germans attributed little if any political value to Arslan and Scheubner asked Leverkuehn to retrieve an official German guarantee declaration from Arslan.[346] When this plan failed, Scheubner kept Arslan under close watch. In the end he got the declaration and ended the cooperation. Scheubner dismissed Arslan who entered officially Nadji's and Haidar's services despite the former conflict. Scheubner attributed part of the cooperation's failure to the CUP. Pursuing Pan-Turkist strategies Nadji and his companions tried to keep out Germans from the Caucasus and suggested to Arslan he should avoid risks by remaining quiet until Ottoman forces liberated the area.[347] Arslan stayed with Nadji's service

---

343 AA-PA, Weltkrieg 11d secr./11, A 5382, Metternich to Holstein, [Constantinople], Feb. 2, 1916 telegram No. 8 enclosure in Wolpmann to Generalstab Sektion Politik, Constantinople, Feb. 19, 1916 B. No. 1081 enclosure in Nadolny to AA, Berlin, Feb. 27, 1916 No. Pol. 6028. Leverkuehn, *Posten,* pp. 108-109.

344 AA-PA, Weltkrieg 11d secr./1, A 5382, Holstein to Embassy, Mosul, Feb. 15, 1916 telegram No. 9 enclosure in Wolpmann to Generalstab Sektion Politik, Constantinople, Feb. 19, 1916 B. No. 1081 enclosure in Nadolny to AA, Berlin, Feb. 27, 1916 1 No. Pol. 6028.

345 DH.EUM. 2 Şb 19-15, Ministry of Foreign Affairs to Ministry of Interior, Feb. 21, 1916 General Directorate for Political Affairs No. 2353-78569; EUM to Mosul province, Mar. 1, 1916; EUM to Constantinople Police Headquarters, Mar, 2, 1916; Şerif (Deputy Governor) to Ministry of Interior, Mar. 5, 1916; Haydar Bey (Mosul governor) to Ministry of Interior, Mar11, 1916; EUM to General Staff, Mar. 19, 1916; EUM to Ministry of Foreign Affairs, Mar. 19, 1916.

346 AA-PA, Weltkrieg 11d secr./11, A 5382, Text of a telegram Holstein to Embassy, Feb. 15, 1916 enclosure in Wolpmann to Sektion Politik des Generalstabes, Constantinople, Feb. 20, 1916 B. No. 1121 enclosure in Nadolny to AA, Berlin, Feb. 27, 1916 No. Pol. 6028.

until the latter's death, whereupon he received no assignments from the Ottoman military.[348]

For the time being, such differences about political strategy remained an academic matter. The expedition faced its first combat in Iran. The joint force occupied Sautshbulaq on December 29, 1915.[349] Scheubner prepared for a defence of the place and the production of equipment. Soon, however, the situation deteriorated. Kurdish tribesmen started leaving and Haidar departed on January 8, 1916 taking with him a part of the troops and artillery. Before leaving, Haidar handed over a considerable sum that had been designated for the raid by the Ottoman government.[350] Goltz had called the governor to the support of allied forces further south.[351] Now, Scheubner who had believed he had some authority over Nadji's troops, came under Nadji's command. This was a visible setback for the ambitious German. His unit was turned into a combat unit, losing its character of a political expedition. Ten days later, it faced the first Russian attack.[352] Encountering superior forces, Scheubner ordered the retreat, bitterly recording that the Kurdish tribesmen were unreliable.[353] Thus, his hopes for local reinforcements had been frustrated. Luckily, cold and snow

---

347 AA-PA, Weltkrieg 11d secr./13, A 18574, Scheubner to Schulenburg, Mossul, May 11, 1916 No. 32, J. No. 36, I No. 194, copy enclosure in Schulenburg to Stellv. Generalstab Abteilung Politik, Samsun, June 19, 1916 No. 31 copy enclosure in Hülsen to AA, Berlin, July 13, 1916 No. Pol. 8543; Weltkrieg 11d secr./13, A 18573, Scheubner to Schulenburg, Bukan, February 25, 1916 No. 19 J. No. 36 Confidential report of the expedition commander No. 3 copy enclosure in Schulenburg to stellv. Generalstab Abteilung Politik, Samsun, June 25, 1916 No. 28 copy enclosure in Hülsen to AA, Berlin, July 13, 1916 No. Pol. 8542.

348 Sarısaman, *Ömer Naci Bey*, p. 512.

349 With entering Persian territory, communications between Scheubner and his superior became increasingly difficult. Schulenburg often received only fragmentary and late information. AA-PA, Weltkrieg 11d secr./11, A 5153, Schulenburg to Stellvertretenden Generalstab Abt. III b Pol., Trapezunt, Jan. 26, 1916 No. 11 enclosure in Nadolny to AA, Berlin, Feb. 24, 1916 No. Pol. 5973.

350 Sarısaman, *Ömer Naci Bey*, p. 507.

351 MA-Freiburg, Nachlass Ritter N 131/2, [Goltz] to Bopp, Baghdad, Feb. 2, 1916 6th Army supreme command No. 437. The document has also been published in Kiesling, *Mit Feldmarschall*, pp. 143-147. Leverkuehn misrepresents Haidar's actions, implicitly suggesting that the governor had abandoned the expedition thereby obscuring the well-known command structure. Leverkuehn, *Posten*, p. 96.

provided some protection from further Russian advances, but in March 1916 the snow melted and with it shelter. Scheubner's situation was uncomfortable. Supplies were a problem as Nadji shared little if any of his. But unlike Scheubner's, the casualties sustained by Nadji's unit had been critical with losses surpassing 50%.[354] Nadji's situation was further aggravated as Kurdish tribesmen had begun abandoning him as well.[355] In his reports to Schulenburg, Scheubner voiced concerns about inadequate defenses against a Russian advance on Suleymaniya or Mosul. He put the blame for the failure of his political work on his dependence on the Ottoman command. Now, he had new plans. He prepared for a raid into Trans-Caucasia, to the Shahsevan tribal confederation that was believed to be ready to rebel if weapons and ammunition were supplied. As before, all looked too good to be true: only supplies and money were needed. Scheubner saw himself as the right man for the job, had 160 mounted men and only needed five month's supplies for about 500 men. But Russian advances put an end to the scheme and Scheubner obtained permission to go to Mosul for further instructions. Once in Mosul, he continued campaigning for a command position. This time he wanted to discuss his plans with Enver Pasha directly. The lieutenant of the reserve saw himself as an important leader.[356]

---

352 AA-PA, Persien 24/10, A 13774, Scheubner to Schulenburg, Sheherkend, Jan. 26, 1916 copy enclosure in Nadolny to AA, Berlin, May 24, 1916 No. Pol. 7690. Weltkrieg 11d secr./15, A 34350, Scheubner to Schulenburg, Mosul, Aug. 23, 1916 J. No. 431 enclosure in Scheubner to Greßmann, Mossul, Aug. 23, 1916 Expedition Scheubner J. No. 436 enclosure in Greßmann to Generalstab Sektion Politik, Baghdad, Oct. 23, 1916 Deutsche Iraktruppe I. No. 5092 enclosure in Hülsen to AA, Berlin, Dec. 16, 1916 copy No. Pol. 12166.

353 MA-Freiburg, Nachlass Ritter N 131/2, Scheubner to Embassy, Penjuin, Jan. 26, 1916 telegram copy enclosure in Metternich to Goltz, Pera, Feb. 2, 1916 telegram 135.

354 MA-Freiburg, Nachlass Ritter N 131/2, [Goltz] to Bopp, Baghdad, Feb. 2, 1916 6th army supreme command No. 437.

355 MA-Freiburg, Nachlass Ritter N 131/2, [Goltz] to Bopp, Baghdad, Feb. 2, 1916 6th army supreme command No. 437. An identical copy of this document has been published in Kiesling, *Mit Feldmarschall*, pp. 143-147. Sarısaman, *Ömer Naci Bey*, p. 508.

356 AA-PA, Weltkrieg 11d secr./13, A 18571, Scheubner to Schulenburg, Mossul, May 11, 1916 No. 33 J. No. 196 copy enclosure in Schulenburg to Stellv. Generalstab Abteilung Politik, Samsun, June 16, 1916 No. 29 copy enclosure in Hülsen to AA, Berlin, July 13, 1916 No. Pol. 8518.

By May 1916, Russian advances had practically ended all hopes for a successful raid into Trans-Caucasia. Now Scheubner suggested the dissolution of his expedition. In case of an Ottoman advance, he and some of his German associates could be attached to the Ottoman forces and perform political work in Azerbaijian and the eastern Caucasus. While remaining either under Schulenburg's or Lossow's command, the group's task would be the creation of political coordination center under Scheubner that would report independently.[357]

By June 1916, the German Supreme Army High Command had aborted plans for the Eastern Caucasian Project and attached Scheubner with his German staff to German forces operating in Persia.[358] The expedition was dissolved on July 31, 1916 with personnel and assets transferred to German forces in Iraq. Scheubner and the Leverkuehn brothers who were seriously ill, were sent back to Germany.[359] They left Mosul on August 28, 1915, arriving in Aleppo on September 4, 1916 where they stayed at the German officers' home.[360]

Scheubner's Final Analysis

Back in Germany Scheubner obtained a copy of Johannes Lepsius' report on the Armenian Genocide.[361] Due to wartime conditions, he did not comment at length on the book, but confirmed his strong interest in it as he had seen the Armenian's misery. He had tried all he could to stop the people's annihilation. Generally, Scheubner thought that the report contained little that was incorrect or biased. He made it clear that

357 AA-PA, Weltkrieg 11d secr./13, A 18572, Scheubner to Schulenburg, Mosul, May 16, 1916 No. 34 J. No. 198 copy enclosure in Schulenburg to Stellv. Generalstab Abteilung Politik, Samsun, June 20, 1916 No. 32 copy enclosure in Hülsen to AA, Berlin, July 13, 1916 No. Pol. 8519.
358 AA-PA, Persien 24/10, A 16389, Nadolny to AA, Berlin, June 20, 1916 No. Pol. 8124.
359 AA-PA, Weltkrieg 11d secr./15, A 34350, Scheubner to Schulenburg, Mosul, Aug. 23, 1916 J. No. 431 enclosure in Scheubner to Greßmann, Mossul, Aug. 23, 1916 Expedition Scheubner J. No. 436 enclosure in Greßmann to Generalstab Sektion Politik, Baghdad, Oct. 23, 1916 Deutsche Iraktruppe I. No. 5092 enclosure in Hülsen to AA, Berlin, Dec. 16, 1916 copy No. Pol. 12166. Leverkuehn, *Posten,* p. 158.
360 Leverkuehn, *Posten,* p. 159. Fliedner Archiv, Auslandsstationen, Archiv II, Äußere Mission, Karton 223, Offiziersheim Aleppo 1916-1918.
361 Johannes Lepsius, *Bericht über die Lage des armenischen Volkes in der Türkei,* Potsdam, Reichsbote, 1916.

deportation was synonymous with extermination and that he had pointed this out to the relevant authorities. Scheubner told Lepsius that he seen the rest of the Armenian people in a desolate condition between Mosul and Aleppo. They could hardly be labelled "human" anymore. If Lepsius was to save some of them, he had to act swiftly. Scheubner was willing to help Lepsius and offered to meet him in Berlin. This was probably an offer to share information not fit to be put in writing.[362]

About two weeks later, Scheubner submitted to the AA a comprehensive report on his observations during the extermination of the Armenians. With few exceptions the Armenian people had been practically exterminated. The murder was part of a Turkish nationalist strategy as the CUP wanted a Turkish Empire based on Pan-Turkism and Islam. If possible, victims were forcibly assimilated, if not they were killed. The CUP took advantage of the war as a suitable moment for the implementation of its plan. Instances of Armenian resistance against the CUP had been exaggerated and used as a pretext for the murders which were mostly executed by Kurdish and Turkish irregulars and gendarmes. In line with massacring of Armenians, Scheubner saw the massive losses of Ottoman Arab army units due to insufficient equipment during the winter campaign. Both weakened the non-Turkish element. A CUP member had told Scheubner: "If we, the Turks, bleed to death in this struggle for the existence of the Ottoman Empire, there should not be any other nation left within it." Thus the Turkish campaign losses triggered the killing of non-Turkish communities.[363]

Not much is known about Scheubner's views on the Armenian Genocide after 1916. Some evidence from 1922, however, suggests a change in his perceptions. In November 1922, Scheubner informed Lepsius that he was not willing to support an appeal to the Lausanne Peace Conference on behalf of the Armenians. He advised Lepsius that the Armenians should better reach an agreement with the Turkish CUP regime, now called "nationalist" and headed by Mustafa Kemal Pasha. Scheubner was impressed by the CUP's successful opposition to the treaty of Sevrès. After all, Scheubner had become a member of the Nazi movement that aspired to the same goal. Scheubner might have realized that his reasoning was flawed, knowing that the CUP and its adherents had maintained their course and not altered their strategies.[364]

---

362 LAH 244-2580, Scheubner-Richter to Lepsius, München, Nov. 18, 1916.
363 AA-PA, Türkei 183/45, A 33457, Scheubner-Richter to Bethmann Hollweg, München, Dec. 4, 1916 Tgb. Z. 243.

Conclusion

This case study addresses a number of key issues related to the Armenian Genocide that are still under debate. The pattern of centrally supervised deportations and the repeated massacres at known killing fields demonstrate that the atrocities were not random acts of violence but part of a genocidal scheme. At Erzerum, deportation orders emanated from the office of the provincial governor Tahsin Bey, while it seems that military authorities issued deportation orders only in areas close to the frontline. In other words, deporting Armenians was primarily the task of the civil authorities. Moreover, it appears that the CUP's party apparatus participated in the execution of the deportation scheme, at least in its initial steps. We are still unable to clearly differentiate between CUP party politics and the actions of CUP members in public office. But the role of the administration was critical as the CUP lacked the manpower and infrastructure for coordinating the systematic execution of the genocidal program alone. Nevertheless, along the deportation routes, CUP members coordinated the killing of Armenian deportees.

The confiscation of Armenian property was a chief objective of the Ottoman government. By May 1915, however, no elaborate preparations were in place at Erzerum that would secure a thorough confiscation. In fact, until June 1915 the provincial authorities had not received specific orders in regard to Armenian properties. Accordingly, they approved local initiatives and sanctioned the Ottoman Bank's or ABCFM's missionaries' storing of Armenian assets. Even after May 30, 1915, when the Ottoman central authorities had issued a first basic outline regarding the confiscation of Armenian property, Erzerum's governor Tahsin was uncertain about what he should do. Only by June 10, 1915, the Ottoman government provided precise instruction to provincial and local authorities. Tahsin's recourse to an improvised arrangement at Erzerum demonstrates that the Ottoman government had not coordinated the confiscation of Armenian property before the start of the deportations. Generally, Tahsin followed orders closely which suggests that the authorities at Constantinople exercised strong control over local affairs. Thus the lack of early preparations for confiscations suggests that the orders for the deportations and confiscations had been drafted at very short notice. Therefore, it appears that no longstanding plan or blueprint had existed to exterminate the Ottoman Armenians. The case of Erzerum challenges notions that the Armenian Genocide was the result of an old conspiracy.

364 LAH 244-2580, Scheubner Richter to Lepsius, München, Nov. 18, 1922.

The study also introduces evidence on the German role in the Armenian Genocide. While we know very little about the role of some German officers serving in the Ottoman 3rd Army, the role of von der Goltz could be clarified to some extent. Goltz had not supported the extermination of the Armenians. He was not associated with anyone involved in criminal activities during the Armenian Genocide. On the contrary, Martha Koch was a leading member of the local resistance against the genocide. She went to extra-ordinary steps to save Armenians known to her, to support deportees, and she attempted to save Armenian orphans by the hundreds. She also used her social standing to counter CUP propaganda within German officers' circles. It can be safely assumed that Koch had not failed to brief Goltz on her own observations and activities. The German consular officers at Aleppo and Mosul were working along the same lines.

Goltz' decision making regarding the resistance at Hazik shows that he had only limited information at his disposal, leading to some confusion concerning the identity of Nadji Bey. When Goltz realized this mistake, he understood that the trust he had placed in Nadji was misplaced and acted swiftly. It is likely that incoming information and his own experiences during his journey from Constantinople to Mosul had exposed Goltz to the realities of the Armenian Genocide and turned him into an opponent of the CUP's genocidal program. Within this context, Scheubner's refusal to join the Nadji's expedition against Hazik appears less as the decision of a lone hero. It was much more an element of a negotiating process between the German consulate at Mosul, the embassy, and the German military authorities on the one hand, and the Ottoman authorities on the other. These negotiations had gone on for some time and at least on the German side had remained under the embassy's control. Thus, Scheubner followed orders and did not act on his own, even if he did not like to see things as they were in reality. His claim that the Ottoman military tried to compromise him and the German side by involving them in a massacre has to be seen with some reservation. If any such plot had existed, the Ottoman Army High Command was not part of it. Instead, Enver rejected German participation at Hazik. On a different level, the fact that the defenders were allowed to survive suggests that the high-ranking elements within the CUP made a distinction between Armenian and other Ottoman Christians, though this might not have been the case at the local and provincial level.

Both Dadrian and Krethlow did not properly evaluate the situation at Hazik. In accusing Goltz they neglected the single most important fact any discussion has to take into account: the command structure of the Ottoman forces. Goltz had no authority at Hazik as the region belonged to the 3rd Army's area. His involvement was limited to decisions concerning the dispatch of troops from his future area of command. Krethlow's claim that Goltz had no humanitarian motives in saving the Armenians at Mosul is not convincing and at best speculative. Like Liman von Sanders at Smyrna, Goltz used the only pretext he possibly could employ to overrule the decisions of the civil authorities, namely, military necessity. To expect Goltz to issue orders on humanitarian grounds within the context of the contemporary situation is unconvincing. It appears that both authors used only part of the available record to produce arguments that would fit their wider interpretations at the cost of academic accuracy.

When Scheubner's mission to create upheaval in Trans-Caucasia failed, his new proposals could not convince his superiors. There was neither sufficient local support for a German raid nor sufficient German or Ottoman troops available. The Russian forces were too strong. Leverkuehn, for his part, tried to present Scheubner's mission as instrumental in securing the victory at Kut over the British and thereby saving the Ottoman Mesopotamian front. He credited Scheubner and Nadji with stopping the Russian advance and possible relief of Kut. Leverkuehn claimed that Halil himself confirmed his assessment while others doubted it. In sum, the expedition was a success as it halted superior enemy forces despite the lack of supplies.[365] In reality however, the affair at Sautshbulaq was not more than a side show of operations in Iran which, in turn, were not more than a side-show of the Mesopotamian campaign.[366]

Scheubner's constant desire for promotions and his repeated attempts to free himself from supervision and turn himself into a somewhat independent commander did not escape the attention of his superiors. Scheubner was certainly not a typical German officer who just followed orders. Scheubner had a tendency to act according to his own preferences. For Ottoman Armenians this was good fortune. Scheubner opposed the CUP's genocidal policy. His attitudes were not as diplomatic as Ottoman provincial officials could have expected from regular German consular officials. Later, Scheubner and his associates did not shy away from personal risks when standing their ground against CUP activists. They

365 Leverkuehn, *Posten*, pp. 126, 151, 157.

366 Ulrich Gehrke, *Persien in der deutschen Orientpolitik während des Ersten Weltkrieges*, Stuttgart, Kohlhammer Verlag, 1962 p. 216. Sarısaman concluded that the raid was not much more than an Ottoman bluff, trying to keep superior Russian forces occupied in Iran. Sarısaman, *Ömer Naci Bey*, p. 511. İlter came to a similar conclusion. [İlter], *Hatıraları*, p. 54.

knew of the duplicity and lethal mentality of these activitists and were willing to make a final stand against them, killing as many as possible. Importantly, Scheubner understood the CUP's larger scheme. The party tried to create what it considered a Turkish state out of the multi-ethnic Ottoman Empire. Thus, Scheubner did not buy into the Ottoman Islamist propaganda at that time, since he understood the government's willingness to let non-Turkish Muslims perish as part of the same policy that formed the basis of the Armenian Genocide.

Appendix 1

An Extended Note from Hilmar Kaiser
(to follow footnote 132)

Between 1922 and 1930 a number of survivors of the atrocities in the Khinis region reached a League of Nations shelter in Aleppo where they were cared for and their experiences recorded. The teenage girl Khazal Sarkissian lived in Khinis at the time of the massacre. In 1922 she recalled her experiences: "Her family was killed by Kourds in their native town. Her mother escaped to Russia. She was married to a Kourd with whom she lived for 7 years. She tried several times to flee but she was not successful they brought her back and treated her very badly." Farfure Amoershadjian was 20 years old when the massacres in the Khinis district took place: "In the beginning of the war her husband was killed, she was deported with her mother in law about two hours far from the city. The caravan of deportation was attacked by Kourds, most of this unfortunate people were killed or wounded. Farfure could flee with another Armenian lady. They went together to one of the environing villages but there they have been caught by officials of the Turkish Government and exiled there again. On the road she fled again, this time she did not go to a village but she made herself a shelter under the ground where she lived a few months. Again the Turkish Government located her and this time she was sent to Haïni. A Kourd from there married her and Farfure lived seven years with him." Siroom Boghossian was 7 years old: "Her father died when she was a little child. During the Turkish-Armenian rebellion a Kourd took her mother and married her. Sirom was allowed to come with her mother to the Kourd's house. During the Russian offensive of that section they were all together deported to Diarbekir. The Kourd and Siroom's mother became ill and died a few days after their arrival in Diarbekir. Siroom was taken by the government and put in a Turkish orphanage where she stayed one year. After this a Turk took her to his house and Siroom lived six years there being the maid-servant of the Turkish family." Satenig Garabedian was 23 years old: "In the beginning of the Armenian deportation her village was attacked by Kourds, most of the people were killed, her husband included. Women and girls were taken to Turkish houses or Harems. Satenig's neighbour, a Turk, took her to his house and married her by force. She lived six years with the Turk. Later she fled to Divrig, there she knew an Armenian family, who was islamized in the beginning of the deportation. She remained two years there doing the work of a maid-servant." Aghavni Movsessian was 10 years old: "When Armenians were deported her mother gave her to a known Turk, hoping to save her life in this way. Four months later the Russian army occupied that region, Christians and Moslems were exiled to Harpoot. In Harpoot Aghavni located her uncle's daughter who was a servant in a Turkish family. The Turkish friend of her mother became too poor to support her and so she was given to another Turkish family. Aghavni served eight years in this family." Satenig Avedissian was just 12 years old: "Satenig, her mother, brother and four sisters were deported to a village named Gouik. There she was separated from her family and given to a Kourd. After six months this town was occupied by the Russian army and before her arrival the whole population had to leave. Satenig and the Kourdish family she lived with came to Ghendja. After being three years in that family the Kourd married her and two years later he died. After her husband's death she worked during 3 years in different houses in order to earn her daily bread." Zanazan and Anoush Merdeyan of Kara Choban village were 14 and 24 years old: "Her native village was surrounded by Kourds in the first days of the Armenian massacres, but the village people resisted against them during the first days. As they had no supply for their guns they were beaten and Kourds occupied the village, killing men, women and children. Several girls were married by Kourds, some sold as slaves. However, Zanazan and her sister Anoosh were taken as servants to a Kourdish family and they remained nine years among the Kourds." Gorun Zakian was from the same village and only 5 years old: "His father was taken as a soldier in the Turkish army and his mother deported with 5 children. Months they were driven to and fro, till they one day were near Severek. There Gorun's 2 brothers were killed. A Kurd took possession of Gorun, and he was a shepherd by thwat man many years." Armenag war only 8 years old: "Armenag was exiled with his parents. The caravan reached "Kouih." There Kourds attacked the people and killed the most of them. Some they dragged away with them, so also Armenag. He stayed with his owner 3 years, then fled to another house, where he remained 2 years. He was illtreated and fled again in another village, where he lived 6 years as a shepherd."[367]

367 United Nations Library, Geneva, League of Nations Archives, C 1601 – C 1603, file 53, 225, 246, 339, 366, 542, 543, 886, 1860. The present author is preparing a study of these survivor biographies.

Deportation of Armenians from Erzerum:
Photographs from German Foreign Office Archives
with original captions.

May 18, 1915 [no further caption].

May 18, 1915 [no further caption].

May 18, 1915 [no further caption].

May 19, 1915 [no further caption].

May 19, 1915 consular employees distributing bread.

May 20, 1915 camp of the deported Armenians.

May 20, 1915 Distribution of bread by employees of the consulate.

May 20, 1915 consular employees distributing the bread.

May 20, 1915, consular wagon during bread distribution.

A German Officer During the Armenian Genocide

A Biography of Max Von Scheubner-Richter

I

Foreword

There are names like Hentig, Wassmuss, Niedermayer, and Klein that are
more familiar to Mohammedans than to Germans, whom they have served
with their daring actions in the Islamic Oriental world. Amongst them
must be included that of Max von Scheubner-Richter. All that has been
published about and by him are his consular telegrams from Erzerum,
printed by Johannes Lepsius in the collection of documents on the
Turkish–Armenian question. The copy I own of this presumably out-of-
print book carries the following dedication:

> To my dear friend and erstwhile aide, Paul Leverkuehn, in
> remembrance of our joint struggles on behalf of the German Shield of
> Honor and our shared dreams about the future of Germany in the
> Orient, 1915–1916.
>
> Danzig, 2nd September 1919.
> Max v. Scheubner-Richter.

A few unadorned words to tell us about the character, convictions and
life of a man, whose heroic death guaranteed his mortal remains a place in
the shining shrine of honor: he rests in Munich, amongst the fallen of
November 9, 1923.

Nevertheless, very little is known about his life and his unceasing services
to Germany during the war and in distant lands. Therefore, as his former
comrade-in-arms, I want to report on a part of this man's life and at the
same time about a little-known part of our war history. I also want to
comment on his virtues, which were often misjudged and seldom liked in
his lifetime, though I came to appreciate them in passing years.

My account is based on my own personal experience, on information
from Scheubner and his collaborators (letters, diaries, draft reports, and
papers of his expedition that are in my possession), as well as from
recollections of his wife, Mrs. Hilde von Scheubner-Richter, to whom I am
most thankful for help.

I must also express my gratitude to the German Foreign Office for
having granted me access to documents related to his expedition and his
work in Riga.

Most of the photographs in this book were taken by members of his
expedition. The view of Sautchbulak was taken from de Morgan's book

Mission Scientifique en Perse (Paris, 1896) with the kind permission of Ernest Leroux publishing house.

The maps in the book have been produced on the basis of the best available maps, particularly on the international map (scale 1:1,000,000) and the German operational map (1:800,000). These were supplemented by Scheubner's expedition papers and log books, which show numerous places, whose names do not figure on currently available maps, to be located with precision. I extend heartfelt thanks to my friend, Hans Doerr, Major at General Headquarters, for preparing the maps, and for his numerous suggestions and cooperation. I also thank Erik Reger, whose elaborate skills gave this manuscript its final form; Paul Scheffer for much friendly advice; Arno Schickedanz, Chief of Staff of the German National-Socialist Party Foreign Policy Committee, who provided me with his recollections of Mr. Scheubner; and Prof. Sarre for his expert advice.

Paul Leverkuehn
Berlin, April 1938

* * *

Rider with Preysing

I met Max von Scheubner-Richter in August 1914, in the barrack-yard of the Bavarian light cavalry.

The old quarter of Straubing* was alive with the martial activities of the first days of mobilization. The 7th Regiment had already moved out; the 5th Bavarian Reserve Cavalry Regiment had been formed and marched out; and now the voices of the Reserve Squadron sang from the Danube (whose waves had once swallowed, for State reasons, the fair daughter of the Bader family from Augsburg), echoing from the steep rooftops of the town:

A lance shall stand upon my grave,
And the white and blue upon it wave.

The Reserve Squadron was mainly made up of older reservists, amongst whom there were also young horses, as well as some younger recruits: about 90 younger volunteers, mostly university graduates, and young men of apprentice age between 17 and 22.

Amongst the volunteers—older, much more mature, and certainly something special—was Scheubner. He was of smallish, agile physique, with a relatively large head that was rather bald, and had a small, dark moustache. These features readily and indelibly impressed themselves on one's memory, even if at the time we didn't entirely realize why. We believed it was owing to his greater age.

He had shrewd brown eyes which, looking out from behind spectacles, betrayed a free and kindly way of interacting with others. I shall always remember the strength of his small, well-shaped hand—a hand accustomed to holding the reins of prudence and will, evincing firmness while at the same time not denying tenderness. I can still hear his pleasant voice with its unmistakable Baltic accent, answering the sergeant-major who took down his personal data.

"Date of birth?"

"January 9th, 1884."

"Place?"

"Riga."

"Riga? Where's that?"

"In Russia."

---

*   Quarter of Munich.

"Russia! Well, we certainly can't enter in a German pay register."

It was totally in keeping with the views of that time to enter false data in a document rather than acknowledge a person could have been born in an enemy country, never mind if he possessed German nationality, as Scheubner did.

Riga was thus unacceptable as a place of birth, yet one had to remain as close to the truth as possible. Scheubner came to an agreement with the sergeant-major, choosing a town in Saxony, from which his ancestors had supposedly migrated to the Baltic.

"Profession?"

"Engineer."

These data were already quite sufficient for the pay register, but back in our quarters he expanded on them. He had studied in Riga. His Student Corps was the Rubonia, which had an ancient fortified tower as its headquarters. But how had he come to Straubing? On finishing his studies, he had moved to Munich where he was happily married and lived in comfortable economic circumstances. As a private scholar he pursued his vocation for chemistry and sports.

He was an outstanding horseman. When we later shared many long rides, he invariably changed the subject whenever talk arose about his riding skills. He claimed to be a poor second to his wife, who was the real expert with horses. And this profound respect for his wife's knowledge and judgment which was often manifested in moments conducive for the expression of greatest personal tenderness, was characteristic of Scheubner. He always manifested the deepest fondness and love for the most faithful companion of his life.

Besides his equestrian skills, he brought something else to the military which made him stand out above all the rest. He had fighting experience. During the 1905 uprisings in the Baltic area, he had participated in self-defense of a landed estate. He had been a member of a Cossack unit. Small wonder, then, that he had begun his military service with the light cavalry as an officer! However, with the lowest military rank, he became our dormitory elder. Among his subordinates were also my brother, Karl Gustav Leverkuehn, Bachelor of Law from Lübeck, and myself, a law student in his fifth semester at Munich University. We had no idea as yet of the close friendship towards which destiny would drive us.

We had all lost hope of a one-year service. There were no longer any special privileges, nor would we have wanted them anyway. We carried out our duties as recruits enthusiastically—even passionately. There were stable duties—brushing the horses six times over. That was life! And then there was riding-school with the old sergeant-majors! They were all fine people, who could hardly understand our ignorance about horses and riding.

"Theile! What do you do in civilian life?" was one of the exasperated questions these expert horsemen would ask.

"I'm a Bachelor of Law," Volunteer Theile would reply.

"And is that the best way you can sit on a horse?" came back the reproachful, accusing retort.

However, no sooner did we manage to keep ourselves in an upright position, we would go to the great exercise square to train with the squadron, practice charges, lances couched, galloping as though the very war depended on the cavalry, singing

> *Is the Bavarian horseman,*
> *Not the most handsome of all soldiers?*

That song may not have sounded very convincing, if our uniforms were taken into account, which were the oldest that could be rustled up in the depot, to which was added the little green bonnet tightly girding our foreheads. However, the people at the grand old marketplace in Straubing seemed not to notice it, but instead must have looked into our eyes: their brightness, their happiness that was as fresh as the cloth of the uniforms was faded, and what could have stoked their fire more vigorously than the news of victories coming from West and East?

Reports from the regiment about its attacks and patrols, about the first Iron Crosses awarded, made the rounds time and again: how the war might soon end victoriously so that we might not even get to the battlefield, too late for the World War! Our most serious concern! The evenings were drawing in, and fogs falling, and then, in early October, bugles began to sound. A generalized hustle and bustle arose: uniforms were handed out, roll calls held, orders given for the transport of troops. . . . and *one* question came from hundreds of lips: are we among them? The volunteers? Not all. Disappointment on some faces, delight on others.

Scheubner? There! There he stands. Inexpressibly overjoyed, though outwardly as calm as ever, savoring the moment, working untiringly with his forward thinking ideas. Where were they already? In France, in Russia? Or even further afield?

For the last time orders were given in the barracks-yard. Horses neighed at the sound of bugles. Gates opened, townspeople thronged the streets— were there so many people in such a small town? All the workshops, every home now lay empty. This was only one more departure of troops, as had happened millions of times before, yet every time it was a unique experience. Once more the town overflowed with music, once more the soldiers sang their bitter-sweet tunes, as the children of the town crowded around them. Then, slowly, a pregnant hush fell, looking back on the past and wondering what the future held in store.

Those who were to stay behind felt it as a misfortune. "The invariable time-piece of Duty..." Never were these words of Max Piccolomini so appropriate. Scheubner, however—our happy Scheubner—was in our Third Squadron!

If marching to battle was favor enough, even more so was it to be assigned to the "Third," the most admired by the veterans and volunteers alike. "The Third" meant enjoying the grace of destiny to a special degree; for the Third, the "Swinging Squadron," was under the leadership of no other than Commander Count Kaspar Preysing, who... well, he was simply "The Preysing."

He was a redoubtable fellow. Strict, very strict. But excellent. An aura of legend surrounded him: he was a truly superlative man, to whom anything but mediocrity was acceptable. When mobilization began, he had given each man in his squadron a knife, to be carried in the leg of the boot. His men were allowed to wear a long beard, or else be clean-shaven; but no other option was allowed. The uniform jacket might be worn open. The men thus behaved and felt different from conventional soldiers. Oh yes, that was Preysing!

His military career was the crowning point of the legend. Thrice wounded, decorated with the Maximilian Joseph Order, the highest award of the Bavarian Army, in the 1916 Romanian campaign. He died on horseback on French soil during the last year of the war.

Have there ever been such fierce onslaughts and intrepid patrols? It was Preysing and his men who carried them out. It seemed as if this man waged war in his own way, like a regimental commander from the Thirty Years' War. It was undeniable that he had a distinct personal style. This aristocrat with rugged features, a hereditary imperial councillor, Master of the Moos, belonged to a lineage that claimed to be of greater antiquity in Bavaria than the Wittelsbachers! According to Hebbel, the Count's ancestors had already shown a particular style in government. It was indeed a Preysing who, though capable of human feeling, firmly placed State morals above Agnes Bernauer's right to life, ordering her to be cast into the Danube from Straubing Bridge. Scheubner was not mistaken in imagining exciting things in store with Preysing.

The regiment was in the area of the Third Bavarian Army, posted in French-Lorraine, in St. Mihiel. The front was at a standstill, and the division's cavalry set up artillery or general headquarters observation posts with patrols, consisting of one NCO and three to six men. On October 30, Scheubner was on duty at one of the artillery observation posts. The initial calm—as so often happened—was delusive. A shell exploded, and the signal was given to open fire. In this letter to his wife, Scheubner narrates the subsequent occurrences.

> The shells burst at every five meters, destroying everything around, smashing through heavy beams as if they were paper. The sergeant and one of the men—the NCO had gone down the mountain carrying a communication—took refuge in a dugout while another officer and I looked on from the edge of a wood. In such heavy shelling it makes no difference wherever one happens to be. Only luck can save one, as no effective cover or protection exists.
>
> A couple of shells exploded very close by, showering us with a hail of shrapnel, branches, stones, and dirt which fortunately didn't injure us. A piece of shrapnel from a grenade struck my helmet. I picked it up red hot and am sending it to you as a souvenir.
>
> There was then a short breathing space during which we relaxed and I made my way to the artillery officer in the dugout. We had just lit up a cigar when all at once we heard another explosion. We got out and a man from the machine-gun unit, an NCO to be precise, covered in blood and calling for assistance, came towards us. The nest dugout had been destroyed. We could hear feeble calls for help coming from it. We hurried to it and started clearing away the heavy beams while shells carried on falling left and right.
>
> A Cavalry auxiliary, Bayer by name, helped me get one of the badly wounded men out, who was then carried downhill by the sergeant. We learned that there were still six men buried under the rubble. I recalled some infantry soldiers who had got away from there in their initial panic (20 men wanted to call the medical orderlies) and in the middle of shell fire we began the tough job of excavation. Unfortunately we were able to rescue only one, who died right away. Of the others only some body parts were left...

The officers' reports praised Scheubner's calm and level-headedness during the incident. Less than a month at the front, and only three in uniform, he had been awarded the Iron Cross. Yet something had happened that troubled his heart: Preysing could not decorate him. Preysing had been transferred to Constantinople a few days earlier. Scheubner was to follow him soon after.

II

Between Turkey and the Caucasus

When the Great War broke out, almost every nation had to ask itself whether Turkey was going to be drawn into the fray or not. If they were, on which side it would it be? Turkey had the courage to forge an alliance with Germany on August 2, 1914, under which plan, in case Germany was attacked by Russia, Turkey would be forced to side with Germany and Austria. Since Russia had not formally declared war on Germany but, on the contrary, it was Germany that declared it, Turkey was under no compulsion to honor the terms of the treaty.

For months it remained undefined whether Turkey would keep out of the war or even opt for the Entente. The cabinet was divided, avoiding a decision until realities overturned its manoeuvres. The German warships *Göben* and *Breslau* arrived in the safe haven of Constantinople and were sold to Turkey. Their commander, Admiral Souchon, entered Turkish service. On October 29, by order of War Minister Enver Pasha, he bombarded the Russian ports of Sevastopol and Novorossisk. At the same time, outgoing Turkish merchant vessels leaving Smyrna were fired at by the British in the Aegean Sea. Diplomatic relations were broken off, and on November 12 Turkey declared war on the "Entente."

The Turkish ministers who had been against an alliance (or at least against an alliance with Germany) resigned. Now all power was vested in those who had really wielded decisive influence on the direction of Turkish policies all along, but whose actions had previously been hindered by their colleagues in the cabinet: War Minister and Vice-Generallisimo Enver Pasha, Navy Minister Djemal Pasha, and Interior Minister Talaat Pasha.

Within the framework of the Central Powers' war objectives, Turkey had three fundamental tasks: the first was that as many enemy forces as possible be kept occupied at the Turkish frontiers, which was a secondary theater of operations. This point had already been emphasized in a letter from Army Chief of Staff, Von Moltke, to Enver Pasha, on the conclusion of the alliance. The second was to advance against what Germany considered the most vulnerable spot of the British Empire—Egypt and the Suez Canal. Finally, to cut Russia off from its allies by land and sea.

The last objective was put into immediate effect by the feverish improvement of the defensive installations at the Straits. However, no danger of attack existed either from the Aegean or the more distant

Scheubner in Erzerum, January 1915.

Mediterranean at that particular time, as with the Entente's attack on Gallipoli later in 1915.

Preparations for the Suez Canal offensive were put in the hands of Djemal Pasha, who had been appointed governor of Syria, and supreme commander of the army there, supported by Lt.-Col. Baron Kress von Kressenstein as chief of staff.

Germany and Austria could provide Turkey only with very limited supplies of war material, as they were separated by the neutral territories of Romania and Bulgaria. Neither could they send troops, but they were able to give effective support in the form of officers, something that had been going on even before the war began. Since 1913, there had been a military mission there under General Liman Von Sanders composed of 40 officers. This mission was now considerably reinforced, and it was owing to the new demand for officers that Count Preysing had been transferred to Turkey. This was because he had already participated as observer on the Turkish side in the Balkan Wars in 1912.

But now the situation and the task were different. His Bavarian military tradition and his personal political orientation, which was not altogether free of aristocratic overtones, could not easily be adapted to the markedly Prussian militaristic character of the mission. As a suitable assignment could not be found for him, he soon returned to Germany and thence to the war front.

He had, however, at the time of his transfer to Turkey, arranged for the reassignment of a certain number of volunteers from his squadron to Turkey, among them Scheubner.

They remained in Turkey and assigned to special missions that resulted from Turkey's first vital task—to keep as many strong enemy forces tied up as possible. It was in both German and Turkish interest to win Persia over to the side of the Central Powers, and to lead this land that for years had been divided into spheres of influence between the British and the Russians, at present scarcely a sovereign nation, to freedom and toward opposition against the Entente.

A mission led by Major Klein was sent by the Political Department of the Chief of Staff to Persia via Baghdad, with the political objective of starting the liberation of Persia on the one hand, and cutting off British oil pipelines in the south of the country on the other. Much more far-reaching were the assignments of Captain Niedermayer and Legation Secretary Von Hentig. They were to travel to Afghanistan via Turkey and Persia in order to persuade the Emir of that country to enter into an alliance with Germany and to attack India.

Quite apart from the Central Powers' common interests, in Turkey's eyes Russia was its greatest enemy. Peter the Great's testament had not been forgotten: to make the church of St. Sophia in Constantinople Christian once again, and the straits Russian. An attack on Constantinople could well be expected, supported by the Russian fleet. However, it could come from the Caucasus as well, where Turkey and Russia had an extensive common border. The Cabinet decided to pre-empt the Russians and attack them in the Caucasus.

While the preparations for this campaign were being put in motion, Scheubner left the Western front and arrived in Constantinople—and at the most opportune moment, for his expertise of Russia and the Russian language was needed at this time. Count Preysing introduced him to Ambassador Von Wangenheim, whose name stood for the August 2nd German-Turkish alliance. He was, for as long as he lived, the very soul of the treaty on the German side.

A successful attack in the Caucasus—and Wangenheim had no doubts as to its success—had to have considerable political consequences, since these regions were not inhabited by Russians, but by a great number of diverse peoples and tribes. Shortly after the beginning of war trusty agents had been active in the border regions of Georgia, the central region of the Caucasus with its capital, Tiflis. These agents reported on the mood of the local population and the preparations for a revolt.

The time would come—and perhaps it was already near—when all the peoples of the Caucasus, particularly the Muslims, would be set in motion and would press for a new national organization. Wangenheim usually received his information from the Turkish Ministry of War, the German Military Mission, or the consul in Erzerum, who was, however, tied to his post during the offensive. Wangenheim must have been interested in having a liaison man who could follow the General Headquarter's instruction. This was to be Scheubner's assignment.

In addition, however, Scheubner was entrusted with a special military task by Military Attaché Colonel Von Leipzig, which had presumably been originally intended for Count Preysing. The oilfields of Baku were one of Russia's main natural resources. To do damage in this region or to obstruct its exploitation by blowing up bridges and railway lines, no matter if the Turkish offensive succeeded or not, was of military and political value—especially if it were possible to sever the pipeline that carried oil from Baku to Tiflis and Batum on the Black Sea. Furthermore, Scheubner was to determine the chances for an advance through northern Persia or elsewhere and, if possible, take charge of such an advance and put it into effect.

For him this was not just a change of scene. He was not merely a soldier who had been transferred from Lorraine to the Orient. From the limited duties of grey fatigues he found himself suddenly at the very core of political planning, at a center of decisions and activities, where he could have some influence. He was now working for the future of Germany not just with weapons but with all the mental acumen he possessed. It was a place where his initiative could be brought into play as he himself wished.

His base of operations was to be Erzerum, a renowned old trading town and important crossroads between Anatolia and the Caucasus, and between the coast of the Black Sea and Mesopotamia, where he would be the only German representative in the 600-kilometer stretch from Trebizond to Mosul. The town was the natural starting point for military and political missions eastwards to the Caucasus and south-east to northern Persia.

The consul who had been in office at Erzerum there when the war broke out, Dr. Anders, had been arrested while on his way through Russia. Because of the interests which the Baku oilfields represented behind enemy lines, an oil expert, Vice-Consul Schwarz, was chosen as Anders' successor. Scheubner was supposed to collaborate with him.

At the beginning of December 1914, Scheubner left Constantinople for Trebizond aboard a torpedo-boat belonging to the convoy of the Minister of War Enver Pasha. In spite of winter storms and fog, the Black Sea was the relatively quickest route to travel. The threatening surveillance of the Russian fleet was a danger for larger vessels, but this time the hunters had no good scent, and the flotilla of men with their bold and wide-ranging plans, their sights set on the far-off Caucasus, slipped by the enemy cruisers.

For his attack on Russia, Enver Pasha assembled the Third Turkish Army (Ninth, Xth, and XIth Corps) in the neighborhood of Erzerum, and two volunteer corps and a gendarmerie division on the Persian border. In addition, troops (36th and 37th Divisions) marched up from Mesopotamia through Mosul to join the Third Army. When the Russians advanced on Erzerum a few days after the declaration of war, the Third Army defended itself under the leadership of Hassan Izzet Pasha on both sides of Köprikoi, on the Erzerum-Kars road.

Enver Pasha, who was set on an offensive success, particularly the conquest of the Russian bastion of Kars, removed the army commander from his post at the beginning of December and took over command of the Third Army himself, with General Bronsart Von Schellendorf as chief of staff.

He decided on a frontal attack against the Russians from the Kara-Killisse-Köprikoi line, stressing the assault in the direction of Kars, while diverting the Ninth and Xth Corps northwards via Artvin to reach the enemy's rear.

Supplies reached the troops along an approximately 700-kilometer route, starting from the Eregli-Ulukishla railway terminal on the northwest edge of the Taurus through numerous mountain passes to Caesarea, and then leading, via Sivas and Erzinjan, to Erzerum. Owing to pronounced differences in altitude (between a thousand and two thousand meters) and the bad conditions of the road with its sometimes crumbly rocky ground, at others its sand-drifts, supplies could only be ferried to the troops with great difficulty and incompletely.

When on December 19 the Caucasus army began its operations, the troops were neither completely assembled nor satisfactorily fed and outfitted. The result was that, without having fought any important engagement, the approximately hundred thousand-strong army fell victim within a fortnight to the intense cold (temperatures ranged constantly 20 to 25 degrees centigrade below zero) and starvation. On January 10 the operation was called off halfway to Kars, with a loss of eighty thousand men. Sarikamish, the furthest point reached, is the name given to the entire expedition.

The diversionary northward march of the Ninth and Xth Corps, which Enver Pasha himself led, was stopped short by storms and adverse weather conditions in the high snow-covered mountain area south of Artvin. The Ninth Corps, whose infantry near Erzerum were made to divest themselves of heavy clothing and backpacks to better negotiate the deep snow, perished almost to a man as a consequence of that measure. The corps staff and the three division staffs were taken prisoners. A division of the Xth Corps under the command of German Lieutenant Colonel Stange managed to take the town of Artvin.

Enver Pasha resigned his command, returned quietly to Constantinople, and never again led troops personally. The heady flight of ideas had been far too hasty for Turkish local conditions: the plans and schemes that had crossed all the mountains, rivers, and deserts, had been much too daring and audacious, far too bold for pathless steppes and endless distances that presented the poor soldiers with hard and terrible struggles before actually reaching the enemy.

Scheubner had arrived in Erzerum at the beginning of the Turkish attack. Consul Schwarz had to leave straight away to confer with General Posselt Pasha at headquarters, and consulate operations were left in Scheubner's hands. When Schwarz returned, it was only for a short time. He left soon after for Constantinople, and in January Scheubner found himself invested with the title of vice-consul, administering the consulate in Erzerum. Around the same time, he was promoted to the rank of Reserve Lieutenant by unanimous accord of the Seventh Cavalry Regiment's body of officers on the recommendation of Count Preysing.

At first, his consular activities were overshadowed by the purely humanitarian assistance he gave to wounded and sick German officers, who reached Erzerum after the offensive. A military hospital was set up in the consulate, affording what scant medical assistance was available, so that the sick and wounded could make the return journey to Constantinople.

Scheubner managed the consular business as well as possible, basing his actions on whatever precedents he could find in the office files. Obviously, it was no easy matter for someone who until then had been a private man and scientist suddenly to be cast in the role of representative of the Imperial German government before the Turkish civil and military authorities.

III

Consul in Erzerum

A consul's position in Turkey was completely different from that in a European country. As the individual national of a European power automatically enjoyed a special status, for instance in not being subject to Turkish jurisdiction, the duties of a consul far exceeded the usual representation of economic and individual interests.

The consular district in which he represented the sovereignty of his country extended over wide areas with poor communications. As he conducted a part of the diplomatic business that otherwise would have been the province of legations, he could claim corresponding honors. This also held true for his public appearances. It did not befit the rank of a consul in a large Asian city to walk on foot, or to show himself without a uniformed *kavass* at his side to mind that no person or animal approached his master too closely on the street. The Russian consul general in Erzerum moved about only by carriage drawn by four horses. His favorite outings were to fortifications: in this way he chose to express that there existed no forbidden or secret parts of town from which he was barred.

Scheubner had no way of acting like him: not only because it would not have been proper, but also because it would have been beyond his budget. Nevertheless, he laid great value on having good riding horses for himself and his elegant manservant, Tahir. When they rode through the town, he on "Pasha" and Tahir on "Kismet," the people stopped and watched them with amazement and respect. His equestrian skills did not fail to impress the Turkish officers as well. By organizing riding events and hunts, he gained their special respect.

His house was always open to visitors. There was still a stock of European wines available in Erzerum, and whatever was lacking could be procured from Trebizond. In short, Scheubner took his representative duties as seriously as he ought to have if we wanted to work successfully in this Oriental world.

In his contact with the urban and rural population, he relied on Tahir to interpret for him. Though the man could neither read nor write, he was a veritable polyglot, who spoke Russian, Turkish, Kurdish, Armenian and Persian—and all of these were spoken in the region. Scheubner was able to converse in German or French with the Turkish officers and officials. Russian was also understood by numerous people in the region.

However, local official business formed only part of his work, and as interesting as it might sometimes have been, it surely was not what appealed to his greatest ideas and inner faith.

Events on the south-eastern front of the Caucasus, where the Turkish Army was operating less successfully, kept the consul busy and in suspense as an observer and a soldier. In mid-January, the Turks took Tabriz, capital of the northeastern Persian province of Azerbaijan, and subsequently Urmia and the border town of Sautchbulak. In this way, they opened up a line of retreat from the north-east toward the south-west along the caravan route between Tabriz and Mosul in case of a counterattack. Though this counterattack was not long in coming and led to the evacuation of Azerbaijan, news of the initial successes had already been so effective that they set the eastern Caucasus—with which contact had never been cut off—in motion. The Daghestanis, composed of Muslim tribes racially related to the Turks, lived there.

Prince Amir Aslan Khan Khoiski arrived in Erzerum as envoy of the Mohammedan organizations of the eastern Caucasus. He announced that revolutionary committees had been set up in all important places with their headquarters in the town of Elizabetpol. They were sufficiently supplied with weapons, ammunition, and money; the movement was to be supported by the Tartar oil-magnates of Baku. Such a revolt, however, could only have lasting success with help of the Turkish Army, and with the provision that Germany would recognize those lands as independent in ensuing peace treaties. Scheubner based his evaluation of the situation on the following military and political considerations.

The Russians' Caucasus army had become weak. The elderly Prince Vorontsoff-Dashkoff, military and civilian governor in one person, had drawn everything that was not truly indispensable and despatched it for service on the threatened European front of Russia. Only those units deemed unfit to take part in the struggle against Germany and Austria were left behind, and thus they were no guarantee of Russian rule in the Caucasus either. Some of these regiments were made up of German colonists from Wolhynia, many of who deserted and passed to the Turkish side and were conducted to the interior of Anatolia where they were given new duties to fulfil. Russian army discipline had also eroded, and the civil administration and police were corrupt. This situation presented a great opportunity for dissatisfied people and revolutionaries for action.

Scheubner didn't have a great deal of confidence that the situation would remain the same. Despite the old prince's helplessness, the Russians themselves would be thinking along the same lines about these matters. It was to be expected that they would gradually bolster and build up this front. This would, however, take considerable time: in fact, it would be impossible if the Russian defeats continued on the German front.

After the Sarikamish failure the Turkish Army could not count on pushing the Russian Army back and reaching the interior of the Caucasus by an attack on its center. They could, however, expect to succeed, via northern Persia, by employing the right wing of the army, and in this way linking up with the revolutionaries. Scheubner expressed these ideas to Ambassador Von Wangenheim, who in turn communicated them to Marshall Liman Von Sanders for further consideration. Von Saunders warmly supported the proposed incursion of the Turkish Army's right wing, which in conjunction with the expected uprising, could lead to a considerable weakening of the Russians.

In parallel with the plans for the eastern Caucasus, the question of an uprising in Georgia was elaborated. This was the region extending from Batum on the Black Sea as far as the valley of the River Kura east of Tiflis. Although the Georgians (or Grusins) had been a part of Russia since the end of the eighteenth century, they still retained their own national and religious identity. At that time, Catherine II allowed their nobility to call themselves "princes." Their number was estimated at 9,000. The grandiose title bore no relation to political influence or commercial importance: very often these princes had no more than a hundred subjects; at other times they were just the members of their own family.

In Tiflis and in all larger towns the Georgians had their committees. They also had emissaries in Constantinople, Berlin and Vienna. In early 1915, the first attempts were made to create a Georgian Legion. While hoping for Turkish cooperation, they also worried about the price they would pay for it. Perhaps it would entail a limitation of their national independence or even Turkish domination. Besides, they had their own Christian Church, closer to the Roman Catholic than the Russian Orthodox, which set them apart from Russia, though they had nothing in common with Islam.

In political and military terms both Germany and Turkey had a common immediate goal, which was to weaken Russia, but beyond that there existed many differences. The Turks wished to extend their own territory, or to only allow the creation of states that would be dependent on them. Germany, however, could only be successful in organizing the Georgian or Daghestani uprisings if it guaranteed them national independence. Scheubner informed the Foreign Office and the embassy of the demands that were made, and he supported the Georgians' own policies as expressed by their leaders in Berlin and Constantinople. With regard to the eastern Caucasus, he submitted an elaborate proposal, outlining the requirements for an expedition. For this purpose he needed German staff. Officers, however, were not to be had, as the German Army had lost too many in 1914—and sufficient replacements had not been trained yet. Scheubner knew how to help himself. He suggested to Ambassador Von Wangenheim that qualified volunteers should be assigned.

While the situation and the resulting measures were being considered in Constantinople and Berlin early in 1915, new developments occurred which drew attention to other matters, so that the Caucasian plans were shelved for the time being. One of these developments was the allied attack in the Dardanelles in February 1915, which concentrated all Turkish forces in that area, so that there were none available to carry out any sort of action in the Caucasus; and, secondly, there was the development of the Armenian question in the Caucasian theater of war.

IV

The Armenian Incident

It was March 1915 and I was in the middle of thundering cannon near Xammes, a tiny village in Lorraine, thinking of my comrades from Straubing. My brother Karl Gustav had changed over to the infantry and was undergoing an officer training course in Germany. We didn't hear much from Scheubner in the Orient. His mind would surely have been occupied with things we would have a hard time understanding.

Then I received a telegram.

It was from Scheubner. He wanted to know if Karl Gustav and I would be ready to accept an assignment in Turkey independent of the military mission. As if I had to think twice about it! I sat down and penned an answer in my and Karl Gustav's names: yes indeed!

The whole of April and half of May went by and I had no further news. I was now in Galicia, some six kilometers from Przemysl. On May 22 the Bavarian War Ministry transferred me to Mackovice, but before going there I had to report at the Deputy General Staff Headquarters in Berlin.

What had happened in Asia in the meantime?

Colonel Khalil Bey had entered the scene—young, lively, adventurously daring, with a brilliant military career—which many attributed to the fact that he was War Minister Enver Pasha's uncle. It was he who shot Supreme Commander Nazim Pasha dead with his revolver during an argument at the end of the Balkan campaign. It was not altogether unbelievable either in this sinewy, proud, and very probably ambitious nationalist—who was to say where his mask ended and the true character began? Djemal Pasha, lord of Syria and Palestine, was a perfect example of self-created power and independence. Why then should Khalil, at the head of an army totally subservient to him, and knowing and dominating the population eastwards to Persia, not dream of an eastern princedom for himself, while the Young Turks Committee found it difficult to exert its influence as far as Baghdad?

At about the same time as I received the telegram in Lorraine, Azerbaijan became Khalil's theater of operations. The Turks had taken possession of the region around Tabriz and Urmia in January. Their luck lasted barely a month. The counterblow was hard and decisive, and they were driven out of the entire region by the Russians in February.

Then Colonel Khalil Bey appeared from Mosul in northern Mesopotamia in March, with a force composed of regulars and gendarmerie contingents. This unit marched northwards to the Azeri town of Khoi. This man, who later had a part in the victory of Kut-el-Amara and the Persian offensive, which the Turks will always consider epic deeds of war, could hardly be foreseen in the spring of 1915. His great advance ended in a resounding defeat, and his retreat skirmishes in May allowed the Russians to cross the border and reach the shores of Lake Van, a mere 250 kilometers southeast of Erzerum.

The dream of delivering a stunning blow to the Russians had ended with a rude awakening, a condition marked by a dangerous thirst for vengeance, which was looking out for defenseless victims—a need for cleansing oneself of all blame for catastrophe by seeking its causes in others. Naturally, he found it where national and religious passions met with an alien body within their own land.

Around the time of Khalil's defeat, eagerly-spread rumors began to reach Scheubner's ears. These rumors claimed that the Armenians had adopted a hostile attitude toward the Turkish troops. He remembered, though, that the only success during Enver's January campaign had been brought about by Lieutenant Colonel Stange, among whose troops were Armenian contingents. Enver himself acknowledged that the Armenians' stance had been absolutely loyal. However, these rumors soon turned into official claims: what a strange contradiction. Had the Armenians suddenly changed? Had perhaps someone provoked them?

In mid-April Scheubner received private news from Van: Armenian unrest, the "Ottoman Bank" being blown up by Armenians. What could one do? What could one believe? In spite of his good relations with them, Scheubner always kept a clear distance from all Turkish officials and officers. This facilitated his judgment and secured respect for his dealings.

The *vali* [governor] of Van, Djevdet Bey, was Enver's brother-in-law. Colonel Khalil, whose campaign was taking such unfortunate turns in that region, had a difficult character to understand. It was almost certain that since they were unable to solve the Russian problem, they would be eager to solve at least the Armenian one. These men, Scheubner immediately realized, were not individuals acting on their whims, but exponents of a group that created or fostered sentiments to expand Islam. They were the Prophet's lieutenants. Their torch was the fire of Holy War, and wherever they operated they carried out their activities under this symbol.

Scheubner cast his eye over many centuries of history. He saw the surge of Islam setting out from Arabia, dividing into streams, one overrunning Asia Minor, the other spreading through North Africa, crossing into Europe through Gibraltar, past the Tarik rock, and flooding half of Spain.

The other current crossed the Bosporus and with its last surge reached the gates of Vienna. He saw them receding, the Christian nations pursuing, Europe returning to the Europeans and, for the moment, the last dam being erected in the Balkan War of 1912. Constantinople and Adrianople, with a narrow strip of land around them, were now the sole remaining Turkish possessions on European soil.

Scheubner did not consider this territorial decline as something decisive in view of Turkey's lasting claim to religious leadership of the Islamic world. Why otherwise had the Young Turk movement not dared proclaim Turkey a republic when they rose up against the corrupt regime of Sultan Abdul Hamid? It would have been well in keeping with their Western ideals. The point was, concluded Scheubner, that it would have made no sense to remove the sultan as a head of state, since, as Caliph, he would have remained the spiritual head of all Mohammedans...

Scheubner deliberated over the incoming reports from Van and drew his own conclusions regarding the current situation. If disturbances had occurred, these were set off by the arrest and subsequent assassination of Armenian notables. These men had enjoyed the greatest prestige among their countrymen. Regardless of whether their arrest had been justified or not, the fact that they had been murdered while in police custody spoke for itself. The real cause was Pan-Islamism and Pan-Turkism.

While the former ideology felt capable of wresting Egypt from the British, Tripoli from the Italians, Algeria and Tunisia from the French, the latter had extended its hands to the Caucasus and the northern coast of the Black Sea, not in order to liberate the local peoples, but to subjugate them, for, according to its ideas, these peoples were of Turkish origin. The very arbitrariness of the idea increased the passion. In reality, Christian communities and nations had always remained along the borders of Turkish territory, as invariably happens in any power whose capacity for assimilation cannot keep up with its territorial expansion. One such nation was that of the Armenians.

Armenians are an Aryan nation, which, around 700 B.C., long before the arrival of Islam, migrated, presumably from India, to the area between central Anatolia and the Russian Caucasus. Conquered by the Persians, liberated by Alexander the Great, with their independence subsequently confirmed by the Romans, and later becoming a pawn in the ongoing struggle between Romans and Parthians, they already looked back on a long and mixed history when they accepted Christianity around the year 300. Byzantines, Arabs, Egyptians and Persians had ruled over them before the Turkish Sultan Selim incorporated Armenians into his empire in 1514.

They had not become worn out with all these conquests, though they finally accepted their lot with resignation, for, as long as their faith and the integrity of their race were respected, they were ready to live peaceably under such conditions.

Armenia prospered through agriculture, trade and a variety of crafts. It was common to find Armenian merchants in Constantinople and all the towns of western Turkey. They were skilful and intelligent, something less noticeable in their Turkish masters. The latter, who had come from the Asiatic highlands, and were probably of Mongol origin, felt these evolving economic differences as acutely as the religious and racial ones.

This did not facilitate their coexistence. However, the situation started to become intolerable only when, during the war of 1877-78, the Russians took over a large part of Armenia, including the monastery of Echmiadzin, the religious center of the Armenian Church, and European powers began to talk about their Christian obligations towards this people. The protection offered Armenians consisted of collective Notes that turned the Armenians into a special nuisance for the Turks. The terms "Armenian secret societies" and "Armenian massacres" by Turks, which came up in turn, did not disappear from European newspaper columns starting from 1890. So what, then? The Holy War had not produced the lively, driving force needed to overtake all Muslims, including those in India. On the contrary, the Allied Powers were now attacking the Dardanelles and threatening Constantinople, the capital. The elements that had been brought forward by the declaration of the Holy War were not satisfied by the order that everything had to be concentrated on the defense of the Straits.

Was it not but a short step for their fanaticism to turn against their own citizens of different religion and race, finding in the small fires the substitute for the great flame that refused to burn? Unrestrained by any annoying interference from Christian Europe, they now sought to finish off Armenia. What a net Scheubner was caught up in! Contradictory claims, unproven assurances, and arrogant judgments, that sought to obscure guilt and soil innocence.

Nevertheless, his grand view of the situation, which I have tried to show in the pages above, was what kept clear in his mind. His innate leadership, respect and commanding decisiveness, as well as his ability to maintain a friendly attitude, suited him well to this Asiatic soil. This was in the face of people who wavered between childishness and carelessness; harshness and good nature; cunning and obstinacy. They were manipulable, in a peculiar light and dark environment, in a difficult-to-gauge combination that is known as the "Oriental." And no doubt a clear head was needed, for events were plunging forward on a headlong course.

In Van the Armenian quarter had been barricaded. More than 200 houses had been destroyed. Would the massacres spread as far as Erzerum? The Armenian population was alarmed; its bishop sought protection from the consulate. The vali of Erzerum, however, followed a more moderate line than his colleague in Van. For now, he limited himself to arrests and house-searches. No incriminating evidence was found, and the majority of the arrested were set free again. Who knows, however, what would happen in the next few days!

The military put pressure on the doveish vali, who did not feel the time had come for a final showdown with the Armenian population. However, Scheubner feared massacre in Erzerum in case new defeats at the front forced Turkish troops to retreat there. "Think of the evil consequences of such disturbances in times like this," he warned the vali.

Tahsin Bey looked uneasy. "Some of the Armenians here are conspiring against the government," he believed.

"Do you have proof?"

"I think so. We will have to deport some of the arrested to the interior of the country."

"Has that already been decided?"

"The decision ought to be made within the next few days."

"I hope it will be possible to prevent massacres here."

This word upset the official, who obviously felt compelled to justify the actions of his colleague in Van. "We suffered two hundred casualties in Van during the uprising, and twice that many injured."

"In the past, you yourself were in Van. Your reasonable attitude, which so far has prevented any crude cases of repression, is the result of your experiences there. And it is also the best guarantee for the peaceful attitude of the local Armenians."

But either a change of heart was taking place within Tahsin Bey, or else he feared the strong arm of the army commander if he persisted. "The Armenians of the border districts," he said, "have fled to Russia and entered the ranks of the Russian army against Turkey—their Fatherland! Others have come to Erzerum. Can you trust them? Who knows what they are plotting. We had armed resistance to requisitioning."

"That happened in remote villages."

"Turks have been murdered. . ."

". . . after demanding the delivery of Armenian girls and women."

The vali remained silent. No expression on his face indicated whether this remark aroused embarrassment or indignation. His next question was only slightly sharper: "What about the spying? What about the destroyed telegraph and telephone wires?"

"I appreciate your experience too highly to consider that you would fail to realize such things are nothing unusual in a border region with a mixed population during wartime," Scheubner replied politely.

The meeting had ended, but something kept Scheubner thinking. It was the reference concerning the fugitives to Russia. It was not the first time that he had heard it. Even before he had heard it, he attributed major importance to Russia's role in the Armenian question. The bulletin board, the reading room, the dissemination of newspaper articles, the posters about the situation on the fronts that he had initiated as part of his consular activities all mentioned it.

At that moment the Armenian bishop was announced. Obviously deeply upset, he entered: the Armenians from the neighboring villages were being driven out and deported to the interior. Babbling in his indignation, at first hardly intelligible, the words flew into the room. Scheubner looked at the old man and gave him time to master his agitation before he answered.

"I'll investigate by what orders and for what reasons these measures are taking place. Yet I must once again remind you that I have no formal right to intervene on behalf of your people and can only appeal to humanitarian considerations as I am forced to keep within certain limits."

"Oh!" the bishop exclaimed, "we know how much your presence has contributed so far to the maintenance of tranquillity in Erzerum! We will never forget the services you and the German officers have rendered us. We are convinced that without your activity there would have been a massacre here in March! We already expressed our gratitude to His Excellency Mr. Posselt before he returned to Constantinople, and I can assure you. . . ." And there followed passionate expressions of gratefulness, which Scheubner cut short.

"Perhaps you are right in what you say about my actions—if perhaps in a different sense than you mean it. It seems that the general feelings of Armenians towards Germans was not very friendly at the outbreak of the. . ."

"I shall not deny that our people entertained distrust. They did not understand how Germany could be friends of absolutist Turkey under whose rule Armenians have suffered so much. Some even doubted whether the Germans were Christians, because they had allied themselves with Muslims. Only a few educated Armenians knew about Germany or the

Germans. Some attended your universities. But the larger part of the Armenian youth have studied in France or Russia. They blamed German influence for the war—and you will understand that a war, with its economic disruptions is considered unpleasant by a people that strongly focuses on maintaining and increasing its wealth. But over the past few months opinion has visibly changed regarding Germans—as Armenians have got acquainted with your officers, your feats of arms. . ."

"Why not rather say 'their better orientation to the general situation of the world'? And this is indeed something I have mostly focused my attention on. For as long as your people got all their news exclusively from biased Russian sources—Turkish publications they naturally distrusted—they got a completely distorted picture of the real state of affairs in Europe. You are surely aware that particularly the Russian consulate in Van is a den of intrigue. No German representation existed there to act as a counterbalance. So it is not totally accidental that Armenian dissatisfaction there made itself felt with greatest vehemence. The weapons confiscated from Armenians may initially have been intended for self-defense in case of a massacre, but their use for uprisings could in no way be entirely ruled out."

"But no bombs or anything like that have been found in Erzerum."

"No. The vali has confirmed that as well. But then it is in Erzerum that I had made arranged for Armenians to be informed of Russian defeats in Europe. Thus, a main reason to express sympathies for Russia through a revolt had disappeared."

The bishop admitted that the Turkish Armenians had looked upon Russia as their natural protector, as Russia had always claimed this right to provide protection. The fact that Russian Armenians had always enjoyed more security of life and better economic conditions had likewise exerted a strong attraction on the masses.

"And was there never any thought that a stronger Russian influence might result in a weakening of Armenian national feeling?" inquired Scheubner.

"This consideration has remained confined to the intellectual leadership, among whom two different tendencies exist: one of them stresses the preservation of our national identity, which is only possible in Turkey, while the other stresses economic interests and religious community."

As the door closed on the bishop, Scheubner remained behind with mixed feelings. He recognized the cultural superiority of the Armenians, without mustering special sympathy for them as a nation and race. Yet one thing compelled him to give his unqualified respect, and he expressed it in one of his reports to the Foreign Ministry:

"Their love for their homeland—this plateau they have inhabited for centuries—is one of their most essential and attractive characteristics. If this were not so, they would surely have been able to avoid many of their woes."

It was only in May that some of their worst troubles occurred. Around Erzerum, Armenian women and children were driven out while the men were serving in labor battalions. They had to leave all their possessions behind without even being allowed to keep the bare minimum for the journey. Nobody knew their destination at that time. The chief concern was to first drive them from their homes. Subjected to all kinds of excesses and without food, they camped by the thousands around the city. Scheubner intervened, making donations, but how could he alleviate such widespread need and misery? The vali claimed to be uninvolved and refused any responsibility for the situation or its consequences. Scheubner telegraphed the embassy in Constantinople. Wangenheim authorized him to make representations to the army commander and to press for humane treatment for the deported. Scheubner announced himself by phone at headquarters. In the meantime the deported people's villages were taken over by Muslim immigrants.

Scheubner was not used to pleading, but to persuading, or else commanding. Standing face-to-face with the commander, he realized the danger of the situation, but also that he could only overcome it through his usual way of acting. He made no secret of his determined opposition to the ally.

"These are military measures," was the reply.

"Is the destination of the deported to remain a secret?"

"The Armenians from the Erzerum plain will be settled along the Euphrates."

"And those of the city? Are they to stay?"

"No."

A pause ensued. The commander mentioned military necessities once more; he was polite—much too polite for the coldness of his words. Scheubner was not intimidated.

"This general deportation is nothing but a massacre," he said. "Due to the lack of means of transportation, hardly half will reach their destinations."

"They will be dispersed in the interior and settled amongst Mohammedans," the commander retorted with indifference, obviously intending to cut short the conversation. But Scheubner insisted:

"No uprising is expected from the local Armenians. So far the deported have been the old men, women and children. Are you going to claim this too is for military reasons?"

"Armenians who convert to Islam will not be deported," exclaimed the commander evasively, without realizing that he had revealed a secret, as, Talaat Bey [Minister of Interior] had also just stated to a member of the German Embassy in Constantinople their plans to use the World War to thoroughly cleanse the interior of domestic enemies, the local Christians.

Scheubner was not surprised. From all other points of view this was nonsense anyway: clearing whole districts of a hard working people, particularly in wartime. Military reasons! Scheubner smiled bitterly: did the commander not realize that such a nonsensical explanation questioned his military capabilities—or his self-respect because he accepted giving such an impression? Whatever it was, there was no point in saying anything more. The leave-taking was particularly polite but cool.

Tortum, where General Headquarters was located, lay some 70 kilometers north of Erzerum. On the way back Scheubner visited abandoned Armenian villages. They had been ransacked, churches and monasteries ravaged. Anything the Armenians had not been allowed to take with them fell as booty to the Kurds, those probably likewise Aryan mountain people, everywhere living mixed with the Armenians but culturally far inferior to them. Their savage instincts had been aroused and was raging. On June 18 Scheubner was forced to telegraph Wangenheim:

> The Armenians deported from the Erzerum plain have been attacked by Kurds and similar miscreants on the road to Erzinjan and Kharput. Most of the men and children were murdered, and the women kidnapped. The government cannot or refuses to do anything to protect the deportees. What steps shall I take in this matter and for the prevention of further slaughter.

Wangenheim instructed him to strongly remind the vali that Turkey's prestige among its friends and neutral nations would suffer from such shameful incidents. "Although we cannot oppose these measures, to the extent that they are justified by war conditions, we must press those involved, also in our own interest, to prevent the slaughter of the defenseless population," wired Wangenheim.

Consequently Scheubner stood once more in the Vali's office. Tashin Bey eyed him uneasily. This Turk was uncomfortable, as he knew only too well that the reproaches were justified, but he was powerless to do anything about it. He feared for his post. All this he had to hide behind a facade of annoyance. The room was completely carpeted, and there was a small bench against one of the walls. There was little else in it—chairs of a venerable antiquity which, once again, were adorned with carpeting. There was a menacing calm in it, as there was on Tashin's forehead. He kept his hands folded in his lap. A loaded revolver might well have been concealed there. Scheubner sat down in the same manner.

The vali expressed his regret for the occurrences. "They are shameful, unfortunately, yes indeed..."

"It would be the duty of the local authorities to prevent them with all means at their disposal, if they wished to avoid serious responsibility for them."

"I will do my utmost to prevent a repetition."

"All depends on what you consider as 'utmost.' Are you aware that your own office's authority is being undermined? Do you realize that reprisals and retaliations on the part of Russians and Armenians in areas occupied by them will be the inevitable consequence of this? Do you understand Turkey's standing in future peace negotiations will be aggravated and will create a renewed cause for the Powers to intervene in Armenian affairs? I must earnestly urge you to forward my representations to the Army High Command."

The vali's ears pricked up, his facial features moved indefinably. He endeavored to give his voice a tone of deep, serious and real earnestness when he said, "Unless you change your stance regarding the Armenian question, I cannot guarantee your personal security here."

"I never asked you to do so," retorted Scheubner with a polite smile.

The vali leaned back a little in his seat, probably painfully aware of the hollow exaggeration of his words. In order to blur this impression, he spontaneously stood up, promising to send a hundred gendarmes to escort the second group of deported Armenians, who were composed of some three hundred women and children. It gave Scheubner some satisfaction when he learned soon afterwards that these families had arrived unmolested in Erzinjan.

Vali Tahsin Bey was surely a man not insensitive to human feelings. At least he had enough administrative knowledge that he shook his head in response to the order to deport the entire Armenian population of Erzerum. All army craftsmen, all chauffeurs were Armenians! It was like chopping off one's own right arm. In this mood he was ready to listen to Scheubner's suggestions requesting to grant some relief. Tahsin granted the deportees a fortnight's grace to prepare themselves and allowed them to take their possessions with them or sell them. Some merchants and notables had the opportunity of depositing wares or valuables with the Ottoman Bank in the Armenian Church. He put ox-carts at the disposal of many families without means. Men whose families had no other male support were discharged from the labor battalions and allowed to accompany their families. And one day the vali appeared at Scheubner's offices with the invitation to accompany him to Erzinjan for a visit to the Armenian deportee camp there. This was not just a token of human respect but in an official sense also a tacit concession allowing outside supervision.

Under the most difficult conditions Scheubner had achieved more than anything that could have ever been hoped. That he reacted indifferently in face of danger to his life gave his deportment the weight and human efficiency that are always found when, in materially limited and conditioned circumstances, a person takes charge of matters without recognizing higher criterion than one's own integrity and sense of justice. His conduct received the embassy's approval even if, in his own estimation, there was insufficient support. He did not skimp on reports, and the present portrait of him is based on these reports. The State Secretary at the Foreign Office, Zimmermann, also expressed his praise. However, by that time, Interior Minister Talaat Pasha was already able to claim that an Armenian Question no longer existed in Turkey.

Indeed! The majority of the deportees met their end in the Kemakh gorge, the first on the Euphrates. No humanitarian aid could reach there, nor did any European eye witness it. All expended efforts, all the consuming representations, could only alleviate the wretches' lot for at most a few weeks. A part of the group of women and children reached the Mesopotamian deserts, where they met the deportees from western Anatolia. Disease and hunger finished off the last of them. The final curtain came down to mark the end of the tragedy—out of 1.8 million Armenians, not more than four hundred thousand survived.

At the few places where the German Empire had representatives (most notably, besides Erzerum, in Trebizond, Aleppo, and Mosul), the German Consuls Bergfeld, Rössler, and Holstein did their part through their own personal intervention, monetary donations, and other humanitarian actions. But what were these few men against the Porte's destructive determination that disregarded even the direct notes from Berlin; or against the wolfish savagery of the Kurds let loose; against the immense swiftness of the ensuing catastrophe, in which, far from European civilization, one Asian nation strove with another in true Asiatic fashion?

V

Departure

On the way from Constantinople to Erzerum we spent the night in Kaisariye, on the northern edge of the Erdjias, the tallest mountain in Asia Minor, where for two nights we exchanged our horse-drawn carriages for a hotel, gaining considerably in comfort from our field beds. We were up before dawn. The Erdjias rose blue-red from its broad base up to its snow-capped peak. The whole of the previous day we had, in fact, spent going by it, traversing fertile plains cut across by little streams which it overlooks, and on the edge of which stands the town of Kaisariye, close by the ruins of old Caesarea. We saw the town from afar, shimmering in the brightness of a sky that promised a beautiful evening, as we came down the winding road emerging from the last mountain-pass.

It was not long before we stood on the walls of Justinian's fortress at the town's center, amid a criss-cross of small bazaar streets, mosques, and the small charming government palace, from which the eye beholds the rubble-studded fields of the imperial Byzantine epoch.

We bought horses and went for a trial ride. The beasts were small, fine, and well broken-in. Pacers. For one chestnut, my brother, Karl Gustav and I paid 23 Turkish pounds, which worked out at something like 460 marks. Finally, we climbed into our large-wheeled, covered wagons, and lay down, sticking our feet out beside the driver over the sides.

The road stretched northwards to Sivas, through the mountainous Kizil Irmak valley, the Halys of the ancient world. Every so often we passed an ancient inn, where travelers used to rest under cool arches and heavy pillars.

We were on our way to Scheubner, as members of the expedition to the Caucasus decided upon in Berlin. This expedition was to divide into a Georgian branch and a north Persian-east Caucasian one. The latter was Scheubner's undertaking. Count Von der Schulenburg, captain of the reserve of the First Field-Artillery Guards Regiment and, until the outbreak of the war, consul in Tiflis, Georgia, had been appointed as the liaison officer of the whole expedition. It was to him we had had to report in Berlin. He was our leader on our trip across Asia Minor. His adjutant was Dr. Schede, previously head of the archaeological station at Moda in Constantinople. Apart from my brother and myself, the others in our company were the military physician of the Reserve Dr. Stoffels, the Baltic volunteer Dr. Schmidt, and Mr. Moser from Vienna.

As Serbia had not yet been overrun, we had to travel through Bulgaria and Romania. Since both countries were still neutral we traveled in civilian outfits and were recorded as civilians in our passports. The Romanians behaved in an unfriendly manner towards German travelers, whereas the Bulgarians were accommodating. One could already sense coming political alliances.

Finally. . . Constantinople. The pressure of the Allied Dardanelles offensive could be felt everywhere. Although the main attack had been repelled, the situation for the Turks remained threatening. They were not nearly as well trained for modern warfare as their opponents. They were short of artillery and ammunition. British submarines slipped through all barriers into the Sea of Marmara. Even the pontoon bridge linking old Constantinople with the Galata quarter had been torpedoed. The tangled city was crawling with enemy spies and accomplices. Night after night one spotted mysterious signal lights: neither trace nor reason could be discovered, although there was no shortage of intelligence agents. They were, however, fully occupied with hunting down critics and doubters. Whoever did not choose his words carefully, no matter whether he was German or Turk, ran the risk of finding himself floating dead in the Golden Horn next morning. . .

We traveled on the Anatolian railway to Ulukishla, and from there made our way in four personnel and eight luggage carriages. As a matter of fact we made surprisingly swift progress with these vehicles. In the first three days we covered more than 200 kilometers over stony, mountainous terrain. When we traveled across boulder-strewn stretches, it was difficult to ascertain whether they were in the process of construction or long since abandoned. Sometimes they were usable only because alongside ran a sand path, which the drivers gladly used. The drivers were agreeable fellows, in the main.

In Nigde we had a bit of trouble with them. We found that one of the carts was missing and another had broken down. But it was precisely there that the local commander so graciously received us at the entrance to the town, so we could not possibly be upset. We were invited to his home for coffee, then we set up a tent, cooked an outdoor meal, and took turns at sentry duty. Then three buffalo-drawn batteries of field artillery arrived at slow pace from Erzerum.

Once we had crossed the Halys, we arrived at Sivas. Behind its Seljuk gates spread the bazaars. The vali lived comfortably. Carpeted rooms opened onto carpeted verandahs, marble walls surrounded a shady courtyard. We paid our respects and were cordially received. In the evening we were treated to a Turkish serenade. In the meantime new teams of buffaloes and ammunition transports arrived. And everywhere were the straggling caravans of Armenians. . .

We turned east. The landscape became progressively wilder. At the entrance to the larger towns we were welcomed by the kaimakams, who were sort of district officials. On their horses they assumed the solemn air of the highest of dignitaries. Occasionally we were advised to travel with loaded guns—many days earlier a cart had been attacked and plundered by a band of 18 roving Armenians. Skirmishes between Turks and Armenians had allegedly taken place in these wild mountain valleys. On one occasion we came across two dead men lying at the roadside, one clad only in a sock, the other with a sack. A little later, in the middle of a clump of bushes and a copse of oaks and dwarf pines lay the body of a little boy with a deep gash above his left eye. Dr. Stoffels estimated he had been dead for about two days. Was he one of those lads who, according to history and poetry, heroically join the battles of men? Or. . . ?

We still had the hardest part of the journey before us. There were days when we were already moving at five in the morning, and we still had to travel on until one in the morning, so as to make it to the next resting place. When we arrived at one of the staging posts we found it was market day. Cattle were being auctioned, and in between sales, the law-court was in session. The most serious cases were solved in a jiffy by means of a cuff or two on the ear. We wanted to stay until noon, but the kaimakam would not leave us alone. He insisted we lunch with him: a lavish nine-course Turkish spread, each course a single bowl out of which we all picked the morsels we carried to our mouths.

Mountain pass followed mountain pass until we reached the Euphrates. The heat increased and our luggage carts were often several hours behind us. From the bald mountain, storms howled down into the near valley. At last we came to the great divide between the Black Sea and the Persian Gulf, where the soil took on a different form, richer and more fertile. In a hollow in the blue mountains nestled the town of Erzinjan. At a distance of about a quarter of an hour from the gates lay the *konak* (government house), where we were received by a group of German doctors. Their hospital was at a still greater distance from the town. It was staffed by six German nurses and as many German male nurses. One evening we all met in the konak. We learned that a few days earlier Scheubner had been here for relaxation. This, and the proximity of Erzerum, made us decide not to stay too long.

Once more we traveled through high mountains alongside the Euphrates, which flowed through beautiful wild valleys, and then again through lush meadows. We came upon a column of Armenians—some 50 children and twice as many women carrying babies in their arms. A few mules were all the possessions they had—and who could tell how long they would be allowed to hang on to them? We had hardly put up our tents when we heard a loud explosion nearby. We were told it had been a road-builders' powder magazine that had blown up. And a whisper was added: "The Armenian did that!" We looked in the direction in which the women and children had disappeared. If their guards had not heard the explosion, they would surely have heard the wind-borne murmur, "The Armenians did it."

This was a land in which greatness and cruelty vied with each other, over whose loveliness hovered the shadow of death. In many areas—and commonly those on which the eye would lovingly rest the longest, typhus claimed many victims each year. One only needed to take a refreshing bath in a gushing stream and one would have been tormented by the thought of the insects that transmitted the disease. Count Schulenburg fell sick with the fever. His life was not in danger, but we had to halt for a day, and only breathed with relief when we came in sight of the first forts of Erzerum: those at the highest altitude on Earth.

The sun was at its zenith, when Scheubner, together with Lieutenant-Colonel Stange and other German officers welcomed us. It was August 6. We had left Constantinople in mid-July.

Scheubner was the same companion as in Straubing, but his impressive, generous demeanor had increased here. He gave us the happy news that Warsaw had fallen. He was already preparing a program for the next few days. It suited him that Count Schulenburg took charge of the consulate. Now he could fully concentrate on the expedition—yet without forgetting that a year had gone by since we had been together in Straubing with the Seventh Light Cavalry. We drank to celebrate it.

Erzerum lay at the eastern end of a wide plateau with an altitude of about 2,000 meters, enclosed on three sides by mountain ranges with an average altitude of 3,000 meters. The city looked magnificent with its impressive mountain scenery, but otherwise it had little of interest. Wholly Asiatic, with its box-like, flat-roofed stone houses, its only outstanding features were the steeples of the Armenian churches and its imposing Armenian mansions.

Although its street life was rather colorful, one could see many filthy stray dogs and smelly cattle and few fine-looking people or interesting faces, except some of the older inhabitants. Often, the soldiers wore Georgian headwear, the *bashlik*, which was a cloth bound round the head in a particular fashion. Constantly, one could see the *tcherkeska*, the peculiar long coat with cartridge-boxes sewn on the breast, and the corresponding fur cap.

The women were practically invisible, as their veils were heavier than in Constantinople, revealing nothing at all. They wore disfiguring gowns with ugly colors, with a sort of black patch covering the face, so that they looked like overgrown insect pupae. Thus, one had to ride out to the steppes in order to discover beauty. From there one could see the town surrounded by great mountains, and on the other side the Armenian highlands with their golden wheat-fields, which lost themselves in the distant chain of blue mountains.

Every morning we would ride for three to four hours round the forts on the bare, treeless heights, or to the villages on the steppe. Next, we practised Turkish orders for an hour. At 1:30 P.M. we all had lunch at the consulate, where correspondence, newspapers, and the latest cables on the war awaited us. In the afternoon we had Turkish lessons with Scheubner's interpreter and learnt to decipher code for the consulate. The rest of the time we spent on tasks related to the expedition.

Scheubner had chosen a house for us, which, however, was not fully furnished and needed fitting out. He advised us to make sure our horses were good climbers so that we could procure others if they weren't. We extended a stable with the help of Scheubner's previous staff. They were Lieutenant Thiel of the military mission, a Turkish lieutenant, a German deputy officer trained at the Jüteborg artillery school and an expert in his speciality, and volunteer NCO Schlimme, previously Consul Anders' assistant, who was now in charge of the expedition's baggage. We needed approximately 40 pack animals and the personnel to look after them.

As personal servants and orderlies we had 10 prisoners of war of German origin from Wolhynia. They were delighted to be out of the Turkish prisoner camp, with its bad accommodation and food, and without anything to do. We were convinced that they would prove themselves excellently, and they did not disappoint us.

In the evening of the third day a reception was held for the new consul and members of the expedition at the vali's residence. We went on horseback and in carriages to the konak. A guard of honor saluted and the corridors were teeming with soldiers and officials. We were escorted to a room where we met the supreme commander of the Caucasus army, Mahmud Kiamil Pasha.

After spending a while smoking and chatting with him, we all went to the large reception hall. A band played the German national anthem. The vali was attired in his official gold-braided robe displaying all his decorations. Almost as youthful as the supreme commander, he looked imposing with his broad figure and full brown beard. Coffee, cigarettes, and ices were served while a band played in the hallway. When we left, the guard of honor stood to attention and a new band marched in.

But who were such honors for? What did the arrival of Count Schulenburg and his company mean?

The plans that had been proposed to the German military and political authorities by the Georgians, east Caucasians, and Scheubner at the beginning of the year were taking shape. Count Schulenburg, as liaison officer for the Caucasus, was the central figure in putting them into effect and the guarantee for their coordinated execution. He also took over the consular duties in Erzerum and the command of the Georgian organization, particularly the Georgian Legion now being formed in Trebizond.

Scheubner was relieved from his consular duties and was supposed to focus fully on the eastern Caucasus. Over the previous months, he had not been idle in making preparations for the task. He was aware that the failures of the Turks had been mainly caused by their unrestrained fantasies. Their massive concentration of troops did not take into account the realities of a war zone that did not permit gigantic steps but required instead small, mobile units able to withstand the greatest hardships, as well as the courage and persistence to keep the enemy busy without seeking an out-and-out victory straight away. If anything, ambitions were misplaced here and lack of restraint was the surest way to one's own ruin. It was crucial to convince the Turkish side and to agree on a reasonable plan for an advance to northern Persia, and from there to prepare and support the revolt in the eastern Caucasus, in Daghestan.

Scheubner found the right Turkish partner for his plans in one of the strangest figures on the Turkish political scene: Omer Nadji Bey.

In the same way that the term "Turk" is hardly definable as regards race, it was also unclear who actually was in charge of Turkish politics. The prominent leaders—Enver, Talaat, Djemal—were apparently not independent. Surely, the "Committee of Union and Progress," representing the Young Turk movement gave them orders, but how this committee was composed never became entirely clear to outsiders. Nevertheless, it had agents and local committees all over the country, whose activities were coordinated and controlled from Constantinople.

The inspector general was Omer Nadji Bey. He was a Circassian born in the Caucasus. In January 1915, he had participated in the conquest of Tabriz. More than for anything else, his heart longed for the liberation of his Caucasian homeland from Russian domination. He arrived in Erzerum in May. Scheubner met him and became fond of him.

At that time Omer Nadji was about 50 years old. He was considerably older than most of the other Young Turk leaders—Enver, for instance, was only 34! Omer Nadji Bey enjoyed the unlimited trust of all Young Turk politicians, and the authority, if one can put it like that, of a prophetic master. Everything predestined him to this role: with his past, during the bad times of Abdul Hamid, he had lived as a political refugee in Paris, and later introduced Enver and Talaat to the Young Turk movement; with his character, he had a winning, unassuming presence, with no hint of personal self-interest or ambition.

He was imbued through and through with French culture, but I remember him remarking how much he supported the government's decision not to send any more young people to Paris because they returned as internationalists, while they returned from Germany as nationalists.

He met Scheubner dressed in a tightly tailored robe with a closed collar, wearing on his head the typical Circassian black lamb-skin cap, with no other soldierly mark than a simple Circassian sword, which was held by a belt hanging from his right shoulder.

One could sense from the conversation that he did not suffer from the lack of judgment and the tendency to exaggeration that so often characterized Turkish leaders and which had cost the country dearly. Scheubner was favorably impressed with his polite European manners, combined with Oriental discretion and dignity. He was completely lacking that trait of cruelty that the consul encountered to be increasingly characteristic of rulers and politicians the further eastwards he went.

"I'm fully aware that a Turkish–German collaboration is indispensable in any Caucasian undertaking," declared Nadji Bey, an opinion not every Turk was reaching so openly. He was a strong supporter of the alliance, and this support was more genuine than Scheubner had become accustomed to hear for a long time. He also indicated that the Caucasian peoples had absorbed too much European culture under Russian rule to be prepared to tolerate complete Turkish domination with all its Asiatic idiosyncrasies.

"This German–Turkish collaboration needs political and military organization," replied Scheubner. "As far as I know, the Turkish government has always insisted that no German officer should command Turkish troops, except by leaving the German Army and entering Turkish service, admittedly in one rank higher than he enjoyed previously. As for me personally. . ."

Nadji interrupted him with a gesture. "I will ignore this," he said. "I'm convinced that I can make some arrangement with our High Command. I would propose that you and I have at our disposal a battalion, a mountain battery, a detachment of Hamidiye cavalry—have you heard of them...?"

"Of course, the Kurdish irregular cavalry."

"That's right. . . . So then, I will ask that these troops be put at our joint disposal. That's what I suggest."

Scheubner remained silent.

"Do you doubt it?" asked Nadji.

"Look—I have enough confidence in you to share a command such as this. But for a multitude of reasons I deem it right to remain more independent. I could accept a joint command if, in addition, I could command a company of a hundred Turkish soldiers, half the battery, and 30 tribal horsemen. This goes against your principles, doesn't it?" he added, as Nadji did not answer right away.

"It will be granted to you," Nadji exclaimed, no doubt impressed by Scheubner's firmness and far-sightedness. "It will be granted to you, never mind that it is usually totally unacceptable."

"What about equipment and provisions?"

"The Turkish government will provide it."

"In that case could I, with German funds, hire more Kurdish volunteers in Persia or Turkey later?"

"You fit them out, and we will provision them."

At first, the Supreme Command opposed Omer Nadji's decision—but without avail. In Turkey, the inspector general of the "Committee of Union and Progress" was more powerful than the commander of an army.

Mahmud Kiamil Pasha put a 500-strong battalion at Omer Nadji's disposal, and a hundred men, one piece of mountain artillery and 30 horsemen at Scheubner's.

While the detachment was being gathered at a camp near Erzerum, news suddenly spread that could have disrupted Scheubner's and Nadji's plans at the last moment. Following the Russian defeats in the European theater of war, Grand Duke Nikolai Nikolaievich had been removed from his post and been sent to Tiflis as supreme commander of the Caucasian army. This surprising change created a completely new situation. In expectation of an attack, Lieutenant-Colonel Guse, Mahmud Kiamil's chief of staff, concentrated all available troops in Erzerum.

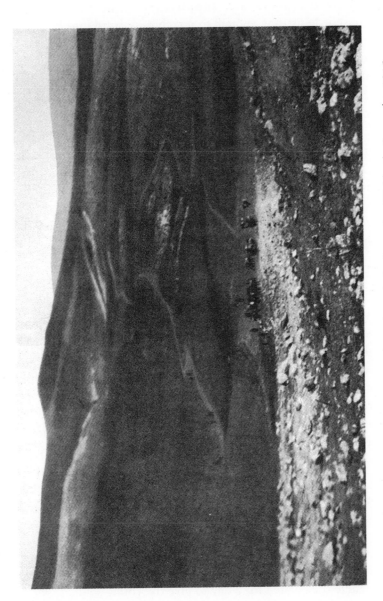

The Scheubner-Nadji detachment marching through the Armenian Highlands, September 1915.

However, nothing happened. Apparently, Nikolai Nikolaievich considered the condition of troops in the Caucasus so poor that he regarded them as unfit for an attack. Instead he preferred to reorganize and, as far as possible, to transfer supplies from the European front. Nevertheless, he felt strong enough to march southward into Persia. There he did not deal with an army like the Turkish one, but with a mere appearance of one, plus disorganized tribesmen. His Cossacks and gendarmerie troops lived off the country. He did not need much ammunition, and the available units were sufficient to occupy northern Persia.

Had Nikolai Nikolaievich's designs for Persia been known in Erzerum in mid-September, no doubt Scheubner and Nadji would have immediately realized the dire consequences this would cast on their own plans. Instead, they shared the delight and relief of the Turkish High Command that the offensive did not materialize, which would have frustrated the expedition from the start. They firmly believed that, with the modest forces then at their disposal, plus the recruited tribesmen, it was possible to invade northern Persia; then, by advancing, they could further strengthen ties with the tribes in Daghestan; and then by supplying them with money and weapons they could support a revolt against Russian rule.

However, would not anyone whose character called for action, tell themselves in such a situation that everything could be managed once the action fully started? Nothing could be won or lost, except if no action was taken at all. In this way Scheubner was right. For this reason he told himself that deficiencies in equipment should not delay the start. The battalion was not as well equipped as it ought to have been. The military regional headquarters in Bitlis and Mosul would have to make up for this. Much was compensated for by the fact that the battalion had in Captain Veli Bey an officer who displayed discipline and rigidity.

Under his command the troops set out southwards at 9:00 A.M. on September 23, 1915, after solemn prayers and a mullah's blessing. They traversed the pass of Palandöken which, at an altitude of 3,000 meters, cut through a mountain range that ends the Erzerum plain on the south. They set up camp on the other side of the pass just below the two forts in the afternoon. After another day's march they got to the Kurdish village of Madrak, where they halted for a day to give the young soldiers, who were not used to long marches, an opportunity to rest.

Omer Nadji left Erzerum and, later the same day, so did Karl Gustav Leverkuehn (or Leverkuehn I as he was called from then on in expedition parlance), with Thiel, Schlimme and Lt. Memduh Bey, a young Turkish officer who had attended school and studied at several universities in Germany. Mahmud Kiamil Pasha had put him at Scheubner's disposal as adjutant and interpreter. This unit made up a caravan of 40 pack animals and 20 drivers. They ran into a cold wind and rain and had an especially exhausting journey through the high mountains with nights when temperatures sank to four below zero centigrade. On September 26 the sun was shining again. In the evening most of the luggage arrived at the Kurdish village of Djemal.

Scheubner, Dr. Stoffels, the interpreter, and myself now left Erzerum with the third detachment. Count Schulenburg, Lieutenant-Colonel Guse and others accompanied us up to the fortified pass. After crossing the Palandöken, we spent the night in Madrak. On the following day we passed the valleys of the Hatran and the Araxes. Towards evening we met up with those who had set out before us in the little town of Khynys, whose pleasant little orchards were a welcome change from the almost bare plateau of the previous days. The inhabitants were mostly Kurds with their tall white caps; the majority of them were, however, generally quite dirty. We had one man sick from the march and two deserters—little in comparison with the losses of the other companies that were all assembling in Khynys.

Scheubner completed his company with 20 recruits, mostly Kurds, and 30 Kurdish horsemen of the Zilan tribe. They were under the command of the chieftain's son, Lt. Abdul Bari Bey. He was dressed in a colorful manner and had a dark, melancholy expression. The way in which he combined refinement and savagery in his appearance could have made him a Shakespearean character—Othello, or one of the courtiers in *Merchant of Venice*. In general, he did not seem to know much about military matters.

The battalion was reinforced by 50 Caucasian horsemen under the command of Captain Ibrahim Bey, and 50 Caucasian infantrymen. During the morning the men were drilled in close formations; in the afternoon they had combat training with the participation of the artillery.

The municipality of Khynys organized a festive dinner in its town hall, decorated with carpets, flags, and patriotic pictures. Besides the local kaimakam, the vali of Bitlis, whom Scheubner had already met as governor of Erzinjan, was present to welcome us. Roast lamb was served from enormous dishes. In the end we had to completely abandon our European table manners. Everybody took a knife, cutting off the piece he liked, and threw the bones under the table, from where the town dogs soon carried them off.

The Khynys Su Valley.

Eastern view of Moush and the road to Bitlis.

The banquet acquired its special significance from the presence of several descendants of the famous Caucasian freedom-fighter Shamil, who had been murdered by the Russians. They were venerable old men wearing long beards and black fur caps. Invoking Mohammed and Allah, they wished the joint German and Turkish troops success with solemn expressions, while predicting, with angry memories of their ancestor's death, the imminent demise of the Russian empire.

On October 2 we left Khynys heading south, arriving in the town of Mush after three days' march.

VI

Bitlis-Siirt

There was nothing more wonderful than the evenings after a tiring march. The sun's last rays poured their loveliest colors upon the mountains, and deep shadows drew their brush-strokes in the deep-cut valleys. Rarely one came across peasants making their way home on their mules, or else, in the distance, saw a caravan of camels heading for a far-off town.

Kurdish villages were a frequent and characteristic sight—although this is a somewhat misleading description, as they were something between an encampment and a village, not quite the former, but certainly much less than the latter. Simple carts with strange tent-like structures on top, populated by dirty, brown-skinned people, flocks of black sheep and calm-looking oxen moving forward. If other nations had settlements, they could be detected from a long way off. Thus, we were surprised, when the soldiers were wading across the Murad Su, the eastern affluent of the Euphrates, and we came upon the clean, solidly built village of Tepekoi. It was inhabited by Circassians who, displaced from the Caucasus, had settled there. Even their tasteful clothing revealed their higher civilization. The men wore fur caps with daggers in their belts.

Scheubner had received news from the Turkish authorities that strong Armenian bands were roving in the mountains to the south. He therefore ordered precautions to be taken during the march. On the evening of October 4 we reached a magnificent bridge, its 12 arches spanning the Murad Su, which had supposedly been built by Sultan Murad during his campaign against Persia. Crossing extensive, desolate steppes, we reached the town of Mush, and the lush, mountainous grass lands.

Mush was a picturesque town stretching uphill, but soon, on closer inspection, the friendly appearance turned into the impression of Kurdish uncleanliness. The many welcomes and invitations by the notables, which we had to honor, pleased us less than the tobacco, grape, and water-melon fields, which satisfied not just the eye.

The detachment rested, but we had visits and receptions. Throughout the day we longed for a quiet hour in camp in the evening. The camp was in a nearby village that had many springs. Scheubner heaved a sigh of relief when, after all the official matters ended, he could sit in his tent and attend to the expedition's affairs. Deep peace reigned over the white tents that glowed in the darkness. The fires cast their light across the green soil, the

The Scheubner-Nadji detachment on Murad Su.

horses, the resting men; the silent silhouettes of the trees stood out against the star-studded heavens above them.

We knew the next few days on the plain would be hot, which was perhaps worse than the demanding marches through the mountains and up and down bad roads. In fact, the next day's subtropical weather claimed its first victim. One of the soldiers died of dysentery.

At noon on October 8 we rested at Kara Lake, a crater probably of volcanic origin, where one branch of the Murad Su begins. Near the lake stood the ancient Seldjuk tomb or *turbe* of Karabedant. The waters of the lake slowly overflow and pour into the riverbed, then flow westward across the plain of Mush, turning southwards at its end. It finally joins the western arm of the Euphrates which has its source in the plain of Erzerum and, after a long journey across the Arabian desert, ends up in the Indian Ocean.

During our march, Scheubner learnt the Russians were again advancing from the direction of Lake Van. He ordered a platoon to accompany him on a reconnaissance ride to Tatvan. On the mountain side we came to a Kurdish village, Sebyan, of the Mukhti tribe, whose chieftain, Hadji Mussa Bey, entertained us. It was him who had stopped and repelled the Russians' winter advance from Van. Again, he knew details of their offensive, so that Scheubner was able to cancel the patrol. The Russians had only been able to advance as far as Sorp, south of Lake Van. There they had been repulsed by Yakub Djemil's regiment.

A tolerably good, if rocky road, led south from the turbe to Bitlis, first steeply climbing to a plateau, then to a pass of about 1,400 meters altitude. Here, the Euphrates basin separated from that of the Tigris. The dormant volcano Nemrud Dagh and the Kerkor mountains could be seen to the north. To the south, a vast mountain range extended into the distance.

A road with telegraph cables along it led from just below the pass, through Tatvan on the shore of Lake Van, to the Russian-occupied provincial capital, Van. The vali Djevdet Bey, married to Enver's sister, had been chased away from there. He was now staying in Bitlis, where we met him at the local vali's reception in our honor.

I had ridden ahead with Scheubner, Dr. Stoffels, and the interpreter Memduh through the wild Bitlis-Su valley, arriving in the town a day before the troops. We were greeted at the town entrance by Turkish officers. We were housed in an imposing stone building that had apparently belonged to an Armenian. We generally had our meals as the vali's guests. In the evening we met in an anteroom where hors d'oeuvre, vodka, and raki, a Turkish spirit made of grapes, were served.

Bitlis was situated beautifully on the mountainsides around the Bitlis-Su. Its architecture was unmistakably Armenian. The massive stone houses, mostly of reddish-gray blocks, were spread out on a number of hillsides separated by valleys, so that the streets often looked like gorges.

For the first time on our march we had strong rain, storms, and thunder. We went to the bazaar, but found many shops shut, as the Armenians had been deported. Kurds with white felt caps and black sheepskin capes were hawking grapes and tomatoes. This was modest activity for a city near the crossroads of the route from Erzerum to Mosul and Mesopotamia and the caravan route that lay from east to west from the Caucasus, through Van to Diarbekir and central Anatolia.

Our Turkish friends had taken care to ensure that we should only be in contact with Kurdish inhabited villages and not see abandoned Armenian ones. But it was of little avail. One could see everywhere that the land had once been inhabited and cultivated by industrious people, but now lay fallow because the Kurds that remained behind were unable to fill the empty space and could not carry on with their primitive tools the carefully laid out fields of the Armenians. Finally, in Bitlis, poverty and need were openly visible everywhere on the streets and could not be hidden from us. Abandoned Armenian women and children lived in greatest penury. But a little anecdote reminded Scheubner of the warning he had received from the vali of Erzerum, and made the rest of us who knew only little about Djevdet's conduct in Van understand the significance of his presence.

There had been an American mission station in the Armenian quarter of Bitlis that had also belonged to a German sister, Martha Kleiss, who had died shortly before the outbreak of war. Her property had been in the hands of the American missionaries Misses McLaren and Shane. We visited them and were astonished that by chance a Turkish doctor was calling on them at the same time. We were even more puzzled when we noticed that the missionaries shared our astonishment—this doctor had never visited them before. It was pretty easy, however, to out-manoeuvre this spy: experience has shown that it was difficult to speak a foreign language and at the same time to understand another foreign language being spoken in the same room. My brother, therefore, had to speak French with a loud and sharp voice, while Scheubner and I conversed with the ladies with a low voice in English.

They pleaded with Scheubner to take care of their protégés, the Armenian children. He would have gladly been willing to do so, and humanity and chivalry demanded such an attempt, but the task was no simple one. Turkey was not at war with the United States: thus, the

American embassy had to take care of its citizens. On the other hand, the Armenian children were part of the Turkish state, in whose internal affairs the Germans could not meddle.

Omer Nadji Bey, his assistant Dr. Fuad, and the valis of Bitlis and Van joined us for dinner in the government building. The news that Bulgaria had declared war produced great enthusiasm in them. It was understandably a great relief for the Turks that the route from Berlin to Constantinople was now open for artillery, ammunition, and anything that was short in supply. It was an animated meal, during which the conversation naturally turned to the alliance and common plans for the future. Dr. Fuad, an ardent nationalist, learnt German with eagerness. Omer Nadji frequently demonstrated his support for the alliance by his constant endeavor to balance differences in a moderating and appeasing manner. In this way, he stood out among the many who so often spoke of duty in high-sounding terms, but never found the time to meet these demands themselves. What was owed to inclination, mood, or moral conviction in Nadji was difficult to determine; he possessed many noble features, the inheritance of his Caucasian blood. Of Dr. Fuad, who was his energetic advisor on political matters, the same could not be said with similar certainty. To a certain extent his sympathy for Germany was genuine, but in order to avoid conflict with him, as a German one had to be frank to the point of rudeness and mainly avoid political matters.

Vodka and Russian hors d'oeuvres were served and, at the table, owing to the festive atmosphere brought on by recent events, there was wine from Siirt. Although the Koran forbade Mohammedans to drink wine, our presence was a welcome excuse to sidestep this ban. Our usually reserved Turkish friends thus became more open and loquacious. Before we could only imagine how incomprehensible and at least embarrassing Scheubner's stance regarding the Armenian Question was to them. But now they expressed it frankly. They considered it simply maudlin sentimentalism, they said.

Omer Nadji exclaimed to Scheubner, "*Un consul avec des sentiments...!*"

Scheubner replied that we could afford the luxury of such feelings and would continue to stand by them for as long as our supreme commander supported it. Turning the matter over, he went on: if they had considered it militarily necessary to chase away the Armenian male population from the war zone, why would they now continue the war against women and children?

With this, it was a simple matter for him to bring the conversation round to the protégés of the American missionaries: the Ottomans' sense of chivalry would not allow them to turn deaf ears to a woman's plea, and certainly not on his suggestion that one of the ladies should be allowed to personally present her plea to the vali.

"No," said our host, the vali of Bitlis—he did not wish to avoid the matter at all.

It was around midnight. Scheubner called a Circassian to accompany me to the American mission and bring one of the ladies to the government building.

There was an eerie silence under the pale moonlight that cast dark shadows over the path. The lady took my horse and I rode the Circassian's, who was leading the lady's horse by the reins on the steep street of the bazaar. I was holding the reins of mine in my left hand, and my loaded revolver in my right. At a dark spot the Circassian dropped his rifle from his shoulder and halted—but we only had a momentary fright. We went on down a steep hill, and up the next until we got back to the hall with the remarkable banquet.

The American lady spoke only English, while the Turks only knew French. In a broken exchange in the two enemy languages, her request to transfer the hundred Armenian orphans to Diarbekir was made and discussed. The vali consented. We were never able to ascertain whether he had kept his word, but we did find out that both Americans had arrived safe and sound in Constantinople. Another American missionary, however, who had left Bitlis for Constantinople shortly before our arrival, died on the way.

When I was saddling the horses the next morning, I noticed my saddle-blanket was missing. While the vali and the other dignitaries were solemnly accompanying us to the city limits, I rode back along the road I had taken the night before, and sure enough found the missing piece in the court of the mission building. I was thus able to take my leave of the two American ladies without the mysterious Turkish doctor getting wind of it and quickly showing up to play the witness. It was foolish to believe that such control would keep the truth away from us. But this strange vacuum that had been thrust so deliberately upon us was a warning. Scheubner advised me to keep my gun hidden under my uniform, as he himself did, and was never apart from it.

We had heard all kinds of things in Bitlis, but never a word about the equipment we had been promised we would receive here. "The supply department is unable to issue anything," was the laconic answer to our question. Nevertheless, we obtained some more information, which, although it did not make our project easier, warded off serious dangers.

Scheubner had hoped to march from Bitlis southeast via Bashkala to Azerbaijan so as to spare us the much more southerly route through Mosul. But now two agents from Daghestan and another from Baku reported on the formation of committees: the Russians had requisitioned and stored all grain from the previous harvest for the eventuality of a Turkish invasion, but they lacked weapons and ammunition. The Russians had posted Cossack detachments not only at Tabriz but also in other locations, so that the only possibility open to us was the rugged mountain road through Mosul and Sautchbulak. The Kurdish tribes in Persia to the west and east of Lake Urmia were prepared to enter German service, but generally they wanted nothing to do with the Turks. An uprising in Azerbaijan would, however, be an indispensable precondition for a revolt in the Russian Caucasus.

The two men from Daghestan were Amir Aslan Khan, Prince Khoiski, and Hussein Agha. They had followed us from Erzerum, whereas the man from Baku had caught up with us from the south, having passed through Teheran. Amir Aslan claimed to have been an officer in Moscow and Tiflis, and wished to be considered the leader of the Caucasian revolutionary movement. He was trusted by the Turks, particularly Omer Nadji, and joined the expedition. As a result of his frequent contact with the Turks, he was a valuable source of information for us. Scheubner could communicate with him in Russian. He was very capable and witty, and a flawless entertainer, but perhaps because of this he spoke a little more than he could afford to. Scheubner felt it was advisable to ascertain more reliable details about the strength of the Daghestani movement. For this purpose he sent the second man, Hussein Agha, back on a mission to bring at least 20 or 25 committee delegates to Sauchbulak, or to meet them on the way to Mosul if the expedition hadn't arrived at its destination.

Scheubner had a sharp eye for such things. When Amir Aslan solemnly saluted the Caucasus, the honesty of his feelings could not be doubted. However, Scheubner had far too much experience to believe all of this. He had also already become familiar with the Caucasian type that constantly made great plans for liberating his country, but at the same time lived at the expense of others, without willing to do anything himself. These were only revolutionary plan-makers, not so much due to calculation, but a certain naiveté.

Between such doubts and hopes, Bitlis disappeared from view behind us. The way southeast was steep and stony, rising to a high pass. The mountain tops were bald and bare, though of grandiose form; the mountainsides were covered with deciduous trees, but not so abundantly as to speak of a wood in the German sense of the word. The mountain region gave the impression of a beautiful, big garden. Scheubner, Omer Nadji, my brother, and I rode ahead of the cavalry. As we came in sight of Siirt, we knew from its architecture that we were now in a more southerly climate and a totally different cultural region. The Arabian houses were built around a central courtyard, and the white outside walls were without windows and often of fantastic shape. Concentrated, closed, without any suburban or isolated huts, the town looked bright and strange in the noon sun. Erzerum, Mush and Bitlis had felt the war, if not right there, at least at close range. But the war had remained distant from Siirt.

At a distance of one hour and a half from the town we were greeted by the commander of the gendarmerie and other dignitaries. Soon a second group of horsemen appeared, and finally, close to the town, the *mutessarif* (local governor) and his entourage. Thus, our party swelled considerably and our entry looked like a great affair, which for the inhabitants it indeed was since they had never seen, in war or otherwise, a German entering the town. Surrounded by women and children, we soon found ourselves in the midst of a large crowd waving flags. The boy scouts were lined up, waving German flags, the colorful, cheerful clothes of the children looked bright, and all streets we rode along offered a joyful picture. The shrill yells of the Arab women might have alarmed us if we had not been forewarned that this was their way of expressing their acclaim. Scheubner especially was the object of ovations when we arrived, as well as on the following days, whenever he showed himself in the streets. A woman was there constantly praying, "God protect this man, a lion against our foes. . ."

It so happened that we arrived on the second day of the Bairam festival. Both events were jointly celebrated, so that the festivities took on a twofold meaning. After the official reception in the konak, we rode up to the gendarmerie building where we were to be housed. The troops camped on both sides of the hills above. The boy scouts again showed up and sang in honor of the alliance.

At the evening banquet, speeches were exchanged celebrating the German-Turkish friendship, and then a little procession of torches came up the hill to the troops' encampment. The torch lights, the colorful crowd, and the moonlit white walls of the town in the background left us spellbound at the image of the Orient unfolding before us that we had seen as children in our fairy-tales.

Scheubner held a reception for all the local dignitaries in the hall of our house the following morning. We shook hands with them and treated them to coffee and the customary candies. Meanwhile, the troops were on

Siirt.

The Islamic monastery of Tillo, near Siirt.

parade outside below a terrace on which a large, open party tent had been erected. The mutessarif made a short speech, and then the Muslim cleric said a prayer in Arabic. Scheubner said much about the good relations between the two empires, which Memduh translated.

Finally, when everything was over, we rode out and visited the Muslim convent of Tillo. It was a few hours' ride from the town, in a locality of the same name in the middle of a magnificent garden. It was founded around the year 1500 by a descendant of the Abbassids who had ruled the Islamic lands from the middle of the eighth to the thirteenth century from Baghdad. The monks were Kaderis, a Mohammedan sect according to whose teachings man has no claim to the work and use of animals. Thus, they are vegetarians, subsisting on what natural products their own work can gain from the soil. As a result they have the loveliest of gardens, with the most extraordinary variety of plants, 40 different sorts of grapes, and such exquisite fruits as one would have a hard time finding elsewhere. Its shimmering white buildings among the green trees had a tremendously festive, promising look in the strong sunlight and blue sky overhead.

We saw the founder's grave and a book of Arabic prophecies that had originated in the convent, which contained the prophecy of a tremendous war in 1914. However impressive all this may have been, the visit we received from the Sheikh of Tillo the following day was more so. They had fitted out their horses with the most incredible accoutrements, and wore venerable white beards, turbans, and long, flowing white robes.

Scheubner had given the mutessarif a donation for the boy scouts, so we were surprised to see them marching to our house, playing music. They approached in the company of dignitaries and many people. There were speeches and songs... Scheubner was then presented with a shaggy goat-hair carpet, a local industry speciality.

Our detachment had by now, towards the end of October, been traveling for almost a month. Scheubner had gradually increased its marching capabilities, discipline had improved, and the question of provisions had been settled. In Siirt, the soldiers were more than happy with the additional provision of mutton and *bulgur* (cracked wheat). Desertions, at first numerous, began to decrease.

Our military drills greatly impressed the townspeople. The artillery was allowed 10 shots for its manoeuvres. The most difficult part of these was the preparation, as we had no ready made shells or grenades, only separate cannonballs and gunpowder. For each shot the powder had to be weighed and put in little sacks, an operation only an experienced gunner like Lieutenant Thiel could hope to carry out successfully with the primitive equipment at his disposal. When Colonel Khalil Bey arrived with his forces, the town of Siirt took on a military look such as it had never seen before within its walls.

Khalil traveled in grand style. The most noteworthy detail of his staff caravan were two mules carrying bathtubs. What was the sense of such luxury? Orientals never bathe in a tub, nor do they wash their hands in a washbasin. This European habit appears quite absurd to them: one could not wash off one's dirt, since it came back, albeit diluted. For this reason they bathed or washed by pouring water over themselves.

In spite of this, the fact remained that Khalil carried two European bathtubs. And that was, apart from everything else, a very complicated matter. Each tub was almost the length of the animal. How could they be secured to the animal's back? The pack-saddle would need to be a very broad one, in order to prevent the tub slipping off. No doubt Khalil Bey did not undergo such difficulties in order to sit in them himself. They could only be meant for the women in the entourage, and then only for non-Muslim ones with European cultural requirements—thus probably for Armenian women.

This ambitious politician and military amateur had commanded a division in the vicinity of Bitlis after his unfortunate invasion of Azerbaijan. As the appointment of Nikolai Nikolaievich as supreme commander in the Caucasus had not generated any consequences, the division appeared to be dispensable. It was thus to be moved to Mesopotamia and become part of the Sixth Army which was then in the process of being formed and whose supreme command was to be General Field-Marshal Von der Goltz. For Khalil Bey, this was grounds for many a fantastic dream. He had that impressive, unembarrassed kindness that his nephew Enver had been praised for. Cheerful and careless, freed from the Russian nightmare, on the way south to fresh achievements, Khalil saw the future in the rosiest colors. The British would lose Kut-el-Amara, then be cleared out of the whole of Mesopotamia, so nothing would lie any longer in the way of an advance on India!

Detachment soldiers at a dance, with Siirt in the background.

The detachment on the march. From right to left: Dr. Stoffels, Memduh Bey, von Scheubner, Omer Nadji Bey.

VII

Down the Tigris by Kelek

The rest taken by Scheubner and the company at Boghtan Su would be the last for some time.

In Siirt he had made yet another donation for the poor, which the town notables acknowledged with a solemn farewell visit to express their gratitude. Then we rode away with Khalil and his staff, followed by our cavalry and one of Khalil's regiments.

We had descended through the valley—the route that connects Mesopotamia with the Black Sea—and along which, in the opposite direction, Xenophon and his Ten Thousand had already marched. We were soon at the Boghtan Su, a torrential river which begins south of Lake Van and receives the Bitlis Su, before itself flowing into the Tigris. By evening we had crossed it. It was now the last week in October, and there was a lot of water which reached up to the horses' and mules' necks. The ford was narrow, and the first to be sent across were the horsemen. They found it relatively easy to keep their horses on the right path. If they slipped down the side of it, they were able to swim to the other bank next to their mounts.

It was more difficult for the pack animals. It was still easy if their load was not too heavy, but it looked dangerous for the animal that was carrying our money in two chests as large as infantry ammunition chests. In one there were 5,000 Turkish pounds, or about 100,000 marks in gold; in the other, silver medjidies to the value of 30,000 marks. With bated breath we watched its first cautious steps as it felt its way across in the deep water: the animal's attentive expression, its pointed ears, its frightened eyes as it waded through the middle of the river, and its relieved, quicker pace as it approached the south side.

We followed the next beast, which carried our chairs. Our *chaydji* had already crossed. He was the man in charge of preparing our tea who, carrying a samovar and tea bags on the right and left of his saddle, would always ride ahead of us to our campsite in order to find a spring and have the tea brewing for our arrival. We were able to calmly observe how the rest of the animals and men crossed over. Our train was rather considerable, as we had to transport everything on the beasts: bedding, table and chairs, tableware, preserves and drinks, summer and winter clothing—everything packed in such a way that neither heat nor cold could affect it, nor water get into our trunks even if at some moment an animal fording a river might be overwhelmed by the current and get washed downstream.

How we enjoyed lighting the camp fires on the other bank. Day was turning into night as the sun, slowly departing from the heath at the river's edge, still warmed the mountain side, then glowing only on the red-grey summit. We finally saw the bright stars in the southern sky overhead. In the meantime the campfires multiplied in the fields along the river and the smell of roast mutton filled the air.

Our tents were soon up: one for Scheubner, then a large one for six men in which my brother Karl Gustav, Thiel, Schlimme, Memduh and I slept. We had inherited it from an Austrian ski expedition that, in 1914-1915, had attempted to carry on this wonderful sport in the Caucasus and utilise it for military purposes.

The next morning, Scheubner left the marching troops. He wanted to get to Mosul sooner. This town was the last chance to provide the troops with winter equipment before the winter campaign on the Turkish-Persian frontier began. After recent bad experiences, Scheubner was much interested on reaching Mosul before Khalil's division, which probably would devour the last available provisions. How right he was in this presumption would soon become apparent.

We stood upon a grass covered hill overlooking the confluence of the Boghtan Su and the Tigris. With mighty arms flowing by long white islands of sand and stone, the swift blue stream rolled towards the sinuous Tigris, the river of paradise and of ancient, majestic Assyria, arriving from the west. A picturesque, broad peak rose at the point of confluence, with solid, well-built houses on it, all around which extended the fertile Tigris valley with its rice, corn and cotton plantations. This was where Scheubner left Leverkuehn I in command of the company and set off with Memduh and me to the tiny village of Til on the Tigris. There, a few kilometers downstream from the mouth of the Boghtan Su, the river turned sharply south, to flow through the mountains into Mesopotamia. But we were obliged to wait a whole day before being able to travel further on. In the meantime we were visited by Omer Nadji, who had some bad news for us. Our ambassador in Constantinople had died of a heart attack.

It was a great loss for everyone caring for the German-Turkish alliance—an irreplaceable loss. Nadji spoke to us all as if we had all lost a dear relative. It was a comfort to sense, here in the East, how the alliance, Wangenheim's masterpiece, had not only convinced politicians, but had become a matter close to the heart of a high-minded man. Nadji remembered the time when the Young Turk movement had ousted Abdul Hamid. In those days all

Tigris valley below Tillo.

A Kurdish village on the Tigris.

western democracies were admired in Constantinople, but Germany was blamed and despised as being Abdul Hamid's friend. Baron Marschall, Wangenheim's predecessor, had watched, hidden behind a window curtain, the screaming crowd rioting in front of the embassy and just said, "That will soon change." And change it did, in the briefest of times. Wangenheim had continued his predecessor's policy, intensifying it, and carrying it to success.

Thus related Nadji, as darkness fell and the *kelek*s, those weird rafts made of sheepskins—which even nowadays are the typical means of transport on the Tigris, as they had been in Assyrian, Babylonian, and Roman times— touched land at the rushing river's stony banks. Nadji could not praise Wangenheim's candidness and reliability enough—characteristics that had made the deepest impression on him, an Oriental, and to which he attributed the ambassador's success.

"With Wangenheim and Goltz Germany has given Turkey two great friends and benefactors. A diplomat and a soldier. And yet, Goltz carried out his duties like a diplomat, and Wangenheim acted towards the Turks always like a soldier."

Night went by and came dawn, with wild ducks and eagles gliding over the river. Dew had settled on tiny thorny twigs that were pleasantly aromatic. The only constant sound was the roar of the waters, drowning the feeble voices of the raftsmen.

We were to travel to Mosul by kelek, a raft or dinghy. The kelek is built as follows. After slaughter, the animals' bodies are pounded till the skin comes loose from the body, allowing the flesh and bones to be pulled out through the open neck. In this way, one is left with a bag whose remaining openings can be bound with gut. It is then pumped up by means of a reed through one opening, which is finally tied up. A special mixture of fat renders it impervious to water. Around 90 of these floating bladders are fixed under a frame made of straight, thin wicker stems, forming a structure of some eight square meters in surface area. Depending on the purpose of the trip, it is loaded with cargo and chests, or else fitted out with carpets. Two large rudders stick out over both sides. These are not used to propel the vessel, but only for steering, docking, or keeping it in the current and away from shallows. Their ends are made of split reeds held together with wicker rods.

This kind of raft traffic on the Tigris is brought about by the nature of the river. Wooden rafts cannot be used because there is not much wood in the area, and besides they would run aground in rapids and bends. Instead, inflated sheepskin bladders easily float above the stony bottom even in shallow places. Should one or more of the bladders tear, the rest of them still hold the structure well above the water, so that the danger of running aground is negligible.

Finally, we were ready to depart by 9:30 A.M. on October 25, 1915. As Khalil and his train needed one more kelek than planned, we had to take charge of 35 ammunition chests besides our own luggage. The kelek was well loaded. We set up a large tent made with strips of tarpaulin to shelter us from the heat of the day and the chilly night dew. On board were Scheubner, Memduh, and myself, with Tahir to wait on us, and two *kelekdjis* to steer the raft. At noon we took on provisions at a village. In addition, Memduh shot three wild ducks that were roasted for dinner over an open fire and served as a feast to celebrate my parents' silver wedding anniversary, which fell on that day.

In this way we traveled over the next three days among imposing mountains, in the coves of which we came upon the occasional village where we could purchase eggs, milk, bread, pomegranates, melons, and a drink made of honey and grape juice. Along straight stretches or gentle bends the kelek kept to the middle of the river, slowly turning on itself in the current.

Near one of the villages, a few Kurds came over and smoked a cigarette with us. But not everything was friendliness. As we pulled in one evening, we came across some Kurdish kelekdjis who not only refused to make room for us, but even threatened to open fire. Although they agreed to let us dock at the bank after a prolonged exchange with Memduh and our own kelekdjis, we decided to go further downstream for safety's sake, and had to continue in the darkness. By the compass and the stars we knew we were headed northwest, while our general direction was southeast. On the Kiepert map, the only more or less reliable one of this region, there was no sign of such bends. According to the international 1:1,000,000 map, which we unfortunately did not then have at hand, it must have been the bend north of Kesta.

The speed of the kelek was considerable, at least greater than that of someone swimming with the current. I found this out from experience one night when I felt like having a dip in the Tigris and fetching some water fowl that Memduh had shot. As I approached the bank, the kelek sped forward in midstream. With great difficulty the kelekdjis steered the raft sideward, a little closer to the bank, in order to allow me to catch up with it, swimming in the cold water.

Incomparably beautiful as this journey was on the whirling waters through the mountain solitude, a waterway very few Europeans had traveled along, where eagles ruled in their true home, we suffered greatly from the heat which was made even more intense by the sun's reflection in the water. Scheubner could only deal with a few of his tasks and reporting. On the second morning we were quite delighted to come to a tiny place, with sulphur springs, in the middle of the wilderness, which some pious donor had made useful for humanity by building a bath-house. Usually, we cast off very early at 4:00 A.M., with the moon still shining, and the cool of the night still holding out.

On the third day we had to pass some perilous rapids. In order to lighten our load and avoid endangering human life, we put the servants and four soldiers ashore who, due to illness, had asked us to take them with us. They marched on foot beyond the rapids, which were at a river bend. We entered the curve at great speed. The kelekdjis worked with full force, all the while loudly invoking Allah's help. We came out safe and sound, but it was necessary to replace a number of the sheepskins afterwards.

The landscape changed. The steeply rising mountains with their rocky peaks gave way to flatter shores, and the hills themselves took on a milder shape. In the early afternoon of that day we reached Jazirat-ibn-Omar.

This town is probably very ancient, and has been known at least since Byzantine times. The local kaimakam resided in its stone-built, imposing government building. He received us on the shore and invited us to stay overnight, as repairs on the kelek could not be completed that evening. Work on it continued well into the night. Fortunately, we were able to leave the ammunition chests. The kelek was fitted with a soft layer of reeds, which made our journey more pleasant.

A day later the village of Rihane was sighted on the left bank. A Kaderi Arabian tribe, (the sect to which the Tillo convent belonged, as described in the previous chapter) had put up their tents close by. Kurds and Fellahin lived in the village. Most were clad in simple robes and Arab headwear. Rihane, however, stood out among the villages of its type, as it was the seat of a sheikh, Hafis Hadji Ullah. We visited him and were very cordially received. He had traveled extensively and was a rather educated man. His natural, dignified posture and manners and refined, aristocratic face reminded one vividly of Homer, personifying natural royalty.

We dined with him sitting cross-legged on the floor, Arab-style. A circular brazen tray of about a meter in diameter with numerous smaller dishes on it was placed before us. Each man reached for the food with his right hand, whether rice, vegetables, or meat. Only the yoghurt posed greater difficulties. We helped ourselves to bread baked in slabs roughly the

Kelek building on the banks of the Tigris.

Loading the kelek opposite Jazirat-ibn-Omar. Lieutenant
Thiel in the foreground

size of pancakes, but more consistent, using them as shovels to scoop up the yoghurt.

At sundown, all the tribesmen met for evening prayers. They recited verses from the Koran individually and in chorus and knelt looking southwest, in the direction of the holy cities of Mecca and Medina. As their silhouettes stood out against the blood-red evening sky, one imagined the minarets and domes of the holy cities across the desert expanses. An infinite solemnity marked this moment of devotion, which unites all the children of Islam in prayer.

Once the riverside again became steep and mountainous, Memduh shot a magnificent eagle. We were badly received in a Shiite village so we had no desire to stay there: we passed by Eski-Mosul—old Mosul—and finally arrived in the city itself on the morning of November 1. We lodged in the old French consulate. On the following day Khalil also arrived, seriously ill with acute appendicitis.

VIII

Politics in Mosul

The site of Mosul could not compete with that of Erzerum. It stands on a plain where the desert road runs into the Tigris, crosses it by a pontoon bridge, and carries on to Persia. Yet the town itself is attractive, with its white Arab-style buildings. It has been a center of transport, commerce and industry since ancient times. The cloth known as "muslin" takes its name from that of the town.

Next to the largest mosque stands a formidable minaret, inclined like the Tower of Pisa, and just as stable. Instead of the round domes one finds everywhere in the Turkish and Arab lands some mosques have scored spires, showing supposedly Persian influence.

In 1915 the town was definitely in a state of transition. New roads had been hastily built through the city, without removing the half-demolished houses, so that entire neighborhoods looked like heaps of rubble.

On the opposite bank of the Tigris was an uncultivated space, surrounded by a low embankment—the site of ancient Nineveh, a bare hill in the middle of the space, and another with a village on top. At its southern tip, where the embankment runs into the river, are the remains of the Assyrian citadel. The village is called Nebi Junus—Prophet Jonas—and in its mosque one could see Jonas' grave.

The battalion reached Jazirat-ibn-Omar at about the same time as Scheubner arrived in Mosul with Memduh and myself, where we made a vexing and unexpected halt.

Displaced Armenians were hiding in the mountainous region west of the Tigris and some of the villages inhabited by Syrian Christians refused to obey the Turkish authorities' orders for requisitions of foodstuffs and recruits. The vali of Diarbekir demanded, on behalf of the government in Constantinople, that Nadji's and Scheubner's troops should be assigned to subdue these villages.

Omer Nadji cabled Scheubner, asking him to place his detachment, including all Germans, at their disposal. Scheubner, however, was put in a very difficult position by this call. He was in no way convinced by the Turkish explanations. On the contrary, he believed that this was not a case of a real revolt, but the hardly unjustified self-defense of a people who feared suffering the same fate as most of the Armenians. If Germans now took part in such skirmishes, the Turks would not fail to make it generally known that it was precisely the Germans who were the leaders against

Christian Turkish citizens. . . . An impression would arise that was exactly to the contrary of what Scheubner had achieved as a consul in Erzerum through strenuous efforts.

In this situation, Scheubner decided to put all his Turkish troops and Kurdish horsemen at Omer Nadji's disposal, but summoned Leverkuehn I, Thiele, and Schlimme immediately to Mosul. In addition, he attempted to persuade the vali of Mosul to solve the conflict in a peaceful manner. After a Turkish attack was repulsed with the loss of 15 dead and 25 wounded, his endeavor met with success. Unfortunately, and contrary to the original plans, the battalion was held up for three weeks and reached Mosul only on December 4, and was only able to rest for four days.

Otherwise nothing had been spoilt. The provisions for the troops in Mosul were insufficiently organized. Khalil's soldiers sold their ammunition in the bazaar in order to still their hunger. Scheubner also found out that his special detachment of a hundred soldiers and his Kurdish horsemen would be forced to stay at the rear of the battalion unless he personally had a say in the distribution of equipment and provisions. Omer Nadji was in a better position—if the military administration had nothing left to deliver, he could fall back on special provisions belonging to the Committee of Union and Progress.

For political reasons, Scheubner was not inclined to ask Omer Nadji for a share in these provisions. He preferred to procure something at a reasonable price, but could not find anything suitable. He therefore obtained materials with the help of the municipal authorities, hired 10 shoemakers, and rented a large building for the German expedition on the outskirts of the town. There he had cheap, long-lasting boots made under Russian–German Isaak Inke's supervision. He also contracted several tailors to make underwear, uniforms, and overcoats, also under the supervision of his own men. As it had become obvious on their journey that the Turkish harnesses for the draught animals were poorly made, causing pressure sores and consequent losses, he had new ones made to his own specifications, which later proved very reliable. Once again we were amazed at his energy and his inexhaustible store of ideas. Finally, he bought more pack animals.

Although these technical preparations temporarily demanded all his attention, political issues remained in the foreground. Many things came together, not always in a satisfactory manner.

Scheubner gathered intelligence on conditions at the frontier and conducted negotiations with the local Kurdish tribes. Obviously, he had to take Turkish wishes into account and, to his great regret, decline a few

Scheubner, Leverkuehn I (right), Leverkuehn II (left), Mosul, July 1916.

favorable offers. The Turks were against an exclusive German command of the tribes. The Kurds, however, due to their experiences over the past three years and also for financial reasons, wanted nothing to do with the Turks. They were only willing to fight under German leadership. With a heavy heart, Scheubner was forced to decline.

There were two chieftains against whom the Turks had no objections. These were Shukri and Hassan Agha of the Abderi tribe. Sinkhi, the paramount tribal chief, was in Tiflis at the time. There he was under the influence of the Russians, which did not please his people. In addition, differences had arisen between Shukri and Hassan and the Russian government. As a result, the tribe had repudiated Sinkhi as their chieftain. He was reputed to be brave. As his family was on Turkish territory, one might have counted on their loyalty. Solemn deliberations were held with Shukri and Hassan. First, they were given 50 Turkish pounds—about a thousand marks—in gold coins to equip their people for a winter campaign. Little of the money ever found its way into any but their own pockets.

All these affairs could have been solved satisfactorily, even if they gave rise to a lot of annoyance and excitement. But suddenly the larger circles began to intersect with the smaller ones, and it was difficult to say if anything good or bad would result from it.

Since Scheubner's departure from Erzerum in September, Turkey's situation had improved. Under Marshal Liman Von Sanders, British and French attacks at the Dardanelles had been frustrated. Now, at the end of the year, it became evident that a renewed campaign would not take place. The withdrawal of enemy troops was only a question of time. In October, the Entente began assembling an army in Salonica, the original reinforcements intended for Gallipoli being moved there. But it was too late to relieve the Serbs. The route from Berlin to Constantinople was open, the Russian Caucasus offensive had not materialized, and the only strategic successes of the British had been repelling the attack on the Suez Canal, and the advance to Kut-el-Amara, about halfway between the Persian Gulf and Baghdad. This, however, was the weakest point of the Turkish position. It was the most remote point from Constantinople and the railway.

On December 6 we were informed by cable that General Field Marshal Von der Goltz, in agreement with German General Headquarters, was to take charge of the Sixth Army in Mesopotamia and had left Ras-el-Ain with his staff in two cars. That was the last station on the Baghdad railway, in the middle of the desert between the Tigris and the Euphrates, 360 kilometers from Mosul. The route to Baghdad passed through Mosul and Scheubner entrusted me the task of greeting the field marshal in his name and that of Consul Holstein. If necessary, I was to act as a guide.

I rode with Tahir and two Circassians westward into the desert, following the cart-ruts that marked the caravan trail. The ground was so firm at this time of year after the blazing heat of summer that cars could go anywhere. Only the dry riverbeds, with their steep banks, had to be crossed with caution.

After riding for an hour I discerned two cars in the distance. It was the field marshal. I reported to him. He briefly inquired about the situation in Mosul and the personalities present there. He then drove on and I followed as fast as the horses would allow. I then saw, out of the corner of my eye, that Tahir, who was behind me, had slid down a steep incline and fallen over with his mount. Fortunately, neither man nor horse were harmed. I caught up with the cars a short way from the city and directed them to the German consulate, where the field marshal was lodged.

His presence brought us joy and relief. Even in the tiniest Kurdish villages we had sensed the unreserved trust his name enjoyed. He knew only too well that he had taken on a particularly difficult task. Conditions in the Sixth Army were deplorable. It had had practically nothing but defeats. The field marshal could not expect obedience or cooperation from its commanders, who saw themselves independent of all orders from Constantinople.

His entourage and the German officers who began to arrive little by little appeared to be much more optimistic than he himself. To our astonishment, we learned that a German artillery regiment was assigned for operations in Mesopotamia and Persia. We really knew all about the local climate and the plan appeared to us as completely impracticable. But it was only one of the many important plans we spoke about. All these words came from men who had never been in these regions and certainly could not assess the difficulties involved. The right judgment was lacking.

Among the field marshal's luggage and entourage was an Irish hunter belonging to one of his aides. Impressed, we watched the gigantic animal, which looked like an elephant next to the well-built Arabian horses. Certainly it was not a considerable drain of transport capacities when the beast was brought here in December and, unable to stand the climate, had to be sent back again in April. We, however, found it inappropriate to see something like this after waiting for such a long time for support from Germany. Unfortunately, it was a characteristic symptom of the privileged status many Germans believed they were entitled to here, arising from a lack of understanding of the local conditions.

More important than such observations was the question of what impact this new command would have on our expedition. The field marshal's interests focused mainly on knocking out the British. Everything else was secondary to him. For this purpose, it was essential to establish efficient lines of communication and supply. From this point of view it was understandable that the field marshal—with a heavy heart, from a soldier's point of view—had had no option but to hand over the command of the *vilayet* of Mosul to the local vali, on whom he depended for the provisioning of his troops, all the way eastwards to Azerbaijan.

This measure altered Scheubner's position fundamentally: his expedition had been based on the plan of moving the extreme right wing of the Turkish Caucasus army through Azerbaijan and advancing to the eastern Caucasus. Now, however, he was suddenly on the extreme left wing of Goltz's Mesopotamian Sixth Army and had for its main objective an attack against the British—at present of no importance. One of his fundamental guarantees in relation to the Turks had been his independence within the combined expedition with Omer Nadji, the visible expression of which had been the exclusive command of a special detachment! Now it was all over. All that was left was a Nadji–Scheubner's expedition under the supreme command of the vali of Mosul. The vali's name was Haidar Bey, a man of Albanian extraction, who was a charming official with no military training and a pronounced talent for intrigue.

That was the unsatisfactory side of the new situation. Nevertheless, Scheubner still had some trump cards in his hand.

From his negotiations with the Kurds and Persians, he knew how much the Turks needed him. All the reports from Persia confirmed it. The trust he enjoyed there found touching expression in the plea of the Persian consul in Mosul that Scheubner take his 10-year-old son as a member of his detachment on his expedition to Azerbaijan, as he himself was unfit to take part in the liberation of his fatherland due to age and illness.

Scheubner had, of course, coordinated his expedition with other German projects in Persia. These had set out from Baghdad on the principal road to Teheran and they had set up headquarters in Kirmanshah. There, under Major Klein, were our regimental comrades who had been transferred simultaneously with Scheubner in the autumn of 1914. Klein also had had to grapple with the opposition of Turkish civilian and military authorities, who—just like the vali of Mosul now—did not wish German influence in Persia and Arabia to become too strong. He did not only have to reckon with temporal leaders either. Islam is split along the Persian frontier into the Sunni Turks and Arabs this side of it, and the Shiite Persians on the other. The latter's shrines, however, are on Arabian territory, south of Baghdad. Before his advance to Persia, Major Klein had negotiated with the spiritual leaders there. Following this, he sent a part of his expedition to the southern border region. This was Lühr's detachment that managed to destroy the pipeline between the Anglo-Persian Oil Company's oil fields and the Persian Gulf.

Wassmuss, who had been the German consul in Bushire on the Persian Gulf before the war, moved south and southwest from Kirmanshah. There, he forced the British to divert and split strong forces, maintaining his position until after the war ended. Captain Niedermayer and Mr. von Hentig, acting as diplomatic representative, went eastward. They crossed the salt desert of Kevir, until then almost unknown to Europeans, broke through the British–Russian cordon at the Afghan border, and appeared in Kabul, the Afghan capital. The emir, hard-pressed by the British and Russians, could not let them stay there for long. Hentig crossed the Pamir plateau, reached Chinese Turkestan and Peking, and returned to Germany by way of the United States: "the hardest trip around the world," as Sven Hedin had called this war voyage. At the same time, Niedermayer traveled north to Russian Turkestan and got back to Kirmanshah disguised as a pilgrim.

In the meantime, Klein and his staff, and the military attaché in Teheran, Count Kanitz, tried to mobilize the Persian national circles and liberate their land from British and Russian influences. If Nikolai Nikolaievich had not unexpectedly increased Russian pressure, it would surely have succeeded. In this way, however, the German and Austrian envoys were forced to leave Teheran and only western Persia remained as a field of operations.

All these enterprises emanated from the Political Section of the General Staff and followed one principal idea: it was in the interest of the Central Powers to keep as many enemy forces as possible tied up in the secondary scene of operations which was Turkey. The expeditions fulfilled this task. Great Britain had been harassed at the gates of India by way of Afghanistan. It was obliged to send troops for the protection of its oilfields in southern Persia. Russian troops were drawn into Persia, thus diverted from other fronts. All this, which the expeditions were able to achieve with untold sacrifice, in a scorching climate, and the most meager of means, belongs to the very greatest individual deeds of the war, on par with the significant achievements of submarine commanders and airmen. As to whether Persia could have been liberated and turned into an ally of the Central Powers, it was obviously a matter that could not be decided by personal efforts alone. Getting nations to revolt without being able to provide them with money, arms and ammunition is a precarious undertaking. Support was lacking from home. Much had been promised, but that was based on a false idea about what was necessary for the Orient and did not take the existing difficulties sufficiently into account.

We met not a few Germans down there, particularly in 1916, who argued that everything in the Orient was a sham, and that the European was under no obligation to honor every promise since Orientals were prone to exaggerate and have a none too high regard for the truth. This was reasoning that flew in the face of all psychology. Scheubner viewed things differently from the very first day of his Oriental enterprise. A large portion of his influence on men like Omer Nadji and, in general, all Turks and Kurds with whom he dealt, was owed precisely to his punctilious fulfilment of promises. For it was in this regard that Orientals accepted the superiority of the European—that he always kept his word.

This was the bottom line as far as Scheubner could see it on the eve of departure from Mosul: it had to be assumed that the Persian question would enter a new phase with the nomination of Field Marshal Von der Goltz, but it was necessary to eliminate British pressure on Baghdad first. The consequences and all that would follow were impossible to assess for the moment even for the field marshal. Thus, Scheubner could not obtain any precise orders from him regarding joint action with Major Klein. At all negotiations, again and again, the concern arose that his influence in Persia would be diminished the moment he appeared there as the vali of Mosul's subordinate. However, as nothing could be done about this, he decided to end the impasse by invading Azerbaijan as far as possible, clear up the situation there, and tie up as many Russian troops as possible.

IX

The Assault on Sautchbulak

Haidar Bey, the vali of Mosul, was most pleased by his new military distinction and had already set out for the Persian frontier when the battalion left under Nadji's leadership. It turned eastward to the fertile district of the Greater Zab river, with its mixed population and tidy, well-kept villages. At Erbil, the ancient Arbela, renowned for the Assyrian cult of Ishtar, they halted to wait for Scheubner.

The little Muhsin, the Persian consul's son, reported in time. On being asked what service he wished to do, he replied, "Write letters for the soldiers and bind wounds." Scheubner took him in. At the same time, the Persian deputy, Major Mirza Khan entered the expedition's services. Two days later, on December 10, the battalion train started under Thiel's command, with Scheubner, Leverkuehn I, Memduh, Mirza, Abdul Bari Bey, little Muhsin, and the cavalry.

Unfortunately, I had broken a rib in a fall from a horse and was forced to remain behind for the time being. Scheubner put me in charge of procuring supplies, leaving me with Schlimme, an interpreter named Jacques Latin, and a few attendants. Our other interpreter, Abdul Hamid, lay in hospital with typhoid fever.

The first impression Scheubner gained in the region east of Mosul was of Kurdish refugees from Persia. They claimed that the Turks had promised them support which they never received. With Mirza's help, Scheubner hired many draught-animal drivers and 18 horsemen under the tribal chieftain Aziz Khan, met up with the battalion, and continued the march to the northeast past Rowanduz after paying Hadji Mullah Effendi a visit, whose beautiful mansion stood in a rich garden, at that time full of flowers, pomegranates, and oranges.

Mirza Khan stayed behind in Erbil to equip the new horsemen and hire additional ones. One must not think by this that the expedition, as it advanced, was continuously growing in size: instead these were usually urgently-needed replacements for deserters and the sick. By the way, Captain Veli Bey had no mercy for cowardly or negligent soldiers and already at the Boghtan Su had had one shot for mutilating himself in order to be discharged.

Passing by the mighty ruins of the old castle of Dir (where Alexander the Great is said to have won a battle), then through diligently-tilled estates, where farmers plowed with asses, producing carpet dyes out of the roots of plants, and through exhilarating, ever steeper and more imposing mountains, Scheubner arrived after a week at the last telegraph post, Rayat. Haidar Bey came to meet him there, informing him that he had already gathered a number of Kurdish tribes. Joint quarters were set up at the frontier village of Darlaman. Haidar's Kurds were there too.

It was with great pride that he introduced an important chieftain, Kareni Pasha, who was said to own 200 villages in Azerbaijan and was always switching his allegiance between the Turks and Russians. . . All this was quite possible. There was no scarcity of aghas or chieftains in the area. Each was the undisputed lord over the men and women in his village and, if he himself could not give proof of his regency, he would attribute the possession of at least 20 castles to his ancestors. . . Kareni Pasha had more important things in store however: four Model 98 German guns, bought by him for 50 Turkish pounds each—that is four thousand marks.

The days and nights got cold. Although Haidar Bey, who loved the sound of his own voice, had mentioned that the battalion would be quartered in houses, nothing had come of this and the men remained in their tents. The sheikh of Darlaman invited Scheubner and the officers to dinner. He was very pious, with a black beard and large hooked nose, and clad in expensive garb. It was said that he received a monthly stipend of 500 piasters from the Turkish government to entertain passing foreign travelers.

All that separated us from Persia now was the frontier pass. We crossed it and camped for the time on Persian soil at the foot of the mountain. On the plain, half an hour's march distant, rose the rock on which the village of Shinova stood. The terrain was ideal for all-type mixed unit exercises. While we had exercised with the individual units on the way, little had been done in terms of combat training. A major manoeuvre was ordered on the morning before Christmas. Scheubner participated energetically, criticizing the fact that the charge had started too early, so many of the soldiers were exhausted by the time they reached the target, at the most critical time. But in the afternoon fever got him and he had to stay in bed. A small thorn bush decorated with colored lights reminded one of Christmas Eve. . .

In general, the Christmas days were dark: Leverkuehn I was ill; there was a shortage of fodder for the beasts; and the promised guns for Mirza's horsemen had not come. Haidar Bey ordered the departure of the infantry, following it with Omer Nadji. In the evening he nevertheless demanded a reinforcement of 40 cavalrymen under Aziz Khan. No one knew what was happening; presumably Haidar didn't either. Mirza arrived from Erbil with 60 horsemen, who were very welcome.

Luckily, on the second morning after Christmas Scheubner felt well enough to take command of the expedition again. The soldiers sensed something was about to happen, but who would have imagined that it would turn out to be such a spectacular gamble?

The infantry bivouacked at 2,000 meters altitude, west of the pass, which was halfway between Lebgin and Sautchbulak. Scheubner and his cavalry overtook them there. There were still about 10 kilometers to Sautchbulak! He rode in a terrible snowstorm, now as the vanguard, and pushed ahead through the pass (2,174 meters) towards Sautchbulak. The town lay surrounded by high mountains, about 30 kilometers south of Lake Urmia (Lake Rezaye), that huge expanse of water 1,300 meters above sea level, 10 times the size of Lake Constance, encompassing the part of the province of Azerbaijan west of Tabriz. In the east and south, the shores changed into wide, swampy plains, out of which rose high mountains, around 20 or 30 kilometers distant from the lake.

Sautchbulak was an important place on the road from Tabriz which crossed the Persian-Turkish border at Sheikhin-Koi, and then led to Mosul, Baghdad, and along the edge of the desert to Syria. Thus the town of Sautchbulak was of considerable strategic importance for the passage from northern Persia to Mesopotamia, the more so as an important route that led southeast via Sakis to Kirmanshah and the towns on the Teheran-Baghdad road. Not without reason had the Russians extended their Caucasian railway from Djulfa to Tabriz, and improved the road to Sautchbulak so that it was fit for truck traffic.

As Scheubner's cavalrymen approached the town, shells from two rapid-firing cannons buzzed over their heads. So—the Russians! A sudden silence. The Russians were evacuating their positions. Scheubner ordered his Kurds to pursue them. The town was stormed and the Russians retreated in a hasty flight—they obviously presumed a whole division stood behind this cavalry vanguard! The Kurds fired. While the Russian infantry was able to cover the retreat of their guns, Russian losses were considerable. Everything had happened so fast that Haidar's battalion had not even come into action.

The cavalry immediately took over security tasks in the city. It was terribly cold and the troops' state of health left much to be desired. Only after several days did it become possible to lodge Scheubner's entire expedition at a caravanserai. Only sentry-posts remained outside the city, where trenches and small fortifications were constructed.

Dr. Fuad became town commander. He set up a postal connection with Mosul and established maximum permissible prices for foodstuffs. The inhabitants accepted the new situation. The regular soldiers' behavior was exemplary, and if the Kurds were blamed for occasional thefts, it was never proven. Envious neighbors could also have taken advantage of the situation. Scheubner completed supplying his troops' equipment and kept them strictly at their duties.

A rumor circulated that the Russians still had spies in the town. Right at the beginning three Armenians were arrested, but the accusations against them proved groundless. The case of a fourth was serious: he was hanged for proven espionage.

After the first week in January 1916, Vali Haidar Bey left, southward-bound, with a company, two guns, a column of cavalry, and many Kurdish units to establish, as he claimed, communications with the Sixth Army, which left Scheubner to think about the local situation. That the Russians' goal could hardly be central Persia seemed quite clear, for to get to Teheran they would use different routes: from Baku along the Caspian Sea through Resht-Kasvin; from Tabriz via Miane-Kasvin. Thus, it was likely that they were planning an invasion of the Mesopotamian plain.

For this the Russians had two remaining options, after the fall of Sautchbulak had cut off the main Tabriz–Mosul route. The first was to attack southward to the west of the lake to Urmia through the Suldus plain in order to gain the Sheikhin-Koi pass, the only one passable in winter, and so get control of the Mosul road. This possibility concerned the detachment very directly, as it meant the severance of our only line of retreat. The second was to advance south, east of the lake along the road from Miyandowab-Saqqez to Kirmanshah, and try crossing the Persian frontier at one of its several deviations—whether by Panjvin, or the more southerly route near Khanikin—in order to reach Baghdad, their ultimate goal.

It was not certain what the Russians would do, so Scheubner took into account both possibilities.

He sent part of the border battalion to the Suldus plain between Sautchbulak and Urmia under Amir Aslan. The famous Kareni Pasha was there as well. These measures were intended against the first of the alternatives mentioned. As for the second, there had already been skirmishes at Miyandowab, 40 kilometers northeast of Sautchbulak, on the road to Tabriz. Scheubner sent a strong patrol there under Azmi's command, with the assignment of carefully watching the situation and reporting back within four days at the most. When Azmi reached the

Miyandowab region, the Kurds had driven back around a thousand mounted Russians. Their tales were obviously not to be believed, yet Azmi ascertained that the Russian cavalry was composed only of Armenians, Caucasians, and Greeks, who had probably not been soldiers for very long. This information was very valuable. Azmi returned with his patrol through torrential rain.

Amir Aslan's services in the Suldus plain were far more doubtful. As time went by one Kurdish tribe after another that faced the Russians disappeared. Amir Aslan gave himself the title of "Supreme Commander of All the Armed Forces on the Suldus Plain" and sent memorable telegrams and reports, not just to Scheubner and Nadji, but also to the highest places. Nothing has become known of his other accomplishments.

Nevertheless Scheubner did everything possible under existing circumstances. In the snowbound mountains communications remained difficult, even for spies who, in other seasons, could easily travel along secret byways; and the land to the east of Sautchbulak was inaccessible. Even on the international map it was marked as not having been mapped. Nor were the Russians any better off—they too had no idea of the strength of their opponents' forces. In Mosul one could hear rumors that it was said in Tabriz bazaar that 14,000 troops under a German were advancing from Siirt. . . Nonetheless, the presence of Germans was unpleasant for the Russians. They put a reward of 10,000 rubles on Scheubner's head, and 5,000 each on my brother's and mine. All our people knew this. Not one betrayed us.

X

Snowed in High in the Mountains of Persia

Left behind in Mosul when the detachment parted, I had been obliged to stay in my quarters for a short time. After that I made my daily visits to the vali's palace, which was located in a large square on the southern limits of the city not far from our house and the German consulate. Negotiation with vali Haidar demanded patience. He resided in a long hall, and the visitor was guided to him by his attendants. He would ceremoniously greet his visitor in a deep voice, as if he was praying. Then he would take tobacco and paper out of a small valise, which we called the "dachshund" among ourselves because of its shape, and roll a cigarette. He would then clap his hands and a servant would take the cigarette to the visitor. It was then the latter's turn to speak. It was, however, considered to be very bad form to come straight to the point; a general introduction was necessary, as if one hadn't any specific matter to hand, and the day hadn't generated any business. Then, at the appropriate moment, the vali would clap his hands once more and his secretary would appear and prepared to write. He held a small sheet of paper in his raised left hand (that had to serve as a pad) and awaited the words that were to come in order to pen them in diligent lines from right to left...

This effort was, however, minimal in comparison with what one had to get accustomed to from Haidar's deputy after the former's unexpected transformation into a military commander. He assumed a far more self-conscious posture and loved to demonstrate his presence less through manners than by a dashing attitude. During the period after the battalion's departure when I was obliged to remain in Mosul, I experienced some mind-boggling examples of this. For instance, the deputy informed the Austrian consular representative in plain words that his power allowed him to imprison him whenever he wished to do so. . . .

Therefore, I was pleased to wish Mosul good-bye once I felt able to travel and had successfully executed Scheubner's orders concerning provisions. This took place on the last day of 1915. Scheubner had just taken Sautchbulak, although I naturally knew nothing about it then.

I commanded two columns: 15 asses and 14 mules. The people with me were four orderlies, three cavalrymen, 12 drivers for the draught animals, the Kurd Zaduk, the Syrian Gabriel, the bandit Ismail Agha and the interpreter Simon of Kelaita.

We spent the first night in the village of Bartella. It was very cold; in the morning the stony ground was covered with frost and a light mist had fallen. One could see the rays of the sun through the haze. It was infinitely calm and not even the animals made a noise. The mist took many forms, sometimes thick, at other times thin. Visibility at a hundred or a hundred and fifty paces was nil. Suddenly I saw mysterious movements in the mist, like those of animals. They appeared, then disappeared, gliding like ghosts. When I approached, I recognised them: it was a long, slow camel caravan. The beasts passed northwards with solemn calm, carrying their burdens along the road from India and Persia to Europe.

We reached Erbil at noon the following day and camped on the field where Alexander had defeated the Persians. I gained the impression that many of the refugees who had gone there were dissatisfied due to the unfulfilled promises made by the Turkish government and were only waiting for spring to go over to the Russians. Only the mountain snows prevented them from doing so immediately.

Unluckily, the rainy season set in just after we left Erbil. The rain surprised us with its ferocity and I had to call a day's halt. From there on unfortunately delays became regular. It was only possible to march on good days. There was no road to speak of. Only a beaten track led northeast to the mountains, and I counted myself lucky to have only draught animals and no motorcars with me.

By endless exertions we worked our way to Deir-Harir. There we met Colonel Ettam Bey, who had managed to recruit troops from the various Kurdish tribes. There were about 200 horsemen and a hundred infantry in all which, considering the length of time he had to carry out the recruitment, was a pretty meager result. Considering, however, the general atmosphere, the numbers were hardly surprising. Kader Bey, the chief of one of the local tribes, visited me and stated quite frankly, "If there were no German officers here, I would go over to the Russians straight away." He had resisted the order to persecute Christians, although the kaimakam of Bashkala, his Turkish superior, had issued the order in writing and threatened him with a summons to a religious court. Kader Bey had written back, he would rather kill Mohammedans, since they all, together, lived off the Christians. . .

I thought a lot as I rode on. Time and again I had heard that the Turks were spreading rumors that the Armenians' deportations were carried out with German approval, and it almost seemed to me that the splendid receptions they always arranged for us along our route were not only meant to glorify the alliance, but had perhaps served to demonstrate the perfect accord between the Germans and the Turks to the Armenian population...

The tremendous significance of Scheubner's refusal to take part in the so-called "mutiny" near Jazirat-ibn-Omar now struck me with its full political import. Moreover, everything one heard about it ever since confirmed the notion that Scheubner had already been fully aware of the truth. The whole "mutiny" had consisted of the destruction of a telegraph cable in an act of self-defense, as the Armenian villages were repeatedly attacked by Kurds, without the kaymakam replying in any way to the calls for help. Immediately before Leverkuehn I received orders from Scheubner to detach himself from the unit, he witnessed the cruelties the very same kaimakam tolerated, allowing the destruction of peaceful villages and the ill-treatment of the inhabitants.

But aside from the Armenians, there were other Christian sects that for centuries had kept their way of life on the border between Persia and Turkey—they were persecuted as well. The vali of Mosul had put down a supposed insurrection of the Nestorians, a Christian sect established around the year 500 in his vilayet. He had destroyed their precious fields and orchards and by displacing them, naturally provided the Russian Army in Persia with a sizable number of volunteers. Never before this difficult ride along the half-obliterated paths near the Persian border had I fully understood this political and military senselessness.

Less than two hours' ride after leaving Deir-Harir another misfortune befell me. My German orderly Luther fell so gravely ill that we had to take him back to Deir-Harir. We waited there in vain for two days for him to recover. Then we left him in the care of a Turkish *müdir* (official), leaving the Kurd Zaduk and two horses with him. In spite of every effort, no medical care could be found. Only much later did I learn from a German doctor that his symptoms pointed to cholera. During the next few days one of our drivers fell with the same ailment. We were forced to leave him behind too.

Our journey became increasingly more difficult. The pack animals struggled and suffered on a precipitous foot-wide path at the base of a mountain along a deep gorge. It was a magnificent landscape: rugged, treeless heights of around 2,600 meters, deep valleys, roaring rivers, with isolated Kurdish villages leaning against the cliffs, and hardly visible in the distance—but I could not indulge in the scenery.

On arriving in Rowanduz on January 12, 1916, I met Ettam Bey once more. He was having trouble with his Kurds as he evidently did not know, either as a man or officer, how to treat them. He was, however, a formidable warrior, the scion of an old Albanian family—a character just made to portray this land. The kaymakam of Zakho, a Laz from the region around Trebizond who had somehow become an official in this district east of the Tigris and north of Mosul, had recently joined his detachment.

Finally, two of Scheubner's horsemen appeared. They brought money and orders. Accordingly, I sent the column of asses back to Mosul and hired 16 horses and mules in the Rowanduz bazaar which, for five medjidies, or about 22 marks, were to carry our loads to Sautchbulak. I left Schlimme in charge of the caravan, and with three cavalrymen, a mule, Ismail Agha, Musa, and the interpreter Simon of Kelaita, went on ahead in order to arrive as soon as possible.

I arrived at Sheikh-Koi in a terrible snowstorm on January 17. It was unthinkable to advance any further in the cutting wind that piled the snow in drifts from the heights. Musa started a quarrel with Simon of Kelaita because he thought the latter had translated something inaccurately. He pointed his gun at Simon and, had I not intervened, would surely have shot him.

The snowstorm raged unabated. A leader of Persian irregulars named Alibeck visited me, and we whiled away the time in tea drinking and polite conversation. Soon, I had had enough of all this and wanted to be on my way at whatever price—but the storm was stronger than us. I left nothing undone to reach the 1,841-meter high pass—in vain. After hours of trying to make way through the snow with our horses, we had to give up and go back to the village.

Suddenly, Ettam Bey turned up as well. He was very cheerful. First of all, he claimed he had been named commander of the cavalry and all the Kurds up to Sautchbulak. Second, he claimed that we were already on Persian soil. These were two reasons for a large party. Ettam and the kaimakam of Zakho drank undiluted raki out of water glasses—that was their trick to get around the religious prohibition of drinking alcohol. When they lifted their glasses, the liquid looked harmless and as clear as water, whereas if it was diluted, it took on a milky color, like absinthe. Therefore it was not diluted and the deception was successful. Which one of them had hit upon the clever idea I don't know, but it was the kaimakam who brought most amusement to the company. He treated his respectfully astonished countrymen to some of his French by tirelessly singing in all possible keys some verses from Lafontaine's fables.

> *Maitre corbeau, sur un arbre perché,*
> *Tenait en son bec un fromage. . .*

The storm howled on throughout the night, and at daybreak it possibly got even worse. We could hardly open the doors. The room we occupied was hardly as high as a man. There was a fire which burnt dried buffalo dung. The acrid smoke wreathed back and forth across the ceiling and only a little of it found its way to the tiny hole that served as a chimney to the outside. Even the unabashed cheerfulness of the Lafontaine scholar was no longer so convincing as, sitting cross-legged on his bed in his ever-so-long night-shirt, he declaimed, *"Maitre corbeau. . ."*

Finally, even the ghastliest of snowstorms must subside, even in Persia, and the weather finally cleared up. Traveling through the pass was obviously inconceivable for the time being. At the same time, more than two-thirds of Ettam's 300 horsemen took advantage of the fair morning to disappear. They obviously considered the way through the valley more hospitable than into the mountains. I feared the worst the moment Ettam inspected his remaining crowd: even this miserable lot was in open mutiny under its sheikhs Mohammed and Djevat. However, all that made no impression on Ettam. He had a few gendarmes with him, whom he reinforced with my few men. With this bodyguard he arrested Mohammed and Djevat and bound them in the room. Then he took his riding whip, drove the remainder into a group, took their weapons from them, and gave them a long talk on their depravity and lack of patriotism.

In the meantime, I had spoken to Mohammed and Djevat. They assured me that they belonged to the bravest of Kurdish tribes and would gladly fight against the Russians under German command, but they had got too little to eat under Ettam and were inadequately outfitted for the winter... Nevertheless, when Ettam reproached them again for their sins, they swore loyalty and subordination to him once more. On the following morning, January 23, they were among the company that moved out.

On account of the shortness of the days, everything had to be ready by 9:00 at the latest. But it was not. Loading the pack animals was complicated by the fact that they now had to carry the guns which soldiers were to carry no longer. This went on until 11:30. Only then did we depart.

There was no sign of a path. Two Kurdish guides went ahead of the column. With their broad shoes, similar to Canadian snowshoes, they left tracks behind them. How should one recover the situation, though, if there were trouble with some of the loads, or an animal slipped off the road, or there was a holdup? Obviously the thing to do, in order not to lose contact with them, was for the caravan to halt till the beast was unloaded, set back on the track, and loaded once more. Our guides were not interested in what went on behind them: not once did they look back and after a few hours they had vanished completely. Vanished without trace, in the literal sense, as they did not even leave footprints!

By 4:00 P.M. it was already twilight. Night fell unbelievably quickly. The moon shone faintly, the stars twinkled cold in a deep sky. The temperature was 20 degrees centigrade below freezing. Dangerous as the snow was, we were grateful for its shiny reflection. And this is where my interpreter, Simon of Kelaita, proved himself a savior in the presence of need: his home was the Urmia plain, on the other side of the pass, and he had the right instinct about which direction we should go. He even seemed to sense what could lie under the snow-covered crevasses and slopes on the way.

I had given him my Anatolian chestnut. He led the horse to the head of the column and pushed it ahead of himself. The beast's instinct was possibly even better than his own. Kelaita held tight to its tail. The snow reached up to the poor chestnut's neck, as the company was getting more and more exhausted. I marched immediately behind Kelaita, with the reins resting on my arm, stumbling uphill, slipping when crossing the bed of a stream, and my white horse following close behind me. How it kept upright in the frozen snow and without once falling on me as we slid down is something I cannot comprehend to this day.

It was equally miraculous that the caravan was able to keep advancing at all, although we had to intervene every few moments when someone would sink in at the edge of the path and remain lying there. Taking into consideration all these adversities, the caravan managed to keep in remarkable order. We lost three animals that, having wandered off the track, tried to get ahead through the deep snow and finally died of exhaustion. Their loads had to be carried by the mule drivers. Finally Ettam Bey was also not able to put one foot in front of the other without help from his people. We could not even think of our frozen limbs, nor did we know exactly where the pain and tiredness was. Anyway, around 9:00 P.M., after the moon had already set, we found quarters in a little village. They were so poor that at any other time we would not have accepted their hospitality. It was impossible to stand up straight in their huts, but any roof over our heads was good enough for us, as long as we were out of the hellish snow and the freezing, open sky.

The next morning was taken up with an inventory of men, animals, and equipment, and we only left at noon. The march through the valley was easier. There was no wind, so we did not have to put up with the dreadful snowdrifts. Five hours later we came to Shinova and heard the sound of

Text in Ottoman-Turkish and Latin script read: "The German officer
Herr Leverkuehn, who on Tuesday February 23rd, 1331, rode first
though the tape in a horse-race held in Bowkan, has been presented
the gold medal. Signing for the Jury: Omer Jemil, Commander of
the Cavalry Section; von Scheubner, Chairman; Amir Aslan.

artillery fire north and east of it. Suddenly the rumor spread that the Russians had recaptured Sautchbulak.

Ettam sent two men in the direction of the muffled noise, which we concluded was the sound of cannon-fire. It was the only patrol sent out during the whole of this march and it never returned.

Next morning we awoke in Shinova and saw a broad valley towards the northeast, that of the little Zab. Soon, we saw a column of pack animals advancing, noticing two guns and around 200 men. We anxiously awaited their arrival.

It was Amir Aslan who arrived from the Suldus plain. He told us he had repelled the first Russian attack on January 22, but the following day he had had to retreat before the second attack. He had no fresh news about Sautchbulak, except that it had been taken by the Russians. Scheubner's and the expedition's fate were supposedly still unknown. He himself had withdrawn to the border as otherwise his line of retreat to Mosul would have been cut off.

This was unwelcome news, made even more unpleasant by the lack of certainty. What would happen if the Russians advanced in the direction of Rowanduz and Mosul? I immediately thought it was vital to establish defenses against attacks from Sautchbulak. Amir Aslan's people were the right unit for this. He had quartered them in the village of Sedava one hour away. Military matters, however, did not concern him. Instead, he had initiated a fierce quarrel with Ettam Bey as to who was in command. Ettam Bey was a colonel, whereas Amir Aslan had no military rank at all and was, moreover, a Russian citizen. He claimed, however, that Omer Nadji and the vali of Mosul had assigned him the supreme command of the left wing.

Aslan was the only one with somewhat regular troops at his disposal. Ettam's Kurds were totally unfit for any combat duty. So I spoke to Aslan. He promised to remain with his detachment at Sedava for the time being, but in case of a Russian advance, he would retreat to Sheikhin-Koi in order to defend the pass.

I used this remark to ask him why he had put up less resistance to the Russians the second time than the first.

"They were far too strong," he replied. "I would have been taken prisoner." He showed me three letters in Turkish script, with Russian signatures. One of them contained a sketch or indication of troop deployments. He had got this from the other side, Amir Aslan said. Fifteen thousand troops from Urmia and a special detachment from Tabriz had marched on Sautchbulak.

I tried to persuade him to meet Ettam Bey halfway to cooperate, but he fiercely shook his head: Ettam was one of those officers installed by Sultan Abdul Hamid and could not read nor write. Three Turkish officers in his entourage, who seemed to be staunchly loyal to him, confirmed this statement. "Very well," I said, "if you do not want to be under Ettam's orders, all the Turkish troops automatically come under his command."

Aslan responded agitatedly. Ettam had wanted to send some of his cavalry men to Sautchbulak—which, in the deep snow meant exhausting the horses, and in the face of the enemy's superiority, certain death for the men. Since Aslan had been given his command by Nadji and was responsible for his people, he would certainly not give them up for any useless resistance.

At least I was able to calm the tensions down during this conversation. As Ettam Bey himself now negotiated with Aslan with great politeness, all seemed to go well. Meanwhile, more troops and guns arrived, among them the famous Kareni Pasha, who claimed to have been on Aslan's right flank. Some of the commanders blamed Aslan for having forced them to give up their lines by his hasty retreat. It seemed useless to wait for this exchange to come to an end. I repeatedly offered myself to Ettam for patrols and other duties. But he had no use for me, thus it was up to me to undertake something on my own. Now, frightful rumors spread: the Russians had ostensibly annihilated the expedition, and both Scheubner and my brother had already been hanged.

XI

Retreat

It proved absolutely impossible to obtain reliable information or to send out a messenger by one of the more southerly passes. In winter, there was not even the smallest pass through the mountains other than the one we had so laboriously come by in the last days—and the passes near Suleimaniye and Panjvin could only be reached by week-long marches.

As I could not hope to have any military use in these snowed-in mountains, the most important thing was now to inform the Army High Command in Baghdad that the whole road to the Tigris plain lay open to the Russians aside from Amir Aslan's small detachment. In addition I had to send messengers to the region south of Sautchbulak, in order to ascertain the fate of Scheubner's expedition and send him whatever he needed in case he was still alive.

Thus I first sent a letter to Schlimme, whom I had left in charge of the provisioning of the caravan; he was to wait. For, if he advanced further, he could fall into the hands of the Russians very quickly. Then I took my leave of Ettam, who carried out the only military deed that I ever came to see: he returned the weapons he had taken from his Kurds after their mutiny and issued the guns and ammunition that were still available at Shinova. His intentions were unclear and I soon had the chance to meet him once more. He had decided to retreat.

Amir Aslan handed me a telegram I was to send Field-Marshall Von der Goltz from the telegraph station at Rayat. It read, following the Russian calendar, as follows:

To the Commander of the VIth Army
Von der Goltz Pasha.

On January 6th, after two days' fighting near Miyandowab, the enemy arrived at Sautchbulak. We fought there for two or three days. The enemy was very strong. According to more or less trustworthy news we had, our troops have retreated to Bane. I was with a tribal detachment at Negada. Mohammed Emin had held out with twenty horsemen.

On 11th January I also advanced. The enemy numbered 6,000 infantry and cavalry. Four infantry battalions and a column of cavalry as well as one piece of artillery were deployed against Sautchbulak,

2,000 cavalry and four guns against Negada, which fired on us until the evening. Following news from my right wing I withdrew to avoid capture with my hundred men and two guns. We had ordered the right wing to join us. It was then four hours away from Negada. Seeing the enemy's strength from a distance, they were unable to offer any resistance. The road from Sautchbulak and Mehmed Shah was cut off by the enemy. They withdrew to Ladshan and the Shinova road. The troops at Shinova retreated to us. The enemy troops advancing from the direction of Tabriz and Maragheb sent against Sautchbulak attacked in four groups: 1. Against Sautchbulak; 2. Mehmed Shah; 3. Negada; 4. Shinova. According to my information the strength of each detachment was two batteries, two infantry regiments, and three cavalry regiments, in total about forty thousand men. We have had no reliable news about Nadji Bey and his troops for the past eight days, either about a retreat or resistance. Following the retreat I had all the troops assemble and join me, in order to take up a defensive position in the Rowanduz valley. Our force consists of four hundred infantry, six mountain guns, fifty volunteers, and some Kurdish tribes. The prospects of resistance appears small.

(signed) the Commander of Suldus and the surrounding area.

Amir Aslan.

If I had hoped to learn from this report something more reliable than from the earlier stories, I had been mistaken. Even if one was well-intentioned and avoided certain conclusions that were to be drawn from this telegram, one would still have to say that it was not exactly a model of clarity. I did not do any better by interrogating some of the sick soldiers who arrived from Sautchbulak before I set out on my return journey. They could only tell me that, on account of an imminent attack, all the sick had had to leave town.

Before I rode from Shinova to Sedava, I gave orders to my two Kurds who were to accompany the pack animal to take the same road. However, I waited for them in vain. Had they lost their way? Had they had a fall, or already been captured by the Russians? Although I had always considered them reliable, I could not overcome the feeling that they had perhaps deliberately taken the way to the Russians. This I would have accepted, except that there were thirty thousand rubles in my travelling bag on one of the pack animals.

However, all other considerations were overshadowed by the question of what had happened to the expedition, to Scheubner and my brother Karl Gustav... What would the final result be of all these confused reports and bad rumors? I felt compelled to get to Rayat, where I perhaps could hope for some report or could try to find out something by means of the telegraph.

The distance the column had needed nine hours to cover I now rode in just two. The track was passable and, if it was still iced over here and there, I never once had to dismount. A short distance outside Darlaman I heard merry laughter behind me. Turning, I saw my two missing Kurds coming towards me along the track from Sedava, with the pack animal and the thirty thousand rubles. I took this as a good omen. The two braves had probably been as worried about me as I had been about them.

At Sheikhin-Koi I met Schlimme with the luggage. I sent it back through Rowanduz, and after a short rest traveled to Rayat. Ettam stayed the night there as well. The only telegram he sent was a request for Haidar Bey to come to Panjvin. I myself added a request for information about Scheubner. We both waited in vain for an answer.

All the villages and roads on the way to Rowanduz began filling up with refugees from the Suldus plain. Carrying what little movable goods they called their own, they sought security on Turkish soil. Some brought, on the backs of patient cows, their meager household items: a cradle, stools, worn-out carpets, jugs, copper bowls. They would drive the beasts forward with blows and yells. The children cried because of the cold as they were practically naked. They cried with hunger, as they had had almost nothing to eat for many days. They cried due to fatigue, having been driven for hours through the snow. If one of them was unable to go any further, a sister or brother would carry the child on their back. Parents carried the youngest. They squatted in the snow for short rests. They were unable to sleep for hunger and exhaustion. They sobbed until some compassionate rider gave them a piece of bread.

One of them had managed to carry a few pieces of dried dung with him from the abundant stockpiles outside the huts, and they lit the pieces with difficulty. Women and children warmed themselves, weeping. But after nights that had to be spent outdoors in the snow, in the mornings there were many a small, emaciated body that no tears or wild laments would ever awaken again... No one took care of cattle that remained behind. No one counted the exhausted animals that died a slow, moaning death, with fear and torment in their eyes. They had to go on, far across the border. When boys and girls were unable to go further, their mothers would goad them on with loud tales about the Cossacks wielding their swords upon defenseless children—was that the only choice open to them, the Cossacks or endless flight? What was crueler? Rumors about the destruction of the villages that they had just passed through drove the tired ones on anew: in their over-excited fantasy the enemy possessed a tremendous speed...

I soon realized how pointless it was to try and get information on encounters and positions out of them. They could tell of numerous things, but generally it was nothing but what the rumors had already spread and lacked cohesion. Where were all these poor people to stay once they had crossed the pass? The mountain villages were miserable and poor. They had scarcely enough wheat and rice for themselves. There was only hope: the fraternal hospitality of the simple Muslim for the destitute, particularly for the believer who approached his door in need. Even if there were many hard-hearted and mean people among the dull-witted inhabitants of Kurdistan, in general the old, unwritten law of hospitality, a characteristic of farmers, shepherds and hunters from ancient times still held good.

I reached Rowanduz after a good day's ride and finally bid Ettam Bey farewell. I breathed a sigh of relief. Despite the exaggerated courtesy on his part, I had practically been his prisoner, as I could not speak or write down a single word outside his control. His Kurds had, by the way, already returned home. Perhaps this was also due to his inability to establish his authority over Aslan. I sent a report to Consul Holstein in Mosul, to be forwarded to Field-Marshall Von der Goltz, but learned then that Goltz was in Kirmanshah, in Central Persia. Thus, for the time being, no orders could be expected from him. Later he acknowledged receipt of Aslan's and my own reports, adding that he was unable to send troops to the border near Sautchbulak, but did not believe that a Russian attack would take place.

I set out for Mosul without further ado with Simon of Kelaita, the two men and the pack animal. At Deir-Harir I visited the müdir to learn from him what had happened to my orderly, Luther, whom I had left in his care when he had fallen seriously ill. He led me up a hill not far from the stage-post and told me Luther had regained consciousness for just a few moments and had died two days later. They had dug a grave for him up there and put stones over it so jackals and wolves could not disturb it at night.

From that spot one could overlook the surrounding hills and the Tigris plain, the battlefields of Alexander's Persian campaigns and, beyond, the vast, vast deserts leading to the holy sites of Muslims and Christians—Mecca and Jerusalem. They had laid out the grave facing Mecca so that at Doomsday the dead man might hear the Angel of the Resurrection and thus enjoy eternal life.

They had looked upon this German as one of their own community, and gone to some pains to ensure his eternal peace. I never felt the existence of a true inner bond between us and the simple Turk more strongly than there, at my orderly Luther's grave, with the threat of invasion at the rear and the endless deserts in front of me.

Deeply moved, I continued my way to Erbil. Deep disappointment awaited me there. I had been certain to find news from Scheubner but there was none. One day after my arrival in Mosul on February 6, the first telegrams from him arrived.

XII

How Sautchbulak Was Evacuated

Vali Haidar Bey had left Sautchbulak at the beginning of January. He ordered that Omer Nadji Bey replace him as "Supreme Commander," as he was called at the time. In view of the arrangements made in Mosul, the absurd situation now was that Scheubner was subordinate to Nadji, from whom he had received in Erzerum explicit assurances of his full equality. Thanks to their mutual respect, which had become even deeper during the past months, relations between Scheubner and Omer Nadji remained friendly and open, and withstood the burden of intrigues and occasional misunderstandings. The initiative and the practical military leadership remained in Scheubner's hands during the difficult time that followed.

This state of affairs can be concluded with absolute clarity from a report he submitted to the liaison officer for the Caucasus. The still extant document reads:

Sheherkend (Persia), January 26th, 1916.

Combat Report

After our occupation of Sautchbulak on 29th December 1915, our primary object was to take all measures for the defense of the town. Omer Nadji and I based our decisions on the following premises:

Sautchbulak is situated in a valley closed in on three sides. Owing to the militarily unfavorable geographical location and the complexity of the narrowly built-up town, a defense of the town itself seemed inadvisable, quite apart from the fact that such a defense would have endangered the inhabitants of Sautchbulak who, in the main, were well disposed towards us. Trenches were therefore dug on the heights southeast, southwest, and northeast of the town.

My suggestion of rendering the trenches suitable for prolonged defense by the construction of shelters, the storage of fuel and animal fodder, and placing distance markers was accepted but not put into effect. During our three week stay in the town I was, by the way, the only one who ordered uniforms, saddles and other equipment for the troops and put the town's available resources to use.

The tribes gathered by the Vali of Mosul were sent as a vanguard to Miyandowab (in the direction of Tabriz) as well as to the Suldus plain (in the direction of Urmia). However, it turned out we could get them to perform military duties as advanced posts and patrols.

I commanded 24 men I had trained as cavalry as well as 50 other untrained volunteer horsemen which I used in the capture of Sautchbulak. Apart from this detachment there were 60 other horsemen who could be considered as cavalry if need arose. Understanding that a strong cavalry force was necessary to wage war in that district, I intended to have my infantry mounted and form, through recruitment and the organization of volunteers, the core of a mounted force.

The Russians had retreated from Sautchbulak to Miyandowab and the Suldus plain, where almost daily skirmishes took place with the advance guards. Amongst the tribes, who could not take further booty, a war weariness soon became apparent, which led to many of them going home with or without leave. On January 8th the Vali went southward accompanied by a company, two cannon, thirty horsemen, and some tribes. From this moment on we were cut off from all news from Baghdad and Mosul, as all telegrams directed to the Vali were forwarded directly to him. Thus we did not know if or when the requested reinforcements would reach us. News of troop withdrawals spread immediately among the tribes; the number of withdrawing soldiers was grossly exaggerated.

On January 18th the Russians advanced near Miyandowab with around a thousand cossacks, two pieces of field artillery, and two machine guns. They repelled the tribes and advanced to Inderkash— two hours distant from Sautchbulak. The border battalion (300 men) and two cannons were sent against them the same day. On that day I had sent a sixty-man cavalry patrol to the village of Chillik in the direction of the Suldus plain. During the night I recalled them and on the 19th advanced with 150 cavalry towards Inderkash. The border battalion had occupied some of the hilltops east of this village. The tribes had also occupied several of the hills in front of this position, but in general remained inactive. On my arrival, Lieutenant Thiel took over command of the two guns. The artillery position was well within reach of enemy artillery fire, but they remained outside ours, so a new position was taken up on a hill further forward. At the same time I sent half of my cavalry to occupy some heights on the left wing, and the other half to the right. In the ensuing artillery duel the enemy alternately bombarded our artillery position and my cavalry on the left. Our artillery was successful in hitting the withdrawing Russian columns. Later I gathered my cavalry and advanced with it. A few

Kurds also joined us from the right wing against the enemy. We dismounted twice for foot combat and shot at the enemy's horses, which were hastily taken away. We were able to advance some four kilometers. As our position was very exposed and it was getting dark, and since we had no fodder for the animals, I withdrew to our original position, where the infantry and the two cannon were also assembled. The infantry bivouacked on the heights. During the night strong cavalry patrols were sent against the enemy. It was very cold and there were sporadic snowstorms on that day. The patrols I sent in the direction of enemy-held villages on the morning of the 20th confirmed that they were in enemy hands. At the same time we received news that the majority of the enemy had marched off towards Suldus. During the night the cold had increased and strong, icy snow showers began. The wind was against us that day and the next, so that the soldiers had difficulty in shooting on account of the snow intermittently blowing in their faces. During the night several of the men of the border battalion, who were very inadequately clothed, suffered frozen hands and feet. As the danger of being outflanked by the enemy could not be ruled out, I considered it advisable to withdraw. The border battalion retreated as well and occupied a position closer to Sautchbulak. On my orders, Lieutenant Thiel handed over command of the two guns, as I needed him for other duties. I rode back to the town, had the animals fed, and went to Omer Nadji Bey to report. On my warning him about the possibility of our forces being outflanked from the west, he stated that the road there was well secured by the 150-man gendarme battalion and the 30 horsemen under Amir Aslan Khan. In spite of the assurance regarding the western side of the city, I decided to send a patrol there as well once the horses had been given a well needed rest and time to feed. However, before the patrols went out, the town was attacked from the west and northeast. About twenty of my cavalry men and a few of my animal drivers, who were lodged in a yard to the west of the town were the first to face the enemy and pushed the Russians, who had already crossed the river, back. They held on until the infantry, including my company, reached the spot. My horsemen and I later occupied a height to the east of the town, as I could not risk a cavalry battle. It was only from there that I was able to gain an overview of the situation. I had my cavalrymen open fire from that position on the Russian troops advancing to the west.

I had ordered Lieutenant Thiel to secure the baggage, which he did under heavy machine-gun fire directed on our courtyard (due to betrayal by a spy).

Lieutenant Leverkuehn I and I rode back to the town to recover our files and money that had been left in his quarters. We were unsuccessful in this, as the pack animal driver had deserted. I was, however, able to enter the town and recover it later that night.

The enemy, who had advanced from Inderkash during the course of the battle, was halted by our infantry and artillery. The guns brought from Erzerum had been rendered useless right from the beginning because their axles had been bent. The Russians directed heavy rifle and machine-gun fire at the town before nightfall.

That night the troops bivouacked on the heights in heavy snow and freezing cold. The enemy strength that day must have been over 1,000 cavalry (two Cossack regiments), an infantry battalion, two field guns, as well as machine-guns.

The battle resumed on January 21st with a fusillade by the Russians who advanced from the direction of Inderkash. The enemy also soon resumed firing from the west and the battle was joined within a short time.

The battalion's train, with my own, withdrew towards the village of Bairam, south of Sautchbulak, during the morning. After consulting with Omer Nadji, I took my cavalry to reinforce the left wing on the plain extending south of Sautchbulak. There I took up a position by a tomb where there were several officers watching the battle. The troops on the left wing, composed of border battalions and parts of the regular battalion, were on the heights southwest of the town. Fierce gun and machine-gun fire was directed against it. I advanced with the cavalry, ending with a gallop under heavy machine-gun fire which slight losses, to the infantry position, where my men dismounted and formed a reserve. I watched the battle, with my officers, from a trench for some time. As I left the position I received the report that the company southeast of us was pulling back, and that Cossacks were on the heights to the northwest, probably with the intention of encircling us. In order to protect the infantry from them and, if necessary, cover its retreat, I rode up the mountains in the west. We found a group from tribal fighters in an observation post there, who told us a troop of about fifty Cossacks had appeared but had retreated. Following this news and as an occupation of the mountain sides was impossible due to deep snow, I rode back to the plain to protect the retreating infantry from being pursued by the Cossacks. However, the Russians contented themselves with keeping the infantry under fire. Then I rode to our artillery position on the eastern heights to see how the battle was proceeding, finding that here too the infantry was retreating. The artillery commander informed me that a general retreat had been ordered. Thus I decided to cover the retreat of the artillery with my cavalry against any pursuing Cossacks. During the retreat our troops were heavily bombarded by enemy artillery. As a result of the cold, their exertions, and their inadequate clothing, a number of soldiers froze to death. Quarters were set up in the village of Usundere, three hours distant.

The retreat continued slowly over the next few days, with some days being used for the troops to rest. The detachment is located in and around Sheherkend, about forty kilometers from Sautchbulak. The sick and the heavy baggage were taken to Saqqez. The detachment has recovered and is in good order. I myself am busy with the further organization of my cavalry.

My losses are: I. Troops: 8 men dead, 20 slightly wounded and frost-bitten; II. Horses: 4 dead, 4 wounded. Among the frost-bitten are the following officers: von Scheubner, Lieutenant Thiel, Lieutenant Abdul Bari, and Lieutenant Memduh.

Von Scheubner-Richter

The tremendous difficulties of this retreat through the snow of the high mountains are only discernible between the lines of this short military report. Along narrow paths, through deep snow, the retreating column headed in single file for Gildeberdan. The night was dark, but the snow shone. It was only later that the moon rose, glowing milkily through the snow clouds. The worn-out train slowly dragged itself across the white hills, now up, then down. Here and there a man would sit at the edge of the path. The falling snow made him white and damp. He did not move, but in his total exhaustion he slept himself into death. A twitching mule lay on the ground, its load strewn all around—weapons and rucksacks, ammunition boxes, spades, pack-saddles. The powdery snow covered it all. The exhausted men murmured and moaned perhaps a complaint, perhaps a prayer. Under their colored headgear one could see the stiff, contorted faces of the Arabs. They had never known what winter could be, and looked horrified into this cold hell. In the twilight cries and shots were heard on all sides... Men strayed from the path and were smothered by the snow. No one went to rescue them—no one could. Nobody could walk away from the path, not even horses. Some compassionate souls shot in the air or shouted with their last remaining strength at the wounded, but often there was no answer; they faded away in a merciful sleep...

Sheherkend, from where Scheubner sent his report, lay some 40 kilometers south of Sautchbulak, and 25 northwest of the Persian city of Saqqez. From a military point of view, the place was unsuitable for a prolonged stay. Scheubner chose instead the little town of Bowkan, 12 km northeast of Sheherkend, where the detachment arrived on the 1st of February. Omer Nadji set up quarters a little further to the south at Karava, 10 km north of Saqqez.

Bowkan lies on the river Tatavi, whose source lies in the mountain range along the Turkish-Persian border. It first flows east, turns north and pours into lake Urmia. Bowkan lies at the very end of the bend northwards, its southern side protected by the almost 2000 meter-high Bedshin-Basar. The Tatavi valley is flanked on the eastern side by a mountain ridge. On the other side of the ridge, perhaps 20-25 km to the west, the river Dshagatu flows north, then a little northwest. The valley between the two rivers, close to the town of Miyandowab, is only five kilometers wide. East of the Dshagatu, the only town of any importance was Sainkaleh, at roughly the same height as Bowkan; and then came a mountainous region that, totally unexplored and inaccessible, was not considered for troop movements.

From Bowkan and through the Tatavi and Dshagatu valleys at Miyandowab, Scheubner threatened the Russian lines of communication between Tabriz and Sautchbulak, and the border pass at Sheikhin-Koi. It was unlikely, if not impossible, that the Russians would attempt to advance on this routs to the Mesopotamian plain and the rear of the Turkish army fighting south of Baghdad, as long as communications with their rear were threatened from Bowkan.

Should they, however, have chosen the Saqqez—Bane—Panjvin—Suleimaniye route, Bowkan was the first defense position, and from where, by a slow retreat, the Russians could have been held up for a long time. Even large contingents may be successfully fought against using guerilla tactics in the mountains.

Admittedly Scheubner's position in Bowkan was very exposed. The Russians could attack him from east, north, and west. Nevertheless he considered that the opportunity to withdraw south, and the advantage that he could attack from Bowkan, Sautchbulak or Miyandowab at any time, was worth the exposed position.

When the Russians attacked Sautchbulak they must have expected that the Turkish occupation forces would try to withdraw to the border, to the pass they had advanced from. Instead they had advanced southeastwards, that is, further into the disputed Persian territory.

Scheubner could not have known at the time how desperately the British government was urging St. Petersburg for Russian troops to go to the aid of the British corps in Mesopotamia. Under the general command of Field-Marshall Von der Goltz, the Turks were making progress. The fall of Kut-el-Amara, where thirty thousand British troops were trapped, was threateningly close. Only from post-war publications, such as the memoirs of British Civil Commissioner for Mesopotamia, Sir Arnold T. Wilson, came bitter public criticism the British felt for the failure of the Russians to help. General Baratov in fact did advance from the Caspian Sea and took the city of Hamadan on the Baghdad-Teheran road on 15th December 1915. However, he had to consider his very long lines of communication. The shortest way to come to the aid of the British would have been from Tabriz through Sautchbulak. Here the Russian troops made no progress, halted by the Scheubner-Nadji detachment. If the two had been unable to accomplish their original plan of going to the Caucasus, they had now found a new task of at least equally great importance—and this one they did fulfill.

XIII

Meeting in Bowkan

Bowkan, that small Kurdish town of about five thousand inhabitants was the trading centre of a relatively large area, and consequently had a strikingly large bazaar. Almost all the goods were Russian or, at any rate, imported through Russia. To judge by the volume of trade at the market, the population of the region seemed to enjoy a fairly uniform, tolerable standard of living. The region was owned—Bowkan and fourteen villages—by a single landowner, 18-year-old Serdar Ali Khan.

He lived pretty much like a fairy-tale prince in his castles. He always wore two medals on his pretty Russian uniform. Any time he went out, he would have a flock of colorful Kurds with him. He exerted almost unlimited power over his subjects, from whom he collected taxes. He will surely remember with mixed feelings that winter's day on which war broke into his princely idyll in the form of Scheubner's riders. His father, who had been court-martialed and found guilty of pro-Russian activities by a Turkish commander, had been shot by a firing squad the previous year. He himself had spent three years in the Cadet Corps in Moscow. His sympathies were certainly with the Russians, and he made no secret of it. This was only natural, as everything above the level of wild, strife-torn Kurdistan, he had seen and experienced in Russia.

In spite of all this, he declared himself fully neutral towards the expedition, showing Scheubner and Leverkuehn unrestrained hospitality. Gradually Scheubner, whose knowledge of Russian stood him in good stead, succeeded in overcoming Serdar's initial mistrust, which in turn alarmed Dr. Fuad, the fanatic Turk. This nationalistic teacher of the young Turkish officers, as one can safely call him, felt no pangs of conscience when his brave Anatolian countrymen perished of their wounds for lack of adequate attention, but watched with hawk's eyes to ensure that German influence would never, under any circumstances, be too great. Therefore he befriended Serdar, using the latter's strong religious feelings, in order to win him over completely to the Turkish cause. It had also been he who had taught Amir Aslan to read and write Turkish, and in general—and this is his undeniable achievement—all really lasting friendships between Turks and Kurds were owed to him.

Karl Gustav Leverkuehn (I)—
drawing by Otto Kursell

Serdar Ali Khan—drawing by Leverkuehn I.

Scheubner, however, hadn't any interest in these petty jealousies, but in getting things done. It was unimportant by whom the Serdar was made to keep his promise of neutrality, so long as it actually happened. In this sense the reports of Russian atrocities against the Kurdish population that came in all of February and partly confirmed had a positive effect. It had been established that the Russians had many unarmed groups among them, who followed the infantry in order to plunder, and these groups had also massacred women and children with the excuse of having been shot at in the villages. Thus, an 8-year-old boy was brought to Scheubner, and the doctor diagnosed serious sabre wounds to his head and hands. The boy declared he had been ill-treated by a Cossack. Such scenes did not fail to have their effect on the Serdar; and if one could not fully deny that he had kept in communication with the Russians at the beginning, he was certainly becoming increasingly friendlier towards Germans and Turks. By referring to him in the bazaar, Scheubner was able to put up a notice reminding the population to do nothing against the neutrality, and guaranteeing them payment for all military purchases.

In general there was no cause for complaints. A spy who had fled had his camels, cattle, and horses confiscated; and a certain mayor, who was rather too eager to spread news about the strength and deployment of the expedition, had his horse taken from him in order to render his indiscreet rides more difficult.

Political propaganda in Azerbaijan had been rendered almost impossible by the Russian occupation. Vali Haidar Bey and Omer Nadji had tried several times to win over some of the tribes. Some refused on the grounds of their close ties with the Russians, whereas others were discouraged by mistakes. For instance, the vali refused one of these tribes time to think things over in the roughest possible manner. On another occasion, while on his way south, he bombarded the undefended town of Sainkaleh, although no Russians were there. This admittedly happened due to a false assumption, but the excuse was of little avail. In addition there were the extraordinary difficulties of transport in this grim mountain winter, which can perhaps be appreciated from the fact that, out of eight postal messengers, seven froze to death on the road. As if this were not enough, the vali had sent the good Russian maps seized during the capture of Sautchbulak to Constantinople to be reprinted without making a copy first. This was the cost of having a man, who had never served in the army, at the head of an important detachment operating under the most difficult circumstances.

The villages were teeming with false news about a Russian advance. No doubt these were systematically and deliberately spread; and Azmi, whom Scheubner entrusted with the assignment of finding those responsible and delivering them up for punishment, was faced with a Sysiphean task. No indication existed of a Russian further advance, yet their proximity called for all imaginable precautions. Scheubner kept permanent observation posts northwest and north of Bowkan in the direction of Sautchbulak and Miyandowab, in Tasekaleh and Üchtepe.

The forces under Scheubner and Nadji now consisted of the Border Battalion under Major Mukhtar bey and the original battalion, made up of three companies, under Captain Veli Bey. The latter was a religious and morally sound Muslim, who prayed conscientiously and regularly. In many ways he was the counterpart of the free-thinking Dr. Fuad, whose lack of orthodoxy he lamented, as he lamented the easy going lifestyle of Nadji who, though in general was admired by him, must have caused him occasional disquiet.

Steadfast on duty, responsible as a leader of his men, fatherly to the officers, to whom he sometimes also showed traces of fine humor, he was more the old-fashioned type of army sergeant than a modern officer. His capacity for retaining what he learnt was remarkable. While he spoke French very slowly and deficiently, the number of expressions and words he employed without any affectation was phenomenal. He was also brave, and shrewd in the choice of defensive positions. All he lacked for greater military undertakings was the educational background. This is why, at Sautchbulak, he sometimes did not give the proper order at the right moment, he hesitated, and finally let the reins slip out of his hands.

The Anatolian soldiers were in general austere and very efficient. In the case of sickness or injury, however, their whole nature changed. Then, one realized that they had not been brought up to put up with and hide pain. A similar lack of upbringing probably explained desertions too. These simple soldiers, mostly peasants from remote districts, were quite childish; this remained the same in regard to their duties, and their attempts to outwit their superiors. If they felt homesick, or something displeased them, they simply ran away. At the same time they possessed many good traits, often sharing their scanty food and pay with those less fortunate than themselves, in true keeping with Islamic teachings. As they were easily influenced, it was important to address them in clear and impressive terms to awaken their enthusiasm for an idea, and demonstrate to them the incompatibility of a weak sense of duty with their religious and patriotic feelings. Scheubner never failed to do this.

Things were very different with the Border Battalion. It had been in the mountains of northwest Azerbaijan for quite some time, mostly consisting of reserves from the vilayet of Mosul and, owing to its composition, almost useless for military purposes. Moreover, only two companies, of about two hundred men in total had been left. The others had been taken away by Vali Haidar Bey, as he had one of the two cannon. The remaining one was unserviceable and had to be sent to Baghdad for repairs. Its gunners were assigned to Scheubner. After a Persian Lieutenant Colonel, Abdul Kader Bey, had joined the expedition with 10 men, he had around 150 to 200 horsemen in his own unit divided into two squadrons of three columns each.

Added to these there were varying numbers of tribesmen from the border districts, sometimes up to two thousand, which were put under Scheubner's charge at Omer Nadji's request. They were Kurds, only with strong Persian traits, and so less hardy than the ones from Turkish territory. Their combat value was small. Still, they mounted splendidly, and their horses' speed was by far superior to that of the Russians. They were useful for spontaneous assaults and routs, but were an obstacle or hindrance for planned operations because of their unreliability. They either did not appear in time, or they did not wait for the time of attack.

As already explained in the chapter on the Armenians, the Kurds, mixed with other populations, inhabited the region from central Anatolia to Persia. However, they kept to themselves in their own humble villages, as Turks, Armenians, and Syrians lived in the small towns and cities of the valleys. It is said the Kurds are the Kardukh mentioned by Xenophon; their language, as a great scholar once explained to me, would be halfway between Old Latin and Lithuanian. Still, I have never known a European who could speak their language, of which there are many dialects.

The Kurds stand at the most primitive stage of culture and do not even have songs of their own. We looked for ornaments or gadgets we could bring back as souvenirs, but all we found were tobacco-pipe-bowls, whose decorations had been made by burning with a red-hot iron. Instead, we came across many cases of ruthless damage against their own people, and in relation to this I would like to mention the case of an agha or noble who—unheard of amongst Kurds—spent three years in Paris and acquired some medical knowledge. He then opened a big pharmacy in which he hung up large posters about leprosy. But Kurdish horsemen devastated it and pulled up the floor, suspecting treasures were hidden underneath.

Women worked in the fields, taking care of the thin cattle. At twenty they looked old and ugly, shy and depressed. Amongst the men, who were relaxed, one came across well-built physiques. They were used to making a large part of their living by plundering peaceful settlements, especially those of Christians. They did not lack courage but had anything but chivalrous characters. One of their proverbs, which one must not forget if one has to deal with them, is, "Kiss the hand you can't cut off..."

The area inhabited by Kurds south of Lake Urmia to the Khanikin-Kirmanshah district on the Baghdad-Teheran road, in which Scheubner's expedition operated, was largely unexplored territory, and even the best maps showed extensive blank areas which meant *terra incognita*. With support from his government, the French explorer de Morgan carried out studies in the area south of Lake Urmia in the 1890s and published, in two splendid volumes, his *Mission Scientifique en Perse*. In it he included Sautchbulak as the capital of the Mukri Kurds' zone.

Soane, an Englishman, traveled in disguise in the area around Suleimaniye, somewhat further south, on the Turkish side of the border, publishing a graphic account of his experiences in his book *In Mesopotamia and Kurdistan in Disguise*. He had great sympathy for the Kurds and held them in higher esteem than we had cause to. We entered their territory, however, at a time when the war between the Turks and the Russians flowed back and forth over their land, intensifying their instincts of robbery and greed. Faithfulness and loyalty were deprived of all meaning: why should these children of nature lean towards one or other of the two powers, when all they wanted was to be left alone to live in freedom? In that sense they felt happiest living under the loose Persian domination.

The case was different with Abdul Bari and his horsemen, as they were from a region south of Erzerum, which had long been under Turkish domination, and so the question of belonging to a power had been unambiguously solved. Nevertheless, their sympathies and affection tended wholly towards us Germans. They fully understood the difference between the greed and lechery of the Turkish leaders, and the simple life, focused on duty, that Scheubner and his men led. They sensed the care and attention of the German officers, whose devotion to their strict, caring leaders created educational opportunities which could have had much greater impact if our assignment had been more precisely defined and consistently supported from home.

Inescapably, Scheubner, who had not been only an officer before the start of the expedition but had been a Consul, had, again and again, to face certain important political challenges. He tried to resolve them loyally in the spirit of the alliance. But he always noticed that his subordination to the vali and later to Omer Nadji was not understood by the Kurdish aghas. One could understand how dangerous it was to put a European, a German, under Turkish command, in a country where external appearances were decisive. Scheubner acted as he deemed appropriate for a German officer, and he did have some success; but to have real influence with the Kurds he lacked the necessary vanity and money. If a Kurdish chieftain offered him ammunition, he had to refer him to Nadji, who paid him with shiny, golden, new Turkish pound coins, re-minted from German twenty-mark pieces... All friendly declarations evaporated—he who paid had the prestige. Not even the politest assurance could disguise to the Kurds the fact that the previously-announced deliveries of German weapons and money always failed to arrive.

The matter would have been worse if military consideration had not compensated a great deal. That Scheubner dominated in this aspect, that his unit was the backbone of the whole expedition, was evident to the Kurds as well.

He worked with Leverkühn I on an exercise manual which was diligently put into practice in Bowkan. Great attention was given to the care of animals, weapons, and the equipment in general. At first such a manual was totally new to the people, but they made sense of it. From this daily drill a force emerged that knew how to adapt to the terrain and was equally capable of conducting patrols, attack or defense.

The tribes adopted a little of Scheubner's and his men's thoughts and ideas, or at least had a feeling of trust. They understood the different nature and superiority of the Germans. After all, Leverkuehn I, who was in charge of training and commanding the forces, had won their hearts. He was considered bullet-proof after he had stood up in the middle of a fight and had, while standing right in the middle of Russian machine-gun fire, written a report. Later I asked him about it and he answered with a little hesitation and shyness: He had seen the line about to give way and thought this might prevent the threat of a flight—which it did. He added, "I also wanted to test myself as to how far one can go with that rotten son-of-a-gun we all have inside us."

While the troops could be fed on local produce or from Turkish stores, there were many other necessities that had to be satisfied by being purchased, especially as we were in Persia as friends, not conquerors. Scheubner had brought about 130,000 marks in Turkish gold and silver coins, but there had been considerable expenses incurred in the form of payments for uniforms, pack-animals, supplies and the troops' pay, not to mention payments made to tribal chieftains and messengers to Daghestan while he was still on Turkish territory. Now he needed horses for his whole unit. I was able to send him a small sum in Turkish pounds, as well as the 30,000 rubles I had worried about so much in the Darlaman Mountains via the insecure road through Suleimaniye and Bane. Scheubner, however, could afford to use Russian rubles in Bowkan bazaar. Who would change the currency in his possession for the Persian tomans he needed? He solved the problem by having the whole civilian population dig trenches in the snow. This displeased the Jewish shopkeepers tremendously. They sent a deputation to him to see if they could buy their way out. During the negotiations, carried on with oriental politeness and length, Scheubner explained that it would be impossible, but that instead of digging trenches they could be helpful to him by changing money and procuring equipment. A rate of exchange was agreed, and both parties were satisfied.

Scheubner did everything within his power to oppose food speculation by fixing maximum prices. He appointed Azmi Bey as town commander and police chief, and secured the consent of the Serdar's administrator for all his decrees. Nevertheless, he lived as if he was on a strange island in the middle of the Persian mountains, with a weak force, opposing a strong enemy, in an atmosphere of distrust, and with allies who liked to saddle him with responsibilities but tried to prevent his receiving information or taking part in political activity. Leverkuehn I was his only real aide and they worked marvellously together, with the spirit of August 1914 and natural dedication to the great cause always in the forefront of their minds.

Leverkuehn I had a poetical and philosophical character, a person at the highest level of education of his time. He admired Scheubner's political intuition and his skill in dealing with people, his natural leadership, his noble and great character. They were bound by the most beautiful friendship that can exist—one based on carrying forward a common objective, a friendship made stronger by shared difficulties and dangers, since they lived under the constant threat of falling prisoners to the Russians, or being stabbed in the back for some vile bounty. What they yearned for was the possibility that during this war a way might be cleared, there in the East, for Germany's future, with their participation. They were always aware that the final decision would come from the Western Front.

Their thoughts were very often there. In my brother Karl Gustav's papers from Persia were the following verses:

Bowkan, April 1916

When the Verdun Offensive Started

Quietly sounds a mighty choir—
Reaching from afar our ear
In this magic Orient here,
To which the West can now aspire.

A cry our breast will elevate:
At what time will the hour knell,
When we can all our people tell
The farthest East does us await?

XIV

Fresh Fighting

The mountains around Bowkan lay in the loveliest March sunshine. The rivers had grown broad and mighty, roaring thunderously through the silent nights. In a field to the west of the town, the Serdar had set up a riding range, where the flags of the allied powers, German states and provinces, now fluttered. A gymkhana was to be held.

Nadji Bey and his officers arrived in Bowkan during the morning. Leverkuehn I, with Memduh as interpreter, led a squadron in different movements. A simulated charge was carried out, followed by a fusillade on foot. Nadji made a spirited speech in Turkish which deeply impressed even those who did not understand the language.

There followed races and jumping contests for officers, troops, and the inhabitants of the town. The Serdar won a gold medal as first prize in the jumping competition for officers. Leverkeuhn I was the winner of a flat race for officers. After lunch there was a revolver shooting competition, in which Abdul Bari took the winner's palm. There were many entertainments for soldiers and the inhabitants of the town.

In the midst of this harmonious event, however, came disquieting reports about the enemy. The activities of patrols and advanced posts had never slackened, nor had the stream of refugees. A Cossack division had approached to within three hours distance from Bowkan, but had retreated. In the last week of February a hundred-man detachment had attacked our advance guard on the road from Bowkan to Sautchbulak. They had been repulsed; but the commander of the post, Musa Bey, a young officer, who had studied Law in Constantinople, had been killed in action with a tribal chieftain and several men. On the same evening Leverkuehn and Azmi rode by chance with twenty riders to inspect the post and obtain reliable information. It turned out that the Russians had withdrawn to Sautchbulak with a loss of 10 men. From then on these skirmishes at advance posts were a daily occurrence, with comparable losses on both sides.

It was impossible to check the persistent reports of Russian troop movements and bridge-building. Scheubner, however, had reason to doubt their accuracy. A patrol made up of tribesmen arrived from the southeast, bringing a letter from their commander, Lieutenant Schadow of the 7th Light Cavalry. It was a painful reminder of the lack of all superior orders that would have made a coordinated campaign possible in the various regions of Persia. At least it was a relief to know that there was another German officer together with Persian Kurdish tribes at Bihar and that consequently the Russian advance on the Hamadan-Khanikin-Baghdad road had not yet advanced so far that the Russians could pose a threat from the southeast as well.

Suddenly word arrived that the Russians had evacuated Sautchbulak on account of an epidemic. This rumor also proved to be only partly true. While there had been many deaths, and one or another unit had moved out, the city was still held by the Russians. While everything remained calm in the north, there were lively Russian movements near Sainkaleh, in the Dchagatu valley, thirty kilometers east of Bowkan. Unfortunately, exactly at this moment, one of the advance posts had to be given up, as the thaw-swollen Tatavi could no longer be crossed by horses. The Russians attacked and occupied several localities. In the latest fighting, which had become more serious, Major Tevfik Bey, one of the most agreeable and capable of the Kurdish leaders, met his death, with many of his people.

Early darkness and pouring rain put an end to the gymkhana in Bowkan. On the 7th March, because of the alarming reports that had been received, Leverkuehn I rode with Azmi at the head of a strong patrol to Aziz Khan's outpost at Uchtepe. The Russians had received reinforcements—two thousand men, Aziz Khan claimed. In the morning, while Scheubner and his company took up a position on a hill north of the town, Leverkuehn I advanced with his patrol, reinforced by Aziz's men. A short while later they were shot at and had to turn back because of thick mist. The enemy followed on other hills running parallel but could not dislodge them from their advantageous position. A counterattack was surprisingly successful when Kurdish reinforcements arrived. The Russians had about 300 mounted regulars, a machine-gun and an artillery piece. Approximately a thousand unarmed Persian tribal horsemen, presumably to take part in looting, followed them. Between 80 and 120 Russians were casualties that day. We were able to verify this because of the number of transport wagons we observed. The not only took their wounded away, but also their dead, to be buried in consecrated ground in Tabriz.

Scheubner's force, together with the population of the town, worked feverishly extending defensive positions. From the south came reports that were impossible to confirm that the Russians had taken Kirmanshah. In the long run all these tales of Russian successes could not fail to make an impression on the Persian population. It was to be feared that the Kurdish tribal horsemen would also flee. Scheubner thus decided to adopt a more offensive strategy. On March 13th he sent Ressa Bey with fifty men to the

Dchagatu river, which was generally the front line between the Russians and the Turks. He hoped to capture one of the most dangerous enemy chieftains, Adjamen Sam-Sam, on the opposite bank. He crossed the river by boat, entered Sainkaleh, but was unable to catch Sam-Sam. In spite of this, the appearance of Scheubner's forces on the opposite bank boosted morale significantly and had a good good political effect on the population. As news from Bihar indicated that the Russians were deploying east of the Dchagatu and in the Miyandowab region, on March 19th the whole detachment carried out a reconnaissance raid to the north, advancing with the main body of troops as far as Rahimkhan. The Russians were thrown back on Miyandowab with heavy losses.

There was fighting all day long on March 20th. The diary records:

Monday, March 20th

Herr von Scheubner was in charge of all advancing troops (besides the soldiers, several hundred mostly mounted Kurds). Ressa Bey commanded the right wing, Mussa Bey the center, Lieutenant Leverkuehn the left wing.

The Russians retreated from the height near Saultepe, (45 mins. from Miyandowab). The hill was taken by Mussa, and then held by the left wing. It had been well prepared for defense by the Russians.

From there, and from the village of Saultepe there was fighting until evening. The Russians fired a considerable number of shells using their artillery as well as their machine-gun. Our losses were 4 dead (Bana-Ashiret), 2 wounded (one of them Azmi Bey, right arm) and 4 horses wounded.

The force withdrew in the evening. Our objective to surprise and disturb the Russians and ascertain the situation in Miyandowab had been achieved.

On March 29th Scheubner, with a small unit, left for Saqqez in order to inspect the supply lines and improve the deficient postal communications. It turned out that he had to continue to the border and finally via Suleimaniye to Mosul, where he arrived in mid-April.

Soon after his departure a new operation was started. The balance of power had inclined slightly in favor of the Turks. Even the Serdar was now training infantry soldiers. They lived in tents outside the town and performed dances at Aziz Khan's wedding accompanied by drums and pipes. As for the Russians, their strength had decreased, at least according to reports from the spies. Nadji planned an attack on Sautchbulak and, in order to conceal his advance northwards, ordered the bombardment of the town of Sainkaleh, east of the Jagatu, on April 5th. The fire was returned.

Leverkuehn I and his riders were placed under Major Muhtar Bey's command who, as leader of the tribesmen, was to keep a part of the Russians busy by real as well as feigned attacks. He had two mountain guns with him, which had to be guarded by Scheubner's cavalrymen, owing to the unreliability of the Kurds.

They first advanced eastwards. Behind the mountains stretched the green plain. The Dchagatu river glimmered in the distance. Major Muhtar of the Border Batallion was a friendly, fat man with scars from several campaigns. The Kurds moved north under his leadership. Leverkuehn I had departed earlier with his horsemen and the artillery along the swollen Dchagatu and across the fertile plain. Here and there they came upon sizable settlements on both river banks. Further away snowy peaks rose over the grey, rugged, pointed mountains. It was a bright spring day. The sky was overcast with large, fast-moving clouds. A strong wind was blowing and there were occasional showers.

It was evening when they arrived at the village of Ermenibulak. The Agha, the tribal head, had a perfect reception arranged. Leverkeuhn I rode to a hill by the river before nightfall to inspect the battlefield-to-be. On his way back he saw numerous flocks being driven back to the village. Lowing cattle crowded among rams, sheep and goats. Calves and lambs were lowing and bleating fearfully. Brown-skinned Kurdish women yelled impatiently at them with rough voices. One realized, however, how much they loved the animals. Some would pick out the lambs and kids from the herd, carrying them safely in their arms. They would fondle the little animals and laugh, showing their incredibly white teeth. Others milked. Calm shepherds walked with their herds—a scene of great peace in the center of a war zone where nearby half-abandoned settlements reminded one of the blows of fate.

On the 7th of April, after another day's march, the troops were in front of Miyandowab, in a plain surrounded by beautiful mountains. Trees could be seen in the distance surrounding the little town. Kurds, dressed in their wrinkled and flowing clothes, rode up from three directions. Many were also on foot, the majority unarmed. They were driven by elation mixed with curiosity, lust for plunder and a dark, religious drive. All these hordes were in constant motion. The color of their clothes glimmered and the barrels of their rifles shone in the sun. Handsome horses pranced spiritedly, neighing impatiently in the morning air. The leaders, riding back and forth, gave orders. The Turkish officers went from one group to another. Shouts, orders, and conversations filled the wide space like the buzzing of bees.

Preparationi for battle was complete. The major had distributed the plan to the chieftains the evening before. The tribal infantry—the ashirets— from the region of Bane, who had expressly requested this task, were to advance against the bridge over the Dchagatu and the Saultepe hill under the command of the Caucasian volunteer leader Mirza. The mounted tribesmen set out from their quarters in Rahimkhan before sunrise and supported the infantry during the initial attack. The artillery detachment was to follow the mounted ashirets. As it turned out, the mounted ashirets left Rahimkhan too late.

The major had expected that the Russians would concentrate all their forces in their positions from Saultepe hill as far as the Dchagatu. He would then be able, using the cavalry, to cut through the line between the Tatavi and the hill to the east of Saultepe and capture the Russian flank and rear. This could only succeed if the agreed plan was faithfully carried out. However, after the mounted Kurds had departed too late, two of the tribal leaders, without waiting for orders, led their men straight to the right wing, and they came under fire in the plain where there was almost no cover. With that the battle began, and the center and left wing came under fire as well.

The various units did not approach the enemy in a disciplined manner. Many shot blindly, out of range of the enemy, who occupied a wide defensive line with strong forces. Artillery was quickly brought forward. The major asked Leverkeuhn I to send a squadron of cavalry to both the right and left, to act as a sort of backbone for the confused melee of tribesmen, who had taken cover as best they could. The remainder swarmed out in front of the guns, whose fire had some impact on a portion of the enemy position. This, however, could not compare with the effect of the Russian guns, which were located in a favourable position on the other side of the Dchagatu and used excellently.

A long drawn-out skirmish ensued. Soon communication between the center and the flanks was cut. One could only just see some of what was happening by using binoculars. Leverkuehn I volunteered to ride over to the left wing and report back.

He was accompanied by a few horsemen. The zone of fire was crossed with maximum speed. The horses, as yet unused to the whistle of bullets, galloped on as fast as they could. The greater part of the Kurds had found good cover behind the houses of an abandoned village. The enemy faced them from a trench on a hill. Leverkeuhn I discussed the situation with the Turkish officer commanding the Kurds, then returned at the gallop. He was thus able to report to the major that a charge would be possible, but it would incur heavy casualties. Additionally, the Kurds' attitude was doubtful, and control of the hill was only worthwhile if a further advance was contemplated. The major shook his head and gloomily asked if a demonstration of strength should be turned into a campaign of conquest?

Meanwhile a second messenger returned from the right wing to report that the regular cavalry were running short of ammunition. He also delivered a garbled report about a ceasefire and a partial Kurdish withdrawal. Leverkeuhn I swung his horse round and galloped to the right flank. He found his men in a tolerable position but the shortage of ammunition was serious. Well covered by the river, the enemy had advanced close to the right flank, from where they were directing well-aimed artillery fire.

Leverkeuhn I was hardly 100 meters from his men's position when he noticed Kurdish riders approaching from the far eastern flank. He went to them and tried, as well as he could, to explain where they should take up positions. It was hopeless to try to drive them back to their old ones. He shouted and gesticulated, as did the interpreter, to no avail. He raged against the fleeing men, lashing them with his riding crop, screeching, screaming and indicating with his outstretched hand the line along the slope they should occupy. The Kurds ducked under his lash, trying to escape it. They stared at him, frightened and abashed, but without understanding of what was required of them.

The enemy noticed worthwhile targets: the bullets whizzed and the artillery fired rapidly and accurately. The wounded staggered back, groaning, while others remained behind moaning. Able bodied men rushed past them in panic; no one wanted to help them.

A general flight soon began. If it continued, Leverkeuhn I and his cavalry would have been isolated and become the useless victims to a superior enemy. He turned his horse, leaving the Kurds, and rushed back to the front line. In the noisy confusion he became separated from his men. He was all alone amidst Russian and Turkish bullets.

Up front he came upon a few stragglers at the front line. Most of his horsemen had ridden off without his orders. Could he have blamed the commander who was also a Kurd? He did not know any better and had only withdrawn when the whole flank had been exposed. He did the right thing in the end.

Leverkeuhn I rode back as well. The major had long been retreating with the artillery...

But what has happened to the units that had attacked Sautchbulak under Omer Nadji to the northeast? They took the town almost without a fight. Only the Kurdish vanguard had briefly exchanged fire with the retreating Russians.

Evidently the Russians had considered themselves not strong enough to counter simultaneous attacks on Miyandowab and Sautchbulak. They had given up Sautchbulak and defended Miyandowab to avoid the risk of losing Tabriz by splitting their forces.

After this Nadji advanced into the Suldus plain to within 30 km of Urmia. In one of the local villages, the Kurds plundered a depot containing Russian uniforms and supplies of tea, sugar, and other foodstuffs. On the other hand, supplies for Nadji's infantry that had made very demanding forced marches began getting scarce, so he was forced to give up further attacks.

It had been ordered that if Nadji was successful, but Major Muhtar Bey suffered a defeat, the latter was to move to Sautchbulak. Communications, however, failed, and Muhtar did not know Nadji had been successful. He heard instead that Nadji had withdrawn to the Leidyan plain close to the border, and then crossed it retreating to Darlaman. At this time the Russians had four to five thousand regular troops, and three thousand Kurdish, Armenian and Persian volunteers in the region south of Lake Urmia facing, on the Turkish side, 1,000 Border Guards near Darlaman and east of it, and Muhtar's and Nadji's detachment, and some reserves near Suleimaniye, altogether about 800 men. Thus it appeared dangerous to Muhtar to go to Sautchbulak. Neither could he remain in Bowkan, as the Russians counterattacked, infantry and cavalry advancing on the town in five columns in a quadrant. Muhtar retreated across high mountains to the border.

On April 9th he reached Gildeberdan, on the 10th Gülolan, Suyenas the next day, and on the 12th Pairasta on the river Kalvi (Lesser Zab.) There was a lot of water in it, as it had rained fairly heavily during the previous days. To cross it with loaded pack-animals, or to trust the guns to a tiny kelek seemed too risky to him. So he had to give up on the original destination, the border town of Serdesht, on the opposite bank. The decision fell on Panjvin, which, however, meant a long and arduous southeastward march.

The region was poor and apparently little traveled, for the inhabitants were shy and the villages dirty and miserable. Paths were steep, stony or muddy, and crossed many deep and roaring small rivers. The only blessing for the eye was the profusion of trees which allowed the impression of barren uplands of Bowkan to fade. They were all happy when finally, on April 16th, they saw Panjvin among its pleasant, gentle hills.

The rest they were hoping for was of short duration. There was a serious shortage of straw and barley in Panjvin, such that the stay there became far too expensive. Moreover, it was ascertained that Nadji had not crossed the border at all, but had returned to Karava, his old quarters. The Russian attack on Bowkan had only been an isolated operation but led to a permanent occupation.

Under these circumstances it was advisable to march back to Bowkan, on the shortest route through Sevan Ben and Bane. The opportunity arose, on the way, to improve the poor supply conditions and to carry out an act of justice at the same time. One of the detachment's messengers had been robbed of five tomans by the agha of one village. The agha had then fled. As punishment, his family had to provide nineteen pack-animal loads of straw and barley.

The detachment had hardly got back to Bowkan on April 23rd before fighting flared up again. This time the Serdar's horsemen also participated in the fighting at the advanced posts. Hadji Baba Sheikh, a man like few in Kurdistan, distinguished himself above all. He came to fight and he rejected all payment for his participation in this "Holy War"—a mindset never seen before in a Kurdish leader. All he asked for was support in case that, as a result of the war, he became needy. Brave and with a high sense of personal pride, he felt very ashamed and it hurt him that his men, like other Kurdish tribes, were so unreliable and took flight so easily. He was greatly revered as the spiritual leader of the Sautchbulak-Sainkaleh-Saqqez region; the populations of the villages he passed through would become ecstatic when they saw him. His understanding and intelligence prevented him, unlike others of his status, from avoiding shaking hands with Christians.

In spite of all the successful skirmishes and bold patrols, it was only too obvious that, on account of the enemy's superior forces, it was impossible to operate here for long. The detachment, in constant contact with, and at times meting out heavy blows to the enemy, withdrew to Bane on May 7th, subsequently crossing the border and establishing its quarters in the Turkish village of Shivkali on May 16th. A patrol under Leverkeuhn I on May 25th found that Bane had not been occupied by the pursuing Russian troops, although a Russian advance unit of 120 horsemen had appeared at Bilek, an hour's distance from Shivkali, as early as May 18th, and skirmishes between the advanced posts had taken place there in the few days following. Daily exchanges of fire were of no importance and were often due to misunderstandings. Other incidents in the rear of the detachment were the cause of more serious worries. The officer in charge of supplies and two soldiers were murdered by Kurds, and the Kurds fought among themselves. Veli Bey sent out several punitive expeditions.

The Russians crossed the River Kalvi, but were unable to take Serdesht. They were surrounded by the local Kurdish tribes and slaughtered or put to flight. The positions now ran roughly along the border. Crossing back over the border was impossible, even further south, as the Russians from the north could easily have cut the detachment off. Thus there was a period of calm.

On the last day of May, Nadji called Leverkuehn I to Suleimaniye. From there he rode, on Scheubner's orders, with Abdul Bari Bey and many men to Mosul. His last impression before separating from the force was a sad one. The following entry in the detachment's log-book, which he carried, shows it:

Thursday May 25th
This evening the horseman Gani died in Shivikal. He was suspected of having warned the Kurds in a village that a punitive expedition was to be sent. By order of Veli Bey he was flogged on the 24th by Turkish officers. He died of the wounds, as the surgeon confirmed. The same evening, the detachment commander inquired into the matter with Veli Bey. The next day he reported the case to Nadji Bey who, according to his later statements, reported the case to a court-martial. There is no point in saying more about this outrageous case.

Friday May 26th
The burial of the horseman Gani took place this morning with full military honors.

Changed Perspectives

At the beginning of February I had established contact with Scheubner from Mosul and regularly informed him of everything important. I also sent him provisions and clothing using mule caravans, as the way was extraordianrily long and difficult.

The telegraph line extended only as far as Suleimaniye on the border, and the Turks did what they could to prevent us from using it. They sent garbled versions of our ciphered telegrams, using a simple procedure that could hardly lead to accusations against the postal workers but which suggested misunderstanding was the cause.

It is well-known Turks wrote their words and sentences from right to left, numbers, however, from left to right. On receiving a coded telegram, the decoder had to begin at the last group furthest out, but read numbers from left to right. The Turks, however, suggested we should write our coded telegrams fully according to our style, that is, from left to right throughout, so that numbers should keep to the general direction. However, if we did that, they would take it down according to their own fashion from right to left. Irreparable confusion was the result.

We had a code we shared only among ourselves. Two numbers replaced one letter, and we always wrote in groups of four digits so that, in this way, each group contained two letters. If we wrote according to our style in groups of four or six in each line, with a little effort the recipient was able to decode the telegram into its original format. If one had, however, as the Turks used to, a variation of between three and six groups per line, which were then mixed up in the manner described, the recipient had to work for hours to make sense of the telegram and often it was completely impossible. Therefore it was difficult to tell how successful I had been in getting vital information on the developments on the eastern front in Turkey through to Scheubner.

Finally, Nikolai |Nikolaievich began the long-awaited offensive near Erzerum and took the fortress. A little later, at the end of February, the Russian General Baratov occupied Kirmanshah and pushed the Turks back to the Paitak Pass, some 25 km from the border. Although Field-Marshall Von der Goltz sent three battalions to reinforce this position, he continued concentrating all his major forces for the battle against the British.

The field marshal died of typhus 10 days before the fall of Kut-el-Amara. His successor was well-known to us, Khalil Pasha, Enver's uncle. He was honest enough to thank Scheubner on a later visit in Mosul for the great services rendered to the 6th Army by the expedition in winter and spring. He explicitly confirmed that its operations had prevented the Russians from crossing the Turkish border at any point north of the Paitak Pass, or attacking the position at Paitak from the flank. It was satisfying for Scheubner to hear these words from someone who was qualified, for he heard very different things from others who were less so.

Even before this I repeatedly had occasion to shake my head in Mosul. Scheubner had ordered me to remain there to organize communications and transport. I resided in the Consul's house and was hardly ever absent: once, I had to leave to recover an armored car that had got bogged down during the rainy season in the desert while on its way to Mosul from the the Baghdad railway railhead; and another time I left with a reserve officer and a Baghdad railway engineer as we tried to discover coal in the Kurdish mountains east of the Tigris and north of Zakho. Indeed, we succeeded in finding good surface coal seams on mountainsides never explored by any European, but transportation difficulties rendered the exploitation impossible. On the way there and back we were the welcome guest of my friend, the kaimakam of Zakho, whom I fondly remembered from the winter days at the border pass.

Otherwise, as I have already said, I remained in Mosul and saw a lot of German officers on their way to Baghdad or to the Persian operation. Mosul became a main staging centre, responsible for the desert route between the railhead of the Baghdad railway and the Tigris, as well as down the Tigris to Samara, where a short railway line to Baghdad began. None of the Germans who arrived had any idea of local conditions. In many cases they did not even wish to learn more about them or be guided by those who had already been working there for some time. More than once, one had to wonder about the principles by which these transfers to Turkey had been made.

Turkish matters were handled at General Von Falkenhayn's Army Headquarters generally by following the suggestions of the military plenipotentiary in Constantinople, Major-General von Lossow. After the successful conclusion of the Dardanelles campaign, Marshall Liman Von Sanders was pushed aside on the coast of Asia Minor. He was reputed to be an uncomfortable man, and certainly was so to many people because of his great ability, as well as his demands on himself and on others. German General Headquarters made a fatal mistake when they did not press for a Turkish front-line assignment for this successful commander; indeed he was not even consulted.

Field-Marshall von der Goltz leaving Mosul by kelek.

Sautchbulak from the northwest.

The Young Turks were ambitious dreamers without military judgment. They overestimated their forces; but what actual forces they possessed they exploited insufficiently due to deficient organization. Marshall Liman Von Sanders, who knew them very well, was sceptical about their high-flying plans. Major General Lossow, who had always been in Constantinople and its surrounding districts, and was particularly close to the Embassy and political circles, had never been in the firing line. He did not display sufficient analytical thinking or enough firmness to oppose the Young Turkish leaders' designs that were full of errors. He was also lacking the necessary sense for cooperating with the Turks under daily conditions. He only dealt with them at higher levels and only in matters with political import.

Liman Von Sanders argued that in the Turkish army Turkish officers should be left to do everything they were capable of, even if only approximately. Germans should be used for special tasks alone. He always had a Turkish chief of staff—Major, later General, Kiazim Pasha. When the Supreme Command in the Dardanelles was given to him, he took on a German Adjutant and a German Chief of Staff, but in general he worked with Turkish officers. On a case by case basis he appointed German officers for special tasks, but these had to work in their turn with their Turkish superiors or subordinates. Field-Marshall Von der Goltz, too, always worked with Turks whom he understood and who understood him very well. His personal influence on commanders, lower ranking officers and the lowest soldiers of the 6th Army was what brought about the heavy defeat of the British at Kut-el-Amara.

Now, however, military assignments in Turkey had apparently become the latest fashion in Germany; and everything had to be done by Germans and according to German rules. Near Constantinople and along the coast of Asia Minor where European culture had had some influence, this could possibly work. In Mesopotamia, however, it struck a definite discordant note.

Scheubner felt most embarrassed by what he saw on his return to Mosul. He had enlisted as a volunteer, and had learnt about war in Count Preysing's squadron, like we all imagine from the idealistic accounts we heard as children. Preysing was indeed a soldier, and no better existed in the Bavarian army.

Next, Scheubner had worked in Erzerum under Ambassador Von Wangenheim, a most remarkable personality. In Lieutenant Colonel Guse, the Turkish 3rd Army's German Chief of Staff, he had admired a man who already embodied, in his appearance, the general staff officer fashioned by

Moltke; who had without much ado cleverly and resolutely carried to success an immensely difficult task, namely the rehabilitation of the army that Enver's militaristic carelessness had destroyed. Finally he had had the luck of finding in Omer Nadji a significant man as an opponent, co-worker, and friend. Fate had granted him all this—it had spared him only one thing—the mediocrity and meanness of human nature. And it was precisely this that, after all the experiences of these months, was to be made up for...

Mirza Khan, one of the Persian officers serving on the expedition, referred to Scheubner when he once exclaimed, "In Persia, one German officer is worth a whole battalion!" And in conversations among the Kurdish leaders one could often encounter the opinion, "There is no truer friend and more active worker for the Caucasus than Scheubner . . . His name will be indelibly written in history the day the Caucasus gains its freedom..." This is the man who earned himself the Iron Cross before he had been in the field for a month; who as the youngest Consul in the Foreign Service had stood his ground in the Armenian question with just as much courage as skill; who had held the advanced position against the Russians the whole winter in the most difficult of circumstances, with comrades and subordinates that went with him no matter what happened—now this man came from his mountains, where he had been like a lord facing nature and the children of nature, down to the flatlands of a dusty and weary order.

Admittedly he had previously had considerable trouble with bureaucratic formalities, but out there in the daily struggle, in the wide open spaces of the countryside he was a complete, exuberant idealist, with a great many plans and activities—and exuberance is a great asset, as Goethe says. What he found in Mosul was plainly incomprehensible to him. He had a deep-rooted belief in the blessings of military regulations and had drawn up an exercise program for Kurdish soldiers. But that the Germans misused the regulations amongst themselves and against each other under the very eyes of the Turks, oblivious of their own dignity as Europeans, which had to be observed with every other European—that made him sick.

One of the best-known personalities in Persia was the German Consul Schünemann, from Tabriz. He had played an important part in Klein's operations in Central Persia: conferring on him the title of a general would not have added a jot to his name. But he had not served in the army before the war, and therefore possessed no rank in the German army. Thus, it was grotesque to hear young, freshly arrived officers without the least experience of the Orient, arguing that one had to instruct Schünemann to wear a uniform, so that he might be granted the rank as a deputy sergeant. Scheubner's experiences with high-ranking officers were not much better when he requested some decorations for his subordinates and comrades. This could not be granted, so shrugging his shoulders, he said: "One has to be where the decorations are handed out, not where they are earned." A high-ranking adjutant asked him amiably how he had organized his personal wine supply. Scheubner could only answer that this problem had never even been talked about on the expedition, and that we nevertheless had always met our duties as hosts in a sufficient and dignified manner.

He, who had really learnt to value his human resources and employ them with the greatest economy, must have been outraged at the thoughtless way resources were squandered on the German side. On one occasion a group of 23 NCOs and soldiers arrived at the Ras-el-Ain railhead, bound for Mosul. Instead of putting a motor-vehicle at their disposal, they were sent on foot, with a camel-caravan, across 360 km of sandy wilderness. The result was that on arrival in Mosul, aside from one man, they all had to be sent to hospital.

This and many other impressions were extraordinarily embittering for Scheubner. In spite of the numerous German commanding institutions that had been arriving in Mesopotamia over time, not only was a firm, coherent strategy lacking, but orders in general as well. The question of what should happen with the expedition simply remained unresolved. As, objectively, Scheubner had to accept that the Turks and Russians were racially different and to take this fact into account, even if he detested it, it was impossible for him to understand—particularly in the presence of Turks—an attitude amongst the Germans which displayed not the slightest trace of the ideal picture he had had as a volunteer.

It was later remarked by many distant observers and confirmed by friends that Scheubner was difficult to approach and difficult to understand. In 1914 he had not been like that. I believe that, if he later appeared that way, it had primarily been brought about by this time from the frontier mountains and the disappointments in Mosul. It was these that changed his view of people in daily life. Only in the circle, and under the leadership, of the one to whom the time before his death belonged, did he once again find the directness to face duties and people which he had lost when he left the Kurdish mountains.

Although none of the various expeditions sent to the eastern border of Turkey ever received the supplies that had been promised, they fulfilled their task. But in so doing, they attracted forces, as they were supposed to, which they could not resist without the promised support. Instead of

Scheubner's expedition's camp.

providing this assistance, it had become a fashion to speak of the Persian operations as failures—probably to gloss over their own mistakes and justify them by means of myths subsequently constructed. Only a very few, like Major-General Duke Adolf Friedrich of Mecklenburg, realized through their own judgment, uninfluenced by the superficialities of Constantinople and General Headquarters, how they had been fought, how they had suffered, and what had been achieved so far in the east.

Duke Adolf Friedrich of Mecklenburg had been assigned the command of a new special mission to Persia, to be made up of four machine-gun units and one artillery unit. That aroused certain hopes. The negotiations Scheubner conducted regarding the further employment of his expedition had, at the beginning of June, when Leverkuehn I arrived in Mosul with Abdul Bari Bey, still not rendered any clear results. Scheubner had suggested a massive organization of Kurdish cavalry units, but found little inclination for it among German officials. In the meantime it turned out that his expedition had, to all intents and purposes, come under the command of the duke, he being the supreme commander of the Suleimaniye sector—news of which must have caused considerable pain to Omer Nadji and especially to Dr Fuad. Finally, much too late, the moment had come when Vali Haidar Bey had to give up his command of the Mosul group. His last official military act was to decorate Leverkuehn I, Thiel, Abdul Bari, and Memduh with the Iron Crescent, a Turkish war decoration.

There were several changes made to Scheubner's detachment subsequently. After an inspection by the duke, the entire column of pack-animals was taken over by his special mission, as well as much equipment from the depot. Lieutenant Memduh was assigned as deputy commander and interpreter to a machine-gun unit, and Schlimme was transferred to the German Mosul Stage as transport leader. Abdul Bari was sent home on leave with the majority of his Kurds, as his father had recently died and he now had to take over leadership of his tribe. Leverkuehn I was once again to lead the cavalry unit, but that did not last long. He fell ill with Papatazzi fever, like Scheubner, and subsequently also with malaria. I myself caught dysentery, soon followed by a serious attack of malaria. In the hot and unhealthy climate of Mosul convalescence took a long time and was even then not complete.

During our illness, Consul Schünemann arrived with some officers from a scouting mission to Suleimaniye. Based on their observations they gave reports that were encouraging for Scheubner's expedition. The numerous Persian Kurds at Suleimaniye warmly remembered our operations and wished for Scheubner's return. However, almost at the same time, we received a sad piece of news: Omer Nadji Bey had died. We mourned him as a man whose presence, amid many alienating and repulsive experiences, remained bright in our hearts.

Once more Vali Haidar Bey became notorious, and this was in connection with a tour of inspection by War Minister Enver Pasha. On this occasion it was emphasized everywhere how good and safe the roads were. Shortly before this, however, one of the duke's special mission transports had been shot at by Arabs, and a guard had been injured, although not life-threateningly. He was hurt when the regional general inspector, General Beck, had been attacked while traveling in his car on his way from Ras-el-Ain. The Vali of Mosul, however, was quick to declare that these incidents had been the work of a Kurdish sect, the Yezidis, who were persecuted as "Devil-worshippers" by the Mohammedans. Needless to say, the Vali planned a punitive expedition against them—once again to exterminate a non-Muslim but peaceful people.

This was our last experience in Mosul. The three of us—Scheubner, Leverkuehn, and myself—had, no longer being fit for service in the tropics, to take home leave, and set off from the town on August 28th, shortly after a friendly call from Khalil who, in his new senior position, remained as sociable, easy going, and comradely as in the days when we had met him in Siirt on the march. Scheubner presented him with a little bear he had bought from mountain Kurds. Khalil and his general staff spent a whole afternoon in the garden of the government building, running around with the funny animal.

With the conquest of Kut-el-Amara, in which he had played a more important role even at the last minute, than could ever have been hoped for, the first part of his ambitious plans had materialized. Now the second part should have followed—the complete liberation of Mesopotamia. However Khalil passed over it and went straight on to the third: to clear the way to India. This step had its own consequences.

In the section of Persia where Scheubner and Nadji had been active— Sautchbulak and south of it—a Turkish unit operated under a German General Staff officer, Captain von Löschebrand. It constituted the left wing of the army group formed by Khalil to recover Kirmanshah and Hamadan from the Russians. The capture of the two towns succeeded; but to achieve this, Khalil had weakened the troops operating against the British excessively, giving the latter time to rebuild and reinforce their lines. He had, however, Enver and the military plenipotentiary von Lossow to blame for this act of negligence. In the winter of 1916-17 the British took the offensive and captured Baghdad on March 11th, 1917. With this the Persian campaign also found its end. In order not to be cut off, the troops there withdrew immediately to the Turkish border.

A few sentences might serve to round off the historical picture. The loss of Baghdad was extraordinarily painful for the Turks. They asked for German help to recover the city. General Von Falkenhayn was supplied for the purpose with considerable funds and a numerous staff of German officers. This project critically depended on military plenipotentiary von Lossow's advice; he was, to use a phrase by von Sanders, "a stepchild of the goddess Strategy." As a result of this focus on Baghdad, much ground was lost in Palestine. At the end of 1917 Jerusalem fell into the hands of the British. Falkenhayn was replaced by Marshall Liman Von Sanders, but Baghdad was never recovered. The front in Palestine, however, withdrew under heavy fighting to Syria and fought to the bitter end in 1918.

On the Caucasus front the Russians advanced from Erzerum to Erzinjan. They also took Mush and Bitlis—the two towns we had passed on our way to Mosul. There the Armenian deportation took its revenge. The land had remained uncultivated, and the Turkish army lost as many soldiers through starvation and cold as in Enver's offensive. After the Revolution, the Russian front slackened. In early 1918 the Turks invaded the Caucasus. In Tiflis a Georgian republic and in Baku a Daghestani republic were proclaimed—bodies imagined by Scheubner when he left with Nadji for Azerbaijan in 1915. These states went down with the collapse of the Central Powers.

We, however—Scheubner, Leverkuehn I, and myself—did not return to Turkey. We crossed the desert sands to the Baghdad railway railhead by wagon, moving mostly by night as it was too hot during the day for either traveling or sleeping. In spite of the enormous strain such a journey put on newly-convalescent men, we enjoyed it as our final time together, drawing closer together in our own caravan.

Coming across a sign in the desert which read "Philipp Holzmann AG" we knew we would soon arrive at our railway connection to western civilization. And so it was. There was nothing there that pointed to the proximity of the famous Baghdad railway; no train station in the European sense, just two sets of rails and many freight cars. We sought out the cleanest among the latter and put our packs and samovar in it, and waited until the train pulled out, which it did in the middle of the night.

At Aleppo, we were warmly hosted in the officers' home run by a German deaconesses. Our impression of this first contact with a German female worker is best documented by the verses Scheubner wrote in the visitors' book at the officers' home:

> We've wandered long—from north to east,
> We've fought, we've won—endured;
> Horrors seen, and so much pain—
> We've never secured our peace.
> But here, where German women's spirits
> Rule—we've been allowed
> To believe everything we forgot;
> Working for the love and peace we've wanted.

From Aleppo on we were able to travel by rail, with the exception of the passes in the Amanus and Taurus mountains. In Constantinople Scheubner and my brother both suffered another attack of malaria. I traveled on alone, but in Berlin had to be taken into hospital with a relapse of malaria. We later heard about our comrades: Lieutenant Thiel had died from some treacherous disease in Mosul. Memduh Bey participated in the campaign in the border zone in autumn, but we never heard of him again. Schlimme was able to return home to Hanover at the end of the war.

After recovering from his tropical illnesses, my brother was sent to the Western front as company commander in the 21st Bavarian Infantry regiment. He was there for the great offensive of 1918 and was able to write one of the most touching poems to emerge from the World War, full of premonitions of impending death. On June 20th 1918 he fell while on patrol against the British positions in the vicinity of Arras. His fate had been fulfilled, as he saw it and never wished it to be otherwise. And the words he dedicated to a friend also applied to him: "A heroic death is the best end for a German."

XVI

Riga

"Munich is quieter now," wrote Scheubner in a letter during home leave shortly after his arrival in late October 1916. "There are many war-wounded on the streets, whose whole outlook is dominated by the military and military uniforms. Civilians are looked down upon, idlers are specially despised, and nearly everyone has been called up. Food supply is the talk of the town, not free of sharp criticism of the government in Berlin. Right on my arrival I noticed with satisfaction the tight posture of the troopers. Even the injured, who however look usually very miserable, salute pretty stiffly. Only the uniforms are sometimes more than poor. The capture of Constanza has produced great enthusiasm and lifted the gloomy mood over the losses at the Somme, in which regiments from Munich were involved... I feel as well as one can among dear friends. They and my wife compete in spoiling me—which one allows with a bit of embarrassment..."

Further on, "I also hope the most valuable gain for us from our time spent together down there will be a lifelong comradeship; and as for gratitude—comradeship precludes or includes gratitude, depending... A few days ago I had the great joy of receiving as my morning greeting the Hanseatic Cross from the High Senate in Lübeck. This was truly moving. The Cross is very nice. It also pleased me that the Senate does not seem to place too much importance on formalities. Anyhow I received the Cross by registered mail."

Despite his urgent need for rest to be fit for service and, if possible, for assignment in the tropics, Scheubner was not spared from having to attend to bureaucratic matters. He not only had to wait for the papers for his leave, but was also pestered from Berlin with many petty inquiries into secondary details about the expedition. Meanwhile he wrote concluding reports, for instance one to the Chancellor on the Armenian question. He also carried on an extensive correspondence concerning further deployment in the Orient, which however remained without result. On December 16th he wrote about it: "Persia does not appeal much to me under the present circumstances. In fact I would be happiest going to Kurland or Poland..." Nevertheless he thought of Turkey with nostalgia—in the same letter he said he was busy finding practical pieces of equipment, and added "should Greßman (then Chief of Staff in Baghdad) wish to have me, I will go there." But things turned out differently.

He resumed working on this doctoral thesis, completed it in a short time, and earned the degree "Dr. ing." (doctor in engineering) at the Technical University in Munich. At the beginning of 1917 he reported back to the Reserve depot of the 7th Light Cavalry in Straubing as fit for garrison duties. The small town in the Danube depression had been less impacted by the shortages of the wartime winter than most parts of Germany, and the time he spent outdoors training recruits with its regularity strengthened him much more than any stay in a sanatorium. Horses and wagons were available for tours into the neighboring Bavarian forest. All in all these months were a veritable refreshment and joy, full of comradeship and friendship.

At the end of March he was transferred to the front as Lieutenant and intelligence officer of the 15th Bavarian Infantry Division. "It is not all that easy for me always to think that I am nothing more than a Lieutenant and have not much say—the nice Persian independence is still too close in memory," he wrote in a letter during the first few days of his new assignment. He participated in the strenuous days and nights of the Aisne offensive. All reports from the front to the division, and thereupon to the higher echelons, went through his hand. In addition he had to analyze the material found in enemy positions, or gained from the interrogation and investigation of the prisoners.

Following the offensive, his work became much less interesting. He specially disliked having to read through officers' and soldiers' letters home as a censor. "My activity is becoming increasingly subordinate," he complained in a letter from this time. "Intelligence Officer without intelligence, Map Officer and now Supervision Officer, Mail control—a hardly pleasant activity it is reading through other people's letters..." Nevertheless he added and this was, indeed, characteristic for his sense of duty, the sentence: "Yet it has to be done, and duty is duty."

"I follow the events in Russia with a most lively interest, unfortunately only passively. I would like to, I could act now for the benefit of Germany. However, old hands are not required.

"If we were in northern Persia now, many things would turn out differently. The Caucasian and Armenian republics would not be so unlikely. Of course, setbacks cannot be ruled out, but radical changes would take place under any circumstance. We Baltians will probably fare worst. We will probably lose our home, and not gain a new one. That is the way it is for particularity, for which there is no room in today's world..."

No matter how justified this internalized pessimism was, in the long run it could not take a hold on a character like Scheubner. Finally his already twice expressed wish to operate in the Russian Baltic provinces came true; admittedly by detours that required several months of patience and hope. Suddenly in July the Political Section [of the General Staff] inquired with him if he would be willing to accept a command in Turkey. He traveled to Berlin, but the assignment offered had no independent character. He turned it down and returned to the front. Straight away he was ordered again to Berlin.

After the shock to the Russian Empire of Kerenski's revolution and its aftermath, the hope for liberation and independence rose among many nationalities in Russia. They sent representatives to Stockholm. Scheubner was asked if he would be willing to negotiate with them there.

He went there and soon found himself in contact with a varied number of partly serious, others partly adventurous individuals. It was not easy to gain a reliable picture of the real situation in Russia and its prospects from the reports of male and female spies or the tainted descriptions of the delegates of national committees. The conferences were very soon cut short. Scheubner, who had already been enrolled as an Interpreter Officer, was transferred to the High Command of the 8th Army, which cooperated with the navy in the capture of the islands of Oesel and Dagoe and the conquest of Riga.

A few days after the conquest, Scheubner came to Riga. At about the same time arrived on the orders of the General Headquarters, Dr. Neumann, a senator from Lübeck who was assigned to "gouvernement" of Riga as a gesture of support for the German Baltic population and the city of Riga, which had once been a member of the Hanseatic League, and whose outward appearance closely resembled that of the other Hanseatic towns of the Baltic. Senator Neumann was entrusted with the task of working on the political and administrative "gouvernement" matters. Scheubner collaborated with him most closely as well as Major Buchfink, the Chief of General Staff of the Riga gouvernement, until the end of the occupation. At the same time he remained directly subordinate to the High Command of the 8th Army. He was named director of the Press Office of the Supreme-East 8 in Riga.

Before the war Riga had been a city of half a million inhabitants, an important port and industrial center—besides St. Petersburg the principal Russian town on the Baltic Sea. Founded by Germans in the Middle Ages, the city had retained its German character despite all oppression in its external appearance as in its people. During the war, however, the German leading class of the population had suffered heavily. The population had dropped to 160,000. The industrial plants had been moved to the Russian interior; bank deposits and with it the operating capital of the merchants and industrialists had been transferred to Moscow. The Russian cathedral, an alien body on this German city's panorama, however, still stood at its place, but the statue of Peter the Great was removed from the entrance. The Russians had put it like a national sanctuary aboard a steamer to bring to St. Petersburg. Peter the Great was not to make it back home, however: the ship ran aground in the Riga bay.

After the fall of the city, the publication of the more than a hundred-year-old German newspaper *Rigaische Rundschau* was authorized. The Latvians were also allowed to publish a paper in their own language, the *Riga Latweeschu Awise*. Both German news services were sent to them by the press department which was also in charge of censorship. But such relatively mechanical work was naturally not Scheubner's cup of tea. But he could not expect military funding for his ambitious activities. According to the old principle that a war should be financed by the land in which it is waged, he requisitioned the municipality's cigarette-tax. Although the municipal authorities, who had been installed by the military, succeeded in getting back half of this income, what was left was still a fair amount. One only has to imagine how heavily people, specially the Balts, smoked on Russian territories. Without their "papirosses" they simply were not happy.

On this material foundation Scheubner organized a very sizable government department. Freed of the need to constantly obtain funding from a higher authority, he saw as his task giving a coherent direction to the political work in those regions stirred up by the war, as well as awakening interest and understanding for Baltic affairs in Germany.

Cultural initiatives reached out to the Baltic from many sides, but the point of contact was at first only negative—censorship. All theater performances, lectures, movie presentations were censored. Nevertheless, this in a way compulsory contact led to requests for support from the press department by the event organizers. Scheubner was only too happy to provide it. Riga began to heave a sign of relief as cultural life flowered again. German and Latvian circles participated equally. Especially the Latvian opera was capable to put on performances of a high musical quality. Half its orchestra was made up of musicians from the former Imperial Opera House in St. Petersburg.

One can easily imagine Scheubner's satisfaction at being able to assist the rebuilding of the Technical University since he himself had been a student there. Now, freed from the bonds of Russian regulations, it took on a new shape after a German model. In the old city tower, the headquarters of his corps, the "Rubonia," Scheubner once again wore his band and cap. Time and time again he discussed there with young students and graduates the most burning questions about the future of his homeland.

He had a staff of sixty collaborators and subordinates from diverse professions. Among them was the best expert on Hanseatic history, the archivist Prof. Dr. Rörig from Lübeck; the well-known art historian, Hans Floerke; Scheubner's comrade from the Rubonial, the Baltic volunteer Arno Schickedanz, with whom he worked most closely until his death; Max Hildebert Boehm, an expert on German minorities; and Friedrich von Vietinghoff, a Balt invaluable for his knowledge of the Latvian language and politics. At the beginning of 1918 I also joined this circle. When Scheubner had asked in writing if I would like to come there, I has declined, as I wished to remain in the West. But he and Senator Neumann had already made an application for my transfer at the Army High Command, so I had to report to Riga. I became Scheubner's deputy and again, as in Turkey, his aide.

Exactly at that time the offensive began by which German forces conquered all of Livonia and Estonia. Scheubner participated in this campaign. The success of the advance through Dorpat to Reval (Tallin) was mainly attributed to his excellent preparations and he soon received the Iron Cross, First Class. The results, however, did not meet his expectations. He wrote about it in later years:

> We remained in contact with St. Petersburg and knew it would be easy to take that city with the help of the German prisoners-of-war who were there, and then we could have concluded a peace with nationalist Russia. The advance on Livonia and Estonia was militarily a walk. The disorganized Russian troops, who had deposed their officers and stood under the command of self-chosen Communist party members, hardly offered resistance anywhere. The capture of Dorpat by a Hussar squadron, which was only later followed by a company of Rangers and a mounted artillery battery, happened so quickly that the Cavalry division sent there arrived a day later. An advance with this division on St. Petersburg, counting on the panic and the general mood there, would surely have succeeded. The Bolshevik spook would have dissolved, and the way would have been open for an alliance between a nationalist Russia and a nationalist Germany. At that moment an order from the Supreme Army High Command stopped the German forces. The German Foreign Office concluded a treaty with the Bolsheviks at Brest-Litovsk. The German Parliament, short sighted as ever, had put the necessary pressure on the Supreme Army High Command to stop any further military operations in the east.

Still, even partial success resulted in strengthening the German military administration, an abundance of new initiatives, as well as a general extension of tasks. Scheubner ran a secret service for the observation of clandestine activities, which was indispensable for a full analysis of the political situation. Through his work in Turkey and Stockholm he already knew about the autonomist aspirations of the peoples on peripheries of the Russian empire. On the one hand they sought success in a cooperation with Germany, while on the other they maintained contact with the Entente. In addition there was the communist group, which saw salvation in its own Soviet state closely allied with Soviet Russia.

During the first years of the Revolution, the Latvians played an important role—Latvian regiments guarded the red Kremlin, for instance. By keeping an eye on the agents, Scheubner was able to determine who pursued political goals behind the mask of civilian activities, to what extent the editorial departments of newspapers were reliable, to what extent they had to be regarded as political centers on the other side of the military divide.

After the conquest of Livonia and Estonia, new newspapers sprang up in the 8th Army's area, German as well as Latvian and Estonian. One of them was the *Baltische Illustrierte Zeitung,* to which Scheubner gave special support. For the orientation of army and civilian administrative bodies he published a digest, Baltic area handbook, followed, starting in April, by *Auszüge aus der baltischen Tagespresse,* (Extracts from the Baltic Daily Press). It reprinted in translation and abridged form every relevant item from the local press. Divided into the main headings "The Future in the Baltic," "Economy," and "Culture" with sub-divisions such as "School," "Church Matters," it was also sent to Germany, where there had only been some interest for the Balts in the eastern provinces. Thus, these accounts reached out to the government department and members of parliament as wake up calls and reminders, particularly because they could be freely re-printed by the German newspapers.

What most occupied people's minds in the Baltic was naturally what would happen there after the end of the war. Those provinces belonging to the German cultural sphere could not fall back to the Russians again, that was clear, but they had only a German elite of about nine percent of the population. It was also clearly politically unacceptable to annex the mass of Estonians and Latvians to the German empire. It was not that there had not been Germans and Balts who entertained such wishes. There were enough people who believed Germany could govern the Baltic provinces with the same force as the Russians. They forgot that Germany was

precisely not Russia but a country standing culturally at a much higher
level, that could not be interested in Russian methods, neither to exchange
one Irrendeta with another. On the other hand, however, the penetration
of Entente influences to turn these countries anti-German could not be
tolerated. It was imperative to keep the right balance. Thus it seemed
advisable to educate the Baltic region under German guidance for
independence and to facilitate this by developing a corresponding degree
of local political expression.

From the still existent remnants of former independence were set up
regional parliaments, to work in conjunction with the German
administration as long as the war lasted. They then asked the German
Kaiser to accept supremacy over the Baltic provinces in a personal union
with the crowns of Prussia and the German Reich. The policy of the
German military and administration was directed for such a program for
the future and its implementation allowed ample latitude to solve specific
questions. The basis for the cooperation between German and Latvian
circles and with the German empire always remained contested.

Some intransigent circles believed they could ignore Estonian-Latvian
influences all together. Personal contacts between Germans and Latvians
and Estonians existed only on a professional basis. Communal relations
were lacking. Yet Latvians and Estonians owed all their cultural assets,
beginning with their letters, to the Germans. The Russian administration,
for its part, had done everything in its power to widen the division between
the two groups.

It is understandable there was not too much love left for Estonians and
Latvians who, in the 1905 revolution had plundered German estates.
Unfortunately, however, the German side for its part lacked most
fundamental knowledge about cultural and economic developments that
had been taking place among Latvians and Estonians in the course of
decades. Scheubner turned his special attention to such issues.

The Latvian rural population was organized in very solid and well-
funded organizations, like consumers' and sellers' cooperatives. All these
groups were united in the Central Agricultural Association in Riga, which
had considerable capital of its own as well as a million rubles savings of its
members. The funds allowed for the maintenance of cultural institutions,
like the local educational associations, the Latvian theater in Riga, and the
agricultural college in Freudenberg near Wenden. The latter published an
agricultural review, *The Baltic Farmer,* as well as a newspaper in Walk
called *Lihdums* (Land Clearing). One of the consumer cooperatives had a
publishing house and a printing-shop, publishing the most widely

circulated Latvian monthly, *Jauna Latwija* (Young Latvia). All of this served to concentrate forces, which guaranteed a rapid rise of Latvian commercial and political life. During the war, however, the well-run private business organization faced an equally well-organized economic control by the State. Scheubner looked for, and found here, common ground which suggested that a favorable development was possible.

The devaluation of the ruble had weakened the Latvians' financial power. The country depended on German deliveries for industrial production. What a chance for setting up natural and commercial relations! However, if this were not made use of before the Peace Treaty, Britain would probably have played the decisive role in imports and exports, just as it was doing in Denmark.

Scheubner clearly saw this danger. He put forth suggestions for first the study and then the penetration of agriculture, trade, and banking. The various administrative bodies, especially those run by men with a background in commerce and baking, responded with lively concurrence and support. The higher echelons of the military authority however reacted differently. These were heavily influenced by the ultra-conservative Sievers-Transche-Oetingen Baltic group, that knew little about the Latvians and cared even less. Yet, still in 1919, Scheubner heard in Königsberg Astaf von Transche, the Secretary of the Livonian Knighthood, express his regret about the "wasted opportunities" vis-à-vis the Latvians.

Thus, when the final collapse became apparent, preparations had been poor. Nevertheless, Scheubner did not lose courage during the negotiations with the Latvian nationalist leaders that started in October. Naturally, the faction tending towards the Entente was sure of victory after the collapse of Turkey, Bulgaria, and Austria; but German guns still dominated the country and the streets of Riga. Scheubner could argue with the Latvians that Germany in association with the German parts of Austria was going to be a more important factor for the Baltic States than the Entente, first of all for their protection against Bolshevik Russia. With this perspective the negotiations were continued. They faltered only on November 9th.

XVII

Saved from the Persecution

From Berlin came the wire: Red flag on the Brandenburg Gate. Then the line broke off.

The Baltic region was caught between two fires; Bolshevism in the east, and apparently also in Berlin. So far the railway still operated. The danger existed that within 24 hours soldiers returning from leave or emissaries of the soldiers' committees would arrive in Riga from Königsberg and Berlin. The question for the officers was: Might and should they maintain order with weapons in hand if necessary?

No order came from above in this respect. Opinions were divided as to how to go about it. We felt we had the right to some sort of clear instruction. On the evening of October 10th Scheubner went together with cavalry Sergeant-Major Scheidemann-Ballenhausen and myself to see Governor von Goßler. We asked him to tell us whether we should make use of our weapons in case of disorder. The more urgently we put the question to him, the less clear the answer. It was only the following day that the Chief of the 8th Army's General Staff, Major Frantz, made up his mind on a clear declaration. He announced that mutineers should be shot on sight.

I want to quickly add here that no such incident took place. Nevertheless it seemed appropriate to voluntarily concede to the army in the East some of the demands that the troops at home had taken by themselves. Soldiers' councils were established. It was possible to put the reasonable elements in charge. No serious disturbance occurred anywhere. Scheubner's press office was altogether spared any trouble.

In the meantime many rumors spread from all sides, but only few reliable news reports. Scheubner decided immediately to publish a new daily for the military, so as to calm them. The first number of *Das neue Deutschland* (The New Germany) appeared already on November 13th, Lance Corporal Diefendahl and Artillery-man Kett figuring as publishers. There was no indication accompanying their names showing that they had been working at the press office so far and would continue doing so. Four weeks later a weekly was added, *Die Richtung. Nordöstliche Blätter zu den Zeitströmungen,* (The Direction. Northeastern Pages on Current Affairs), published by Schmidt and Müller, Riga, Pauluccistrasse 21. It was the address of the press office.

About this time I received a telegraph calling me for an assignment in Lübeck, my home town. On Scheubner's advice I accepted it. As I left I was of the firm belief that the Entente's support for the new Latvian state guaranteed the security of the Baltic area. I watched the British warship that had been lying in the harbor for a few days—full of bitterness at this visible expression of our defeat, yet confident the British cannons could easily defend the town, and the British flag would not withdraw from this outpost against Bolshevism.

But the hopes placed on Great Britain proved deceptive. The warship left. Shortly after Christmas it became clear the German Eastern Army could not hold out after the collapse at home. The German government had recognized the provisional Latvian government under Utmani. The member of parliament August Winnig was sent there as envoy. He was familiar with the local conditions, as he had been in the Baltic since October.

When the Army High Command moved from Riga to Mitau, Winnig thought he should follow it and the Latvian government, which had also moved there. He asked some of the German officers if they would take over his representation in Riga, as far as this was feasible with the upcoming Latvian Bolshevik government. Scheubner accepted the task. First Lieutenant Grimmert, Lieutenant Moser, and of Scheubner's defunct press office, Corporal Koch and Lance-Corporals Kett and Tenner, and Baltic volunteer Arno Schickedanz, stayed with him. His friends beseeched him to leave Riga, as he was one of those who were still known for the suppression of the 1905 uprising and would probably be the target of hate and revenge. But he stood by his plant to make in the interest of the Baltic and Germany even the supreme sacrifice.

In the first place he had to look after the German citizens still in Riga, many of them sick or wounded in military hospitals, and arrange for their repatriation. The High Command left the city on the night of the 29th and 30th of December. The next morning his Baltic employees brought to Scheubner the German flag that had waved on Riga palace. The Legation was set up in Posselt's house. Scheubner had all files brought there that had been, orderly or disorderly, left in the palace. The following night there was uninterrupted shooting all over the city. Plundering mobs sacked the depot. One could see the light signals from the sector that was or should have been the front.

President Stujka took over the government in the name of the Soviet State of Latvia. Scheubner went to see him. Stujka informed him he couldn't recognize a German Legation and ordered him to immediately leave Riga. After lengthy negotiations Scheubner obtained a period of grace until January 15th. During the next days he dedicated himself to having

German nationals provided with protection certificates and arranged for their transport. But on the fourth day a delegation of German communists visited him, who demanded from him to immediately cease his activities. They threatened to arrest him: they could only recognize a Communist Germany, the representation of which only they themselves could be. The principal demand was, however, the funds Scheubner had received from Winnig, which they somehow had gotten wind of.

The house was searched, but nothing found. Shortly before Scheubner had distributed the cash among several Baltic houses that were known to be loyal to the German cause. Meanwhile the harassment continued until Stujka finally prevailed over the German communists. The evacuation of the 2,500 German nationals and a number of Balts was completed within the prescribed deadline. For the evening of January 14th the Latvian government provided a train for Scheubner and his staff, together 22 persons. All met at the station except Scheubner and his wife. At the last moment, he had been arrested by the German communists.

Frau Von Scheubner wanted to accompany him to prison. A German sailor prevented her from doing so. He explained to her that, if she would be in prison with her husband, she surely would not be able to do anything for him, nor would anyone else. If she remained out of prison, however, she might perhaps be able to free him. This made sense. Together with the other members of the German representation equally barred from leaving, Mrs Von Scheubner worked for her husband's permit to return to Germany. She went to all the neutral embassies and consulates, but they either lacked the courage or the will to lift a single finger. Thus, the only avenue left was approaching the Latvian authorities directly. Mrs. Von Scheubner took the step without hesitation.

Time was pressing, Scheubner's life was in serious danger. Rosa Luxemburg and Liebknecht had been shot in Berlin. The German and some of the Latvian Bolsheviks demanded the execution of Scheubner, the German representative. He was sentenced to death by a revolutionary tribunal. During mass gatherings and noisy street demonstrations his head was called for. It was like a miracle that Stujka felt strong enough to oppose all this. He ordered Scheubner's release.

Ordered, however, did not mean carried out. The subordinate offices obliged only unwillingly. With each of them Mrs. Von Scheubner had long arguments. As a consequence of the revolution, enormous disorder prevailed, accompanied by unlimited bureaucracy and a grotesque faith in the omnipotence of stamped paper. The functionaries who had been flooded could not do enough to imitate the Russian bureaucratic system of countless edicts and decrees, under which the country has suffered so long. Finally all the names and stamps necessary for departure were united on one sheet. Scheubner was to pick up the document at his local police station. How to get there, though? He was still held in the police prison on the Alexanderstrasse! The distance from the precinct to that street seemed insurmountable. The indefatigable Kett got into a hefty argument with the precinct Commissioner, who had, however, something good about him. For Kett succeeded in quickly snatching safe-conduct. The document was properly accepted at the police-station. That very same evening the entire legation left Riga in the direction of Dünaburg, as the railway connection to Mitau had been cut.

Mrs. Von Scheubner had collected all funds again. From the numerous house searches she had learned that they went through everything except the chamber pots next to the wash-basin. In there she had hidden the bank notes for a long time, until she could find a new cache in the provisions prepared for their departure. In the butter box, in the bread, in the sausage, the jar of honey, everywhere bills were hidden. And so they all left luckily Riga.

Riga, that is. But now came Dünaburg. Stujka's Latvian-Bolshevik regime had no more say there. The papers issued by him lost all effect. The whole company was again captive and surrounded by enemies who brought them to their headquarters. When Scheubner entered the chief commissar's room, he recognized to his greatest astonishment the previous chief of a Latvian student corps from the Riga Technical University. The latter, with whom he had often attended social occasions, put, unseen by others, but luckily immediately noticed by Scheubner, a finger to his mouth. Scheubner understood him and pretended to face a complete stranger. A long argument ensued, with the result that Scheubner and his company were given new safe-conducts.

This permit turned out to be a veritable Open-Sesame. At subordinate offices where it was read it produced the impression that the group was a delegation of the Latvian Bolshevik republic in Riga. Consequently, the traveling party was everywhere respectfully treated. It was given a Pullman railroad car and arrived in all comfort in Vilna. From there it had to travel 90 km by sleigh to the German border at Koschedarie. On January 28th 1919 the group arrived in Königsberg.

XVIII

The Struggle for the Ostmark

It could be expected that, in early 1919, the troops holding the line against the Russians in the Baltic and Lithuania were able to protect East Prussia from a Russian tide. But only if Bolshevism did not gain control behind German the lines and offer a hand to the Russians.

In Berlin, the immediate Bolshevik threat could be considered as eliminated due to the energetic intervention of the army and the "Freikorps." Now it was imperative to re-establish governmental authority in every part of the Reich, especially in the imperilled east.

August Winnig, former envoy and plenipotentiary for the Baltic region, was appointed Imperial Commissioner for East and West Prussia, and the areas still occupied by Russians. In this way all executive power had been concentrated in a single hand and, since, Winnig was a member of the Social-democratic party, the latter organization's cooperation for subsequent measures had been guaranteed.

With his knowledge of Baltic conditions and his experience with the Bolshevik regime in Riga, Scheubner put himself at Winnig's disposal. He was a great help not only for his knowledge of Russia and the border states, but also in detecting and monitoring all links that crossed the border into Germany and, naturally, had their first impact in East Prussia.

In Königsberg a group of sailors had taken over the leadership of the workers and soldiers committee (the Soviet) and occupied the Palace. At the beginning of March, the volunteer units and the remnants of regular forces in East Prussia were assigned to the cleaning up Königsberg. After some limited preparation by the artillery, it was possible to take the palace and put an end to the sailors' rule. The palace became Reich Commissioner Winnig's office. Scheubner immediately participated in the organization of conservative forces that were mustered into the homeland service, and in lining up volunteer units from these circles.

The governor of East Prussia was Mr Von Batocki, and the Landeshauptmann, Herr von Brünneck. Both headed an old Prussian administrative body and fully supported the struggle for national self-preservation in the face of advancing Bolshevism. The central government in Weimar and the Prussian government in Berlin were indulging in optimism about the internal and external development of Germany, such that it became difficult—almost impossible—to cooperate with them or just receive support for the hard pressed east. Besides, they allowed considerations based on party politics guiding all their decisions. There is no need to explain how much this hampered a united campaign of the conservative forces. Simply put, party rivalries were mixed with matters of a purely national character.

For several months, Scheubner officially joined the staff of the Reich Commissioner as a political assistant. From March to June I worked with him there. Later, the official ties were cut, and Scheubner gained independence as chairman of the East German homeland force. In view of the menacing dangers, to which many shut their eyes, he founded the "Eastern Political and Economic Information Service," which emphasize the catastrophic impact of Bolshevism on the economy. The weekly *Klarheit* (Clarity) was the organization's organ and soon achieved a circulation of 15,000 copies.

In West Prussia people's councils for the protection of the threatened Germany sprung up. But they were countered by a parliamentary committee set up by the government party. It was an unnecessary division of forces and a source of considerable discord. Scheubner worked against it with all his energy. His goal was coordination for East and West Prussia. He succeeded under very difficult circumstances: The founding of the "Central Committee for the Ostdeutschen Heimatdienst" in Danzig seemed to announce a turning point. Scheubner took on the chairmanship. In May 1919 he moved to Danzig.

At about that time the state of the so-called peace negotiations already clearly revealed that the government's optimism was totally unfounded. In the future, the East would have to defend itself not only against Bolshevism but also against the peace treaty.

For some time contact had been established between all national circles of the East, from Silesia to East Prussia. Earnest men considered whether the East should not declare independence if Parliament and Government accepted the Peace Treaty. Scheubner was convinced energetic action had to be successful. Neither, however, Winnig as head of the executive power nor general von Below, as military chief in command, could make up their mind and take the initiative for such a grave step. The East was subjected to the Peace Treaty, and the Homeland force faced new challenges.

Scheubner dedicated himself with special devotion to the preparations of a referendum in East and West Prussia. Not many words are needed here— the result testifies for him. But because the voting districts were administered by Entente commissions, and the territories falling to Poland were excluded, the work's focus was so much on the individual regions and, besides, under such varied conditions, that the Centre could not have immediate impact and adequately respond to arising necessities in the long run. Scheubner realized this in time and withdrew. He wrote a report on his activity, under the title "Concerning the Struggle for the German East Marches" which was printed as a manuscript. Nowadays only one copy of it is still extant. It is reprinted as an appendix to this book.

Besides the reasons mentioned, Scheubner's decision to resign was also brought about by a change in the personal and in the political conditions in the eastern provinces. This change took place with the Kapp putsch in March 1920. At the time of this event Scheubner was in Berlin. Although he had no knowledge of the plans and their timing of their execution, he did have, due to his manifold connections, enough acumen to foresee a violent confrontation. As soon as Kapp and Lüttwitz had occupied Berlin, he was asked to take over the organization of the intelligence service and of propaganda.

He discovered that no preparations of any kind had been made in this respect. He succeeded to put a printing-shop in operation and keep it going in spite of the general strike. However, the first step had hardly been taken when Kapp's government collapsed and he left Berlin. Scheubner went one more time to the Chancellor's palace. Going through the empty rooms, he came across the visitors' book. He destroyed it in order to protect the people whose names figured in it. As a matter of curiosity, he took with him the decree signed by Kapp by which full executive powers had been conferred on Lüttwitz.

As soon as he managed to get some overview of the situation in Berlin, he telegraphed Winnig and warned him in careful words to make no decisions that could not be retracted. However it was too late, as Winnig, forced to make a decision by the military officials, had declared his allegiance to Kapp. In his book, *Heimkehr* (Return Home) he has explained at length all of this. As a consequence of his decision, his retirement was inevitable, a grave loss to the national cause in the Ostmark. The local influence of political parties grew from dependence on the Berlin government, their claims and quarrels increased, and national matters stepped back.

XIX

Anti-Bolshevik - National Socialist

In the final stages of his activity in the eastern provinces, as Scheubner began asking himself what task he would take up now, his collaborator Arno Schickedanz told him about his correspondence with his Baltic student comrade Alfred Rosenberg. The latter was negotiating with south German companies in Munich that were considering sending a committee to the Crimea, where the White Russian General Wrangel was fighting. Scheubner traveled to Munich and was introduced by Alfred Rosenberg, industrialist circles, and White Russian emigrés who were in contact with Wrangel. The result of the negotiations was that Scheubner was placed as head of a commissions charged with establishing communications with Wrangel in the Crimea.

On the adventurous journey there he got acquainted with the White Russian Organization in the Balkans. At Wrangel's headquarters the appearance of a German, even if he had come without a government assignment, caused considerable sensation for the Entente. The attempt to establish cordial relations between White Russia and Nationalist Germany was correctly assessed by the Russian side and bore fruits for Scheubner's later work.

Germany's situation was, however, too hard pressed to render the Russian army any real assistance. Moreover, Scheubner realized that those in Germany who had assigned him his cooperation mission were following more of their own egoistic interests than serving national interests. Apparently there was no intention o collect funds in Germany for supporting Wrangel. In Crimea Scheubner made himself independent of his German principals, purchased a cargo of cotton to be sold in the Balkans, and returned with it on a small ship. On the way the ship ran into a storm, suffered damages, and almost sank. Instead of heading for Constantinople, Scheubner had to put in at Varna, but he was able to sell his cargo and so financed his trip back.

While this journey met with no immediate success, it had enriched Scheubner's knowledge of Eastern affairs. Through his own observation he had reached the conviction that the White Russian forces, properly supported under unified command, would still be in a position to liberate Russia from Bolshevism. He made it his special task to convey this conviction, and to unite the White Russian circles in Europe.

He settled to Munich and founded there an economic and political newsletter called *Aufbau* (Construction) with Arno Schickedanz, his long-time collaborator, at his side from May 1921. As the central organization of White Russian forces functioned, he himself headed the German section and General Biskupski the Russian section of the German-Russian Society. He was aware that any liberal, western form of government was impossible in Russia. He wrote to me at that time:

"I am more convinced than ever that in Russia only two forms of government are possible: Bolshevism or Tsarism. Whoever believes any social revolutionary or kadet circles can last in Russia is barking up the wrong tree."

He managed to organize the exiled Russian nationalist circles dispersed all over Europe and gathered them at a congress in Reichenhall. Grand Duke Kyril released a manifesto drawn up by Scheubner, wherein Grand Duke Kyril substantiated his claims to the Tsarist throne and made himself the center of all nationalist Russian efforts. It was a clear success. Even the political situation was not unfavorable, but the incipient enterprise encountered determined internal opposition in Germany and counter moves from the Entente abroad, which suggested to the White Russians circles in exile, specially in Paris and the Balkans, that Nikolai Nikolaievich was the pretender to the throne.

With internal circumstances in Russia still in a state of flux and Russia remaining an unknown quantity regarding foreign policy, the German government started political cooperation with the Soviet Union at Rapallo. Scheubner, however, saw Germany's good only in collaboration with a nationalist Russia, and not that of the Third International. He wrote in the *Aufbau-Korrespondenz:*

"If the Soviet government in Moscow today stages Russian armies against Poland, it will not be in order to aid Germany. It will do it simply to strengthen the communist movement in Germany, to finally destroy national Germany and to replace it with a dictatorship of the proletariat, that is, in this case, a dictatorship of Jewish Bolshevism. In Russia as well the army has not realized yet that it had not been created for Russian national interests but likewise for those international Jews of world domination. In this case as well the Russian people must recognize its internal enemy."

And about the same time one can read in another article:

"If the nationalist Russian circles do not to pursue a day-to-day policy, but a far-sighted national policy for the future of their fatherland, they must direct all their efforts to Germany's liberation. They must seek to convince their French friends of the madness of their present policy of violence towards Germany."

Scheubner's efforts were directed mainly to foreign policy, in accord with his experience and talent, but in Königsberg he had to deal with internal political matters. His position was clarified in a discussion Winnig writes about in his book, *Heimkehr* (Return Home). The discussion took place in the difficult days of 1918. Scheubner told how much he had once been inspired by Naumann's ideas and how he had become a socialist on account of them—a national socialist, apart of any party loyalty; and therefore he had always felt as a maverick, regarded and rejected with distrust as a reactionary by some, as a red by others. But misfortune matured us for this idea and within five years a new Germany arose.

He has already known that a new spirit had to infuse the good traditions of pre-war Germany, to make them revitalizing and constructive. The moment came in 1916, when one day he came down from the Kurdish mountains to the Mesopotamian plain. Just as he had become convinced in the struggle for the national ideal in the German East, that the new Germany could never be created by the parties of the Weimar Republic, he had seen equally clearly that the nationalist circles had yet to get rid of much dead weight clinging to them from the days of Kaiser William. Sometimes he remarked to a friend, "Nationalism exists with and without stand-up collars. I have chosen the second." And in the *Aufbau-Korrespondenz* he wrote:

"The numerous show-offs among the national leaders fight each other, each with a Bismarck-patent in his pocket, yet not one has the candor to acknowledge, 'We too have failed, because we have not been leaders of German national essence, but wanted to be leaders of a class and a caste; and thus we have been shipwrecked in our endeavors."

He never assessed the governments, were they socialist or middle-of-the-road or right-wing, by their programs or their composition. He only saw their indecision and did not allow himself to be deceived by their nationalistic bombast:

"For as long as the government's words are not followed by deeds, nothing will come of the much yearned-for 'Peace and Order,' for it will mean the peace of the grave and the order of the graveyard for the German people!"

His continuous biting criticism resulted in a legal charge against him at the state supreme court in early 1923, which he published in the *Aufbau-Korrespondenz*:

The State Tribunal versus the 'Aufbau-Korrespondenz.'
'Clarity' denounced!

"The State Tribunal for the protection of the 'German' Republic, has accused the publisher of our correspondence, Dr. Von Scheubner-Richter, on account of the article 'Clarity' in this year's issue No. 3, of January 17th. The charge was brought about by the re-printing of the article by the 'Deutsche Wacht' (German Lookout) in Saxony. The gentlemen of the Saxon government apparently felt personally referred to by the following remarks in the said article:

"'So-called German republican administrations have not been able to do anything better, in the four years since the republic was established, than combating with all power of the state every patriotic movement in Germany and persecuting all nationalistic-feeling men whom the shame brought upon the fatherland cannot leave indifferent, and to assure the further destruction of the German people by internationalist Marxist thinking.'

"We will inform our readers about the continuation of this matter."

Shortly thereafter the plaint was withdrawn. The *Aufbau-Korrespondenz* informed its readers:

"Proceedings Cancelled!"

"According to a communication from the State Attorney's office in Dresden dated 9th of June 1923, the case against Dr. Von Scheubner-Richter as editor of the 'Aufbau-Korrespondenz' at the State Court for the Protection of the German Republic has been suspended. As we had mentioned in No. 16, the complaint against Dr. Von Scheubner-Richter was made as the author of the article 'Clarity' in issue No. 3.

"We congratulate the State Attorney in Dresden for this sensible step, by which he has at least spared himself an embarrassment. As the events taking place in Germany and in the world in general since the publication of the article 'Clarity' have borne out only to clearly Dr. von Scheubner-Richter's statements. Nor could the Leipzig Law Courts could ignore this fact.

"A conviction of Dr. Von Scheubner-Richter by the State Court on purely technical grounds, however, while simultaneously acknowledging the correctness of his contentions would not have exactly raised the prestige of the State court or the governments, particularly that of Saxony. These considerations will surely have played a not unimportant role in the Dresden State Attorney's decision."

How, Scheubner imagined the design of things differently from the government, he expressed in his characteristic way in the depiction of conditions prevailing in Germany, which he concluded with the words:

"The 'German' governments view all of this with benevolence or neutrality; and when former Chancellor Cuno, a man of good but weak will, tried to put a stop to it, at a wink from Moscow and the golden International he was deposed, and left—a typical representative of Kaiser Wilhelm's Germany—without having made the attempt, with sword in fist, based on the patriotic movement, to hold out and thus save national Germany."

The realization that a liberating foreign policy was impossible without inner firmness took ever greater hold of him, and became the focus of his work as an editor. At the beginning of 1923 he wrote:

"The German people stand alone; and it will be their last, but greatest, self-delusion before death to think someone could or would help them if they do not help themselves. The rise of Germany and the German nation from current shame and defenselessness can only take place if first of all anything is ruthlessly and indefatigably eliminated from Germany and the ranks of Germans that is guilty of the destruction of the German people's body and the German nation's strength. A united national front facing abroad can only be formed once such an inward-looking front has been created at home. The organization of this inner front, however, is depended on the integration of the whole racial essence of the German people on a national and social basis. It depends on the ruthless struggle against everything alien within the German people's body. It depends on Germany's ruthless cleansing of all elements inimical to her, and which oppose the racial union of all German tribes. Only if these preconditions are met, if such a racially, nationally unified Germanness has re-emerged, will we be able to ally ourselves with those other nations that do not wish for Germany's destruction but feel bound to us by common interests. Only then will we be in the position of entering alliances without being a plaything in the hands of others. The inner renewal of Germany is the precondition for her outer liberation. And this inner renewal can only take place under the slogan: 'Ruthless struggle against anything alien and unhealthy in our people's body', and the realization that, 'It is necessary that I live! But so it is necessary that the German nation lives in a free and great German Empire!'"

At this time he had fully oriented with regards to home politics: Adolf Hitler and National-Socialism had become the focus of his life and work. In October 1920 he had met Hitler through Alfred Rosenberg. On

November 22nd he and his wife attended for the first time a meeting at which Hitler spoke. Both immediately joined the National-Socialist German Worker's Party, but it was only in early 1923 that a close collaboration developed. On Hitler's request, Scheubner took over the position of leading the fighting squads, in which all the Bavarian patriotic groups and associations were united in a common struggle with the National-Socialist German Workers' Party under Hitler's leadership.

In the National-Socialist movement and its leader, Adolf Hitler, Scheubner found his domestic goals fulfilled and the uncompromising activism he himself had displayed in all his undertakings, the spontaneous daredevil attitude that met his own temper. Here were men of his own kind and persuasion; here was activism without consideration or restraints, without half-measures or illusions. In his *Aufbau-Korrespondenz* Scheubner professed fully to the movement.

"The way to Germany's freedom only leads along a long road of realization of all deceptions the gullible German people have given into and still so. All illusions about the solidarity of the international proletariat; all illusions that it is sufficient to be peaceful, so as to bring peace to the neighbors as well; all illusions that a people will be treated justly if they are themselves just; all illusions that alien people will not allow the destruction of the German people; all illusions about help from Great Britain or Russia or America—all these irresponsible dreams and illusions must go. The whole German people, every single German, must know that we are on our own, and altogether on our own; that only our own strength can save us or else—that we shall perish as a nation. Only the bitter realization of our total isolation will help us to realize, free of all illusions, our own strength and the strength in the unity of the the people cleansed of everything alien, ready to fight it out to a new life—or die fighting. The people's Germany is ready to take up this struggle with faith in the German people, to whom a new prophet has been given in the person of Adolf Hitler. He has understood to awaken the German soul and deliver it from the chains of Marxist thinking. People's Germany knows that its worst enemy is disunity in its own ranks, and it wishes to overcome this enemy by a concentration in a combat association, a patriotic combat association, to the ranks of which belong all those who, with glowing heart, wish for a new, free Germany, and who are ready to give their material belongings and blood for it. And the people's Germany knows that it will lead this struggle not for Germany alone but for the fate of Europe and, perhaps even the fate of entire history of the world to be decided on German soil. For, on the outcome of this struggle will depend whether national culture, racial

Max Erwin von Scheubner-Richter's sarcophagus in the "Ever Watchful Sentries" Temple of Honour in Munich

peculiarities, and Christianity will still prevail, or whether all of this will be melted down into an international pulp. And the battle will be fought under the slogan 'There the Soviet star—here the swastika.' And the swastika will—triumph!"

The passive resistance in the "struggle of the Ruhr" was a bad expression of what the patriots of 1923 and especially the war veterans among them had in mind. They wanted to actively intervene leading Germany back to the national idea. They hoped for a victory of the national idea in Russia. With national Germany, supported by a nationalist Russia, they hoped to take from the western powers what the Treaty of Versailles had torn from Germany. The national forces of Germany were still shattered, inadequately led by short-sighted leaders who could not see beyond their local group.

"Today we are without weapons. Not only that, we have no planes or tanks, no artillery or mortars. We have no army to speak of, but are also without weapons in spiritual terms, as we no longer have a unified German will, and we are without leadership for:

"Wherever German leadership steps forward, it crawls out of every nook and cranny with eager diligence to make sure no German man rises to stand at least a head above the other intellectually dwarfish figures.

"It is bitter having to say this, and more so having to fight against it only with the pen rather than the sword. But perhaps even the pen will be of some use to us if it contributes spreading the realization that the inner renewal of Germany is the precondition of its outer liberation."

This realization grew hand in hand with needs. Events pressed for armed battle and its preparation. The combat squad led by Hitler was the first focus of national unification. If he could be merged with the army and police force to a single movement, the German question could be settled from Bavaria. That was the program Hitler, Ludendorff, and Scheubner agreed upon and for a few short hours on the 8th of November 1923, the Bavarian government, the army in Bavaria, and the police under Kahr, Lossow, and Seißer appeared to be committed to joint action. Yet by next morning Kahr's government had broken its word.

On the evening of November 8th Scheubner had dressed in his uniform of his light cavalry regiment and entered at Hitler's side the Bürgerbräu beer-hall. He had picked up Ludendorff while Hitler conferred in a side-room with Kahr, Lossow, and Seißer. He took part in further deliberations with the men of the Bavarian government and was present at the meeting where they pledged their allegiance to the nationalist cause under the leadership of Adolf Hitler. Even after they had broken their word, Hitler and Ludendorff, and with them Scheubner, did not give up the matter. They were convinced that an attempt had still to be made and promised success in appealing to the patriotic sentiment of the population by staging a rally. Scheubner marched with Hitler and Ludendorff was at the head of the column. At the Feldherrnhalle (Commander's Hall) the state police fired. Scheubner shouted at them trying to end the shooting. But before he could be heard he was hit by the fatal bullet. He fell at the side of Adolf Hitler, in uniform, with the Iron Cross on his chest.

* * *

The last time I saw Scheubner was in the summer of 1921. Towards the end of 1923 I traveled to America for a long stay. There I read news of his death in front of the Feldherrnhalle in Munich on November 9th, 1923.

I thought of the years of friendship that had begun amid the sounds of soldiers' melancholy songs, which spoke of dying for the fatherland. I saw the mountains and streams of Kurdistan in my mind's eye, the Bolshevik hordes who wanted his death, the years of bitter toil after the Capitulation. I saw Scheubner's smile and felt again the pressure of his handshake like on so many moments of leave-takings, when we never knew if it might not be the last. He had never given thought to his safety. I knew he had been of the same belief as his friend Karl Gustav:

"A heroic death is the best end for a German."

Max Von Scheubner-Richter's mortal remains were laid to rest at the Forest Cemetery in Munich on November 17th, 1923. After the Nationalist rise in 1933 they were transferred to the Royal Square in Munich, where all the fallen of 9 November 1923 are, by order of the "Führer," Adolf Hitler, united as Sentries on Eternal Watch.

SELECTIVE INDEX

Harry Stürmer, *Two War Years in Constantinople: Sketches of German and Young Turkish Ethics and Politics* [Revised and Complete Edition] with annotations and an introduction by Hilmar Kaiser. London: Sterndale Classics, 2004, 160 pages, illustrations, index

This book is an insightful critique of German imperial policy in the Near East by the correspondent for *Kölnische Zeitung* in Constantinople between 1915-1917. An energetic journalist, Harry Stürmer kept close watch over developments in the Ottoman capital and in 1917 published a devastating critique of German and Turkish policies with interesting revelations about the genocide of Armenians.

His original German work was published in neutral Switzerland. Since the German Foreign Office could not provide an adequate response to Stürmer's account, it tried to suppress the work by buying its translation rights into European languages. Since it did not manage to buy the English rights in time, Stürmer's book appeared in English in 1917.

In this revised edition of the original German translation, Dr. Hilmar Kaiser provides a critique of Stürmer's work. He identifies contemporary reports by Stürmer in German archives and uses them for an informed appraisal of the book. Kaiser also identifies passages which were left out of the original German to English translation. These passages have been identified and appended to the present work.

Eberhard Count Wolffskeel Von Reichenberg, Zeitoun, Mousa Dagh, Ourfa: Letters on the Armenian Genocide, ed. and intro. Hilmar Kaiser, London: Gomidas Institute, 2nd ed. 2004, xxvi + 64 pages, paper, maps.

Eberhard Count Wolffskeel is the only German officer who served in Ottoman uniform known to have been directly involved in the killing of Armenians. He personally led the attack on the Armenian quarter of Ourfa and showed exceptional zeal when doing so. He comes across as a callous man, and a racist, who takes great pride in his military prowess and his lack of compassion for Armenian victims. As his letters show, his involvement in crushing the Armenian resistance in Ourfa—when this community's turn came to be deported and destroyed—makes particularly disturbing reading.

Rafael de Nogales, *Four Years beneath the Crescent,* London: Sterndale Classics, 2003, 356 pages, illustrations, index.

This work is one of the most incredible accounts of World War I by a former officer of the Ottoman Army. Rafael de Nogales was a Venezuelian mercenary who fought against Russians on the Caucasian and Persian fronts, as well as British armies in Iraq and Palestine.

In May 1915 Nogales commanded Ottoman artillery batteries bombarding Armenians besieged in the city of Van. The Armenian issue had a great impact on him, as he witnessed the slaughter of thousands in Van, Bitlis, Siirt, and other parts of Ottoman Turkey. Although Nogales was an anti-Armenian, his memoirs nevertheless provide invaluable insights into the destruction of Armenians in 1915.

Four Years beneath the Crescent also gives insights into the general Ottoman war effort, relations between Turkish and German allies, and much more.

Nogales' account complements that of Scheubner-Richter in the eastern provinces of the Ottoman Empire.

NOTE: *Two War years in Constantinople* was originally published in Spanish in 1924 and translated into English in 1926.

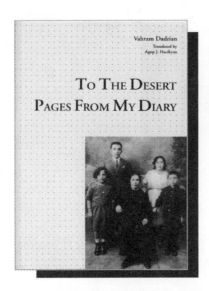

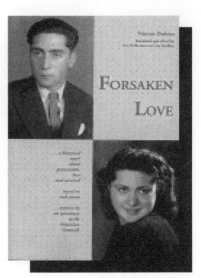

Vahram Dadrian, *To the Desert: Pages from My Diary*, trans. Agop Hacikyan; ed. and intro. Ara Sarafian, London: Taderon Press, 2nd ed., 2006, xvi + 410 pp., map, photos, fold-outs.

Vahram Dadrian, *Forsaken Love,* translated and edited from Armenian by Ara Melkonian and Ara Sarafian, London: Taderon Press, 2006, x + 326 pp., map.

Two related books by Vahram Dadrian, an eyewitness survivor of the Armenian Genocide. These works—a fascinating historical source and a gripping historical novel—allow us to examine the relationship between historical testimony and literature.

Dadrian was one of the first Armenian survivors who tried to integrate a whole novel against the background of the 1915 genocide. As his diary shows, his novel was intimately informed by the author's own experiences, as well as the experience of other survivors he met between 1915-1918.

Both works were originally published in 1945, after the author had left Turkey and settled in the United States.